Praise for
THE AURA COLOR WHEEL

"Embrace the full spectrum of who you truly are with this fabulous book! Through Helen's Aura Color Wheel system, you will be guided to uncover your soul's gifts and express them in your life today."

— **Rebecca Campbell**, best-selling author of
Your Soul Had a Dream, Your Life Is It

"Author, artist, and spiritual teacher Helen Ye Plehn is truly a force of nature! *The Aura Color Wheel* is a groundbreaking tool for healing and transformation, offering a compelling approach to personal growth and empowerment."

— **Dougall Fraser**, cosmic coach and author of
Your Life in Color

"Helen Ye Plehn offers readers an empowering and comprehensive system to identify and understand your aura, soul gifts, and soul wounds. Helen's fascinating personal story and astounding client experiences throughout the book bring this unique system to life! *The Aura Color Wheel* is ideal for anyone seeking deeper insight into their aura and the depth of wisdom it provides."

— **Cassie Uhl**, author of *Craft Your Own Magic*
and *The Ritual Deck*

"Helen has crafted an innovative system for understanding and working with aura energies rooted in healing work, art, and the colors of the aura. *The Aura Color Wheel* is so much more than a book . . . it's a guide to understanding yourself on a soul level. Each archetype is tailor-made to help you heal, grow, and connect with spiritual tools to support your journey ahead. If you're looking to break through self-doubt, fear, or other obstacles that are holding you back from embracing your authentic self, this is the book you've been waiting for!"

— **Ashley Leavy**, founder of the Love & Light School of Crystal Therapy
and author of *Cosmic Crystals*

"*The Aura Color Wheel* is an original and innovative book, filled with wisdom and guidance on every page. From the opening paragraphs of Helen's personal journey to the magic of each and every soul color, you'll be captivated by the depth and breadth of this system of self-discovery. Everything is tied together with practical advice and tangible tools you can use to transform your life, from meditation and crystals to feng shui and psychic development."

— **Nicholas Pearson**, author of *Crystal Basics*
and *Crystal Healing for the Heart*

"A light on the spiritual path! *The Aura Color Wheel* is like a trusted guide, illuminating the path for spiritual seekers ready to uncover their deepest truths. Helen's compassionate voice and innovative system make this book an indispensable tool for those on the journey of self-discovery."

— **Elaine Glass**, author of *Get Quiet* and founder
of the Nemus Code™

THE AURA COLOUR WHEEL

What Your Soul's Aura Reveals About Your Inner Gifts, Wounds and Lessons

HELEN YE PLEHN

HAY HOUSE

Carlsbad, California • New York City
London • Sydney • New Delhi

Published in the United Kingdom by:
Hay House UK Ltd, 1st Floor, Crawford Corner,
91–93 Baker Street, London W1U 6QQ
Tel: +44 (0)20 3927 7290; www.hayhouse.co.uk

Text © Helen Ye Plehn, 2025

Cover design: Claudine Mansour
Interior design and composition: Greg Johnson, Textbook Perfect
Interior illustrations: Helen Ye Plehn

The moral rights of the author have been asserted.

All rights reserved. No part of this book may be reproduced by any mechanical, photographic or electronic process, or in the form of a phonographic recording; nor may it be stored in a retrieval system, transmitted or otherwise be copied for public or private use, other than for 'fair use' as brief quotations embodied in articles and reviews, without prior written permission of the publisher.

The information given in this book should not be treated as a substitute for professional medical advice; always consult a medical practitioner. Any use of information in this book is at the reader's discretion and risk. Neither the author nor the publisher can be held responsible for any loss, claim or damage arising out of the use, or misuse, of the suggestions made, the failure to take medical advice or for any material on third-party websites.

A catalogue record for this book is available from the British Library.

Tradepaper ISBN: 978-1-837-82428-1
E-book ISBN: 978-1-4019-9544-7
Audiobook ISBN: 978-1-4019-9545-4

10 9 8 7 6 5 4 3 2 1

This product uses responsibly sourced papers, including recycled materials and materials from other controlled sources.
For more information, see www.hayhouse.co.uk

The authorized representative in the EU for product safety and compliance is Penguin Random House Ireland, Morrison Chambers, 32 Nassau Street, Dublin D02 YH68, Ireland. https://eu-contact.penguin.ie

Printed and bound by CPI Group (UK) Ltd, Croydon CR0 4YY.

*"Knowing others is wise,
knowing yourself is enlightenment."*

*— **Lao Tzu***

*To my father, who once told me I am his light.
To my daughter, the light of my soul.
To my husband, the lighthouse for my path.
To all the light workers and seekers on the path,
embody your light.
Together, we light up the world.*

Love and light,
Helen

CONTENTS

Introduction: Your Soul Incarnated Here to Evolve. 1

Part I: Auras and Soul Gift Archetypes
Chapter 1: What Are Auras and Chakras? 13
Chapter 2: Your Go-To Aura Layer Health Guide. 22
Chapter 3: The Aura Color Wheel and the Nine Soul Gift Archetypes. . . .43

Part II: Finding Your Soul Aura Color
Chapter 4: Visionary Archetype 77
Chapter 5: Entrepreneur Archetype. 92
Chapter 6: Healer Archetype 107
Chapter 7: Artist Archetype. 122
Chapter 8: Reformer Archetype 136
Chapter 9: Entertainer Archetype 151
Chapter 10: Researcher Archetype 165
Chapter 11: Teacher Archetype. 180
Chapter 12: Warrior Archetype. 194

Part III: Spiritual Tools for Your Aura Health
Chapter 13: Meditation and Journaling 211
Chapter 14: Ayurveda 224
Chapter 15: Feng Shui 231
Chapter 16: Living with Nature's Cycles 237
Chapter 17: Crystal Healing. 249
Chapter 18: Connecting with Your Spirit Team. 266
Chapter 19: Developing Your Psychic Abilities 284

Epilogue: Flowing with Your Rainbow 299
Endnotes 301
Further Readings and Resources 303
Acknowledgments. 306
About the Author 308

INTRODUCTION

YOUR SOUL INCARNATED HERE TO EVOLVE

Have you ever asked, "Who am I?" "Why am I here?" and "How can I be happy?" I asked these questions after going to the ER in 2011 for severe anxiety and depression with panic attacks. At the time I was a Ph.D. student in tourism and hospitality management, and my research area was human sensory experience design. For example, how can Disneyland encourage their customers to stay longer and return to the theme park using sensory cues (sight, sound, smell, touch, and taste) to create and evoke memories? I had finished all my Ph.D. courses and published three peer-reviewed academic articles. At the time, the department had a policy that a Ph.D. student could graduate after publishing six academic articles instead of a dissertation. I was almost there and on track to be a professor. I was engaged to my husband, and our wedding was imminent.

Everything seemed perfect from outsiders' eyes and society's standards. But I wasn't happy—I was lost and confused. I was under a lot of the "publish or perish" pressure. During a psychological evaluation at my therapist's office, she noted that I was a free spirit and questioned why I was in a Ph.D. program conducting data analysis. Although I could manage the technical aspects of statistics and data, my heart longed for creativity and freedom. One time while presenting my research findings to professors and peers, everyone asked about the beautiful background image on my PowerPoint. I explained it was a perspective painting I had drawn of the Schuylkill River Boathouse Row historical neighborhood in Philadelphia. They were surprised to learn I wasn't in architecture school. This moment reminded me of my childhood dream of becoming an architect. When I was growing up in 1980s China, societal and family expectations made it seem nearly impossible for a woman to succeed in architecture while balancing work and family life. All my life I had worked hard to achieve what society and my family wanted for me: a high-paying, stable job; a nice husband; and a family.

I want to share with you my quest to answer these soul-searching questions, which resulted in writing this book. My wake-up call led me to quit my Ph.D. program and begin a deep spiritual self-discovery and self-healing journey. I became an avid student of spiritual wisdom and the soul for more than a decade, and I now have extensive knowledge about Western and Vedic Astrology, Enneagram, Numerology, Feng Shui Birth Element and Kua Number, Human Design, and Gene Keys for self-discovery. I became an aura intuitive, certified yoga and meditation teacher, Ayurveda practitioner, Vedic astrologer, Theta healer, certified crystal healer, and angelic channeler.

Professionally, I returned to school for a second master's degree in architecture and interior design, becoming a licensed architect and interior designer in California. I reconnected with my late father, a second-generation Feng Shui master, traditional Chinese painter, and calligrapher, and became a third-generation Feng Shui master and professional intuitive painter. In 2013, I founded See Beauty Design LLC to offer Feng Shui interior design. I could read the energies of spaces and their inhabitants, creating custom surface pattern designs aligned with clients' Feng Shui Birth Elements and Kua Numbers. In 2018, See Beauty Design evolved into Helen Creates Beauty LLC, encompassing my expertise in intuitive painting and crystal grid art, Feng Shui interior design, holistic healing, and spiritual teaching. As a professional painter, interior designer, and crystal healer, I became increasingly clairvoyant and sensitive to energies and aura colors.

As I searched for happiness and fulfillment, meditation became my medication for anxiety and depression. My first meditation experience

Introduction

was during my yoga and meditation teacher training led by Ed Zadlo at Yoga on Main in Philadelphia. He is a direct student of Dr. David Frawley, founder and director of the American Institute of Vedic Studies. I cried like a baby after my first group meditation session. I felt something bigger than me holding me the whole time, an energy of unconditional love. Since then, meditation has become my daily go-to more than the Asana (physical poses) practices.

I began with the 21-day meditation challenge app with Deepak Chopra and Oprah Winfrey, which is mainly primordial sound or mantra meditation with one point of focus. I've tried mindfulness meditation, transcendental meditation, and Vipassana (insight meditation). When my mind became quiet enough and I noticed the "invisible" energy, I incorporated crystal healing into my meditation practice. I became a certified crystal healer and advanced crystal practitioner with Ashley Leavy at the Love and Light School of Crystal Therapy.

I've explored all the major meditation techniques, from traditional to new age. No matter which meditation technique I choose to practice, it all leads to Oneness—the feeling of connectedness with everything and everyone around you. At the beginning, it's just a matter of quieting the monkey mind and relaxing the body. As you continue practicing, you notice you can stay longer in that quietness, the silence or space in between thoughts and emotions. When this happens, you begin to sense beyond your physical body and tap into what is known as the invisible (to our physical eye) quantum field. You can feel that you are vibrating in a higher frequency, just like the hummingbird fluttering its wings so fast they become invisible. The closest thing to this is the travel of light. At an energetic level, you are not your physical body; you are a light being. You become a channel of light; you begin to have glimpses of all the light beings in the cosmos. You become one with the Universe and everyone and everything around you. It's like Rumi once said, "You are not a drop in the ocean. You are the entire ocean in a drop."[1]

After six to seven years of daily meditation practice, I began to see visions in my third eye chakra, an energy center in the middle of our foreheads (I will discuss this in detail in Chapter 1). I saw glimpses of my past lives, spirits in different forms, and my future self, sometimes in holographic form. In the spiritual world, it is known as the kundalini awakening, where you feel a surge of energy rising up from the bottom of your spine to the top of your crown. I then continued my spiritual studies with various spiritual teachers. To sustain a high vibrational living, I incorporated Ayurvedic dietary recommendations for my dosha and Chinese traditional medicine, which I grew up with in the form of teas and supplements.

During a period of past-life regression work and deep spiritual awakening in 2022, I realized the answers to the questions, "Who am I?" "Why am I here?" and "How can I be happy?" from our soul's perspective. *We are all souls here to walk a human path. Our purpose for incarnating on planet Earth is to evolve—to offer our soul gifts, heal our soul wounds, and learn soul lessons we haven't resolved from our past lives. How can we be happy? Well, by consciously choosing to align our intentions and actions with our souls' evolution path: sharing our soul gifts with the world to be of service, healing, and learning our soul wounds and lessons.* We will likely incarnate again and again until all our soul wounds are healed and lessons learned. When our souls reach this point—the ancient sages call this "enlightenment"—our souls exit the incarnation cycle, and we can choose to remain in the spirit realm or incarnate on planet Earth again to help other souls ascend. This is our souls' ascension process. "En-light-en-ment" is the process of embodying light. Our soul's purpose is to evolve, clear all the blockages, and return to this harmonious full-spectrum rainbow of light. But how do we do this? How do we discover our soul gifts and identify our soul wounds and lessons?

THE ORIGINS OF THE AURA COLOR WHEEL SYSTEM

In 2022, I channeled a systematic and dynamic self-discovery system with my spirit team, the Dragon's Eye. There were four key deep channeling experiences to the process. The first deep channeling experience was during a "remembering my soul gifts" meditation. A 19th-century English philosopher named Herbert Spencer showed up as a spirit guide of mine. He developed Social Darwinism, applying Charles Darwin's evolutionary theory to the study of society. He told me I should write a book on soul evolution.

Then in a subsequent meditation, I was shown the ceilings of Hathor Temple at Dendera, Egypt. I haven't been to Egypt in person, but the vision was so vivid, and I confirmed it with Google Images later. I saw the Dendera Zodiac calendar on the ceiling, which consists of 36 "decans," or spirits, around the circumference, symbolizing the 360 days of the Egyptian year. It is considered the only complete "map" of the ancient Egyptian sky. The 36 decans correspond to the 36 Soul Aura Color profiles in the Aura Color Wheel system.

I was also guided to explore the significance of the number 36. Historically, the number 36 in Jewish traditions holds a profound meaning: the Midrash recounts that the original light, created by God on the first day, lasted for precisely 36 hours before being replaced by the sun on the fourth day. Additionally, the Torah emphasizes the importance of kindness toward strangers through 36 mandates. The belief in 36 righteous individuals, known as "Lamed Vav Tzadikim," in each generation upholds the world's existence. During Hanukkah, 36 candles are traditionally lit on the menorah over the eight-day festival, not counting the shamash, or helper candle.

Another deep channeling experience occurred during a cosmic origin meditation. A crab appeared in my vision. It was walking on a rocky planet radiating turquoise-blue rays of light. I drew the image and googled the meaning. A picture of the Crab Nebula showed up, and I felt chills and goosebumps throughout my whole body. This planet was my home. I was a Pleiadian star being before I came to Earth after my home exploded (now the remains are called the Crab Nebula). Pleiades is known to be a central hub or "school of learning" for all extraterrestrial souls. This school is said to evoke incredible nurturing talents, heal feminine and masculine energy imbalances, and hone creative energy. The Pleiadians are souls from the Pleiades cluster (also known as the Seven Sisters) in the Taurus constellation. They are creative, intuitive, and dedicated to raising the vibration of the planet and sharing new consciousness through creation. Pleiadian Starseeds create, write, speak, or channel.

THE AURA COLOR WHEEL

I channeled the Aura Color Wheel system in the following four to six weeks. During this period, I began to perceive holographic images in my third eye vision, revealing people with different aura colors around their hearts. The stronger aura layers appeared more vibrant, while the soul wound aura layer was weaker or barely visible. It was as if a prism reflected the stronger aura layer colors while absorbing the weaker ones. This vision formed a 12-color additive color wheel, each color having two tints, representing the 36 Soul Aura Colors, spinning in the ceilings of the Dendera Zodiac calendar. For about two weeks, I remained in a channeling state by meditating, praying, researching, and engaging in automatic writing, with minimal food and water intake. Interestingly, despite the limited intake, I slept a lot and received a wealth of information and insights while in the Theta state during sleep.

Our personal Soul Aura Color reflects the composition of our soul gifts, soul wounds, and soul lessons. When we offer our soul gifts, heal our soul wounds, and learn our soul lessons, more strong aura layers are added to our personal auric field. In the ascension process, we say that our light quotient (the amount of energy that our light body absorbs, carries, emits, and embodies) has increased. The more we do spiritual work and heal ourselves, the more light quotient we have in our auric field. When we are fully healed from our soul wounds and have learned our soul lessons, we exit the incarnation cycle—this is what we call enlightenment in spirituality. We become light beings like most ascended masters, such as Buddha and Jesus, who have incarnated as humans with physical bodies but obtained enlightenment during their lifetimes.

HOW THIS BOOK CAN HELP YOU

I have used this Aura Color Wheel system to heal my clients and help hundreds of students find and live their purpose with joy and fulfillment. I also teach the theory and techniques that I include in the book in my signature Flowing with Your Rainbow online spiritual course, which has brought major transformations to my students and named me a visionary educator on MSN.com.

Introduction

Some of my personal experiences may sound mystical or even esoteric to you, especially if you grew up in the traditional scientific educational system like I did. But it won't diminish the benefit of using the Aura Color Wheel system for self-discovery. I want to remind you that we are spiritual beings having a human experience but not the other way around. Therefore, we are ready to connect with our soul's guidance the moment we are born. I use the Aura Color Wheel on my nine-year-old daughter for her healing and soul-gift building. This book will teach you how to discover your Soul Aura Color, so that you can understand your soul gifts, soul wounds, and soul lessons in this lifetime. This self-knowledge and consciousness will help you:

- identify and share your soul gifts with confidence to live a fulfilled and abundant life;
- bring conscious awareness to heal your deep soul wound on all levels of consciousness—physical, emotional, mental, and spiritual—so that you are free from suffering;
- learn your soul lessons, so that you can remove any blockages from manifesting your best life;
- choose consciously to shapeshift into a different Soul Gift Archetype or embody multiple Soul Gift Archetypes simultaneously with your free will to manifest your wildest dreams!

For example, my student Jessica struggled with low self-esteem and confidence, stuck at a government job that she hated for the sense of security. After a year of practicing the spiritual tools recommended in this book, she became a professional painter and musician, living her dream life. Helping others find their purpose is my purpose. The Aura Color Wheel offers a proven method, so you don't need to spend a decade searching for it.

HOW TO USE THIS BOOK

This book has three parts. In Part I, I explain what auras are and how they relate to our chakras. I also introduce the nine Soul Gift Archetypes and the Aura Color Wheel and help you identify your archetype. Once you know your archetype, you can read the corresponding chapter in Part II to determine your Soul Aura Color, so that you can discover your soul gifts, soul wound, and soul lessons. Finally, in Part III, I share my favorite spiritual tools for maintaining your aura health and connecting to your spirit team for soul-aligned guidance, so that you can ultimately embody every aura layer, become a rainbow light body, and attract all good things into your life.

This book is your companion for ongoing soul growth. Use it to identify your archetype and Soul Aura Color and harness your soul gifts. Leverage the knowledge of aura layers and chakras to understand your soul lessons or wounds, and utilize the tools provided to balance your aura layers. As you heal and evolve, return to this book to discover your new archetypes and Soul Aura Colors. Increased self-awareness and the use of your soul gifts for service, along with preventative care for aura health, will attract opportunities, synchronicities, and the right people, making life flow easily and happily.

Knowing my Soul Aura Color is Tangerine with an Artist Archetype transformed my life. It reassured me of my gifts and helped me overcome imposter syndrome. Realizing I was born an Artist Archetype made me regret not following my childhood dream of becoming an architect. This simple yet powerful perspective shift allowed me to embrace my true self without apology, aligning my actions with my soul's purpose. When I fully surrender to my soul and spirit guidance, things manifest effortlessly. My first client, a wedding gown boutique owner, appeared before I even finished my business formation paperwork. I received this book contract after following my soul's guidance to channel the book and discovering an e-mail about Hay House's writers' community contest.

Understanding that the Tangerine Soul Aura Color has a soul wound in the blue aura layer powered by the throat chakra (see Chapter 7) explained my childhood conformity and physical symptoms like

Introduction

nosebleeds and frequent strep throats. This awareness now guides my self-care, focusing on balancing my throat chakra.

When facing adversities, knowing the soul lessons associated with my Soul Aura Color helps me identify issues before they become major problems. This self-awareness allows me to live in the present, avoiding anxiety and depression, and empowers me to make conscious choices. Oprah Winfrey's wisdom about recognizing life's "pebbles" before they become "bricks" applies here.[2] This self-awareness is profound because it places me in the driver's seat of my life instead of being a victim of my life circumstances.

Recognizing my Soul Aura Color's evolution to a full spectrum of rainbow aura unlocks my potential, eliminating fear and connecting me with my soul and spirit guidance. Life flows with joy and fulfillment. I can literally shapeshift into any archetype when my aura layers are healthy and strong to manifest all the good things in life.

Knowing who you are, why you are here, and how you can be happy is an internal job. You can't find the answers from your therapists, coaches, other successful people, or even your parents. Your personal energy composition through your Soul Aura Color holds the key to unlock this information. The more self-knowledge you have on your unique energy composition and how to keep your Soul Aura Color balanced and whole, the more purpose, joy, abundance, love, and fulfillment you find in your life. If you continually return to your soul and spirit team, the next right action guidance will forever be your internal GPS. The Aura Color Wheel aims to equip you with this self-knowledge to unlock your full potential and live your soul's purpose with joy and fulfillment.

PART 1

AURAS AND SOUL GIFT ARCHETYPES

CHAPTER 1

WHAT ARE AURAS AND CHAKRAS?

Light is our soul's essence. Beyond our physical body, humans are energy bodies made up of aura layers. An aura is the three-dimensional egg-shaped electromagnetic field around your body, powered by your main energy centers, or chakras. Your aura color is the light energy you radiate. Everything on Earth radiates energy, and energy is information that vibrates. Everyone's energy is vibrating at different amplitudes and frequencies, thus corresponding with different color waves or the aura colors that surround us. Our aura has layers like an onion, and each aura layer is powered by what's called the chakras, which are wheels of energy along our spine.

Chakra energy manifests in various forms—physical, emotional, mental, and spiritual—and each can become imbalanced. For instance, Miranda experienced pain in her left hip, thighs, and lower back. According to the chakra characteristics descriptions in Chapter 2, this indicates imbalances in the root and sacral chakras, as hips and thighs are governed by the root chakra, and the lower back by the sacral chakra. The left side of the body relates to Yin energy: feminine and hormonal issues. When a chakra imbalance manifests physically, Ayurveda (see Chapter 14) is my go-to recommendation. I suggested Miranda check her Ayurvedic Dosha. She discovered her Kapha was elevated and did a cleanse with recommended diet and herbal supplements. After two weeks, her pain was gone.

Another client, Laura, came to me wanting to know when she would find her soulmate. I asked her to take the Soul Aura Color quiz and found she had a soul wound in her heart chakra. Through deep conversations and Theta healing sessions, we uncovered her self-limiting belief that she didn't deserve to be loved. This was an emotional, mental, and spiritual manifestation of a chakra imbalance. We worked on self-compassion, inner child healing, clearing limiting beliefs, and shadow work with the assistance of Archangels Raphael and Chamuel. After 18 months of soul healing and integration sessions, she found her soulmate.

After identifying your Soul Aura Color, you will learn about your soul wound and soul lessons aura layers. Even your soul gift aura layers can become imbalanced or need strengthening. Understanding the characteristics and holistic energy medicine and soul healing practices (Chapter 2) is crucial for self-healing.

For example, a typical blocked orange aura layer healing session might include: wearing crystals like tangerine quartz, amber, vanadinite, or orange calcite; drinking carnelian crystal elixir; eating orange foods; drinking jasmine or orange blossom tea; self-massaging with tangerine, orange, or geranium essential oils; practicing bridge yoga poses; listening to 417-Hz solfeggio frequency; meditating facing west; calling in Archangels Gabriel and Raguel, nature spirits, and the fairy realm for spiritual guidance; living according to the Wheel of the Year, moon phases, and days-of-the-week energies; releasing stuck emotions; setting healthy boundaries; and cultivating creative flow.

THE THREE TYPES OF AURA COLORS

There are three types of aura colors: the mood aura, the personality aura, and the soul aura. The mood aura color can change and shift rapidly, and it frequently depends on our mood, the people we are with, and the environment we are in at the moment. This color normally shows up around your face. The personality aura color is semipermanent. It's mainly the composition of our soul gifts' aura colors when we were born. This color can be influenced and often changes until we become a teenager and have a stronger sense of self.

It is relatively stable during our adult years, but it still shifts if major events happen in our lives. This aura color typically shows up around your head. The Soul Aura Color is deep within our souls, and it's the most permanent aura color of the three. It comprises the energy of our soul gifts, soul wounds, and soul lessons. It changes only when deep healings and learnings have occurred, and we incorporate these healings and learnings into our daily actions for a period of time. It mainly radiates from our heart chakra, so it typically shows up around our heart. This is the aura color we will focus on in this book.

Of course, the three types of aura colors can overlap, and sometimes two or three of them can be the same during a period of time in your life. They just radiate in different areas of your body.

One of the most common requests I receive from people when they know I am an aura color intuitive is to immediately ask for a reading. I can detect someone's mood or personality aura color quite quickly; however, it takes me longer to accurately identify their Soul Aura Color. This is because sometimes your current soul lesson energy is even weaker than your soul wound energy. For example, I was at a friend's dinner party, and a new friend asked me where her soul wound was located. I could sense her fear and insecurity, and her aura color was lacking red, so I said the red aura layer was her soul wound. However, after she took the Soul Aura Color quiz, she discovered her soul wound was in the blue aura layer. But at the time she was indeed experiencing a sense of doubt and insecurity, which was the soul lesson she was learning; this lack of red aura layer energy was so strong that it made me think it was her soul wound. I strongly urge you to take the quiz in the book to identify your Soul Aura Color, because most aura readers can intuitively pick up what you are working on but might not be accurately identifying your soul purpose if they don't spend enough time with you.

HOW TO SENSE YOUR AURA

Although it may take some spiritual practices like meditation for you to "see" or perceive aura colors, you can *sense* your aura layers easily. Here is a simple step you can follow to sense the energy around you.

THE AURA COLOR WHEEL

How to Sense Your Aura

Hold your hands out at your sides and, keeping them at an arms-length distance with your palms facing your ears, slowly move your arms and bend your elbows horizontally with your palms toward your ears (see image above). When you sense a slight buzzing, a small electrical charge, and warmth—almost like sparks—that's where the outer limits of your aura merge into the cosmos. As your palms keep moving inward toward your ears, every time you feel a slight resistance that emits a rippling sensation—like air blown from a very weak fan—that's the edge of each aura layer. The innermost edge of the aura layer (red) will almost touch the hair. With more practice, this will become easier.

WHAT IS YOUR SOUL?

Since I use the word *soul* to describe this more permanent aura color, it's useful to clarify here what I mean by the soul. According to the dictionary, it means "the spiritual or immaterial part of a human being or animal, regarded as immortal." I agree with this definition and would add that it is the light energy that enters your body when you are born. It contains all the memories of your past lives. It's housed inside of your heart chakra, one of the most important energy centers along your spine.

Merkaba is the vehicle of our light body and soul. It is an Egyptian term translated as Mer (light) Ka (soul) Ba (body). It resides in our heart chakra and interlinks our light, soul, and physical body. Our Soul Aura Color predominately radiates here. The sacred geometry Mer Ka Ba has two opposite interlocking tetrahedrons spinning in opposite directions in our heart chakra. In a two-dimensional drawing, it looks like three triangles laid on top of one another rotating 180 degrees. It's known as the chariot of the soul and must be activated to achieve ascension, to graduate from human school and return to the light source. Here's an illustration of this sacred geometry:

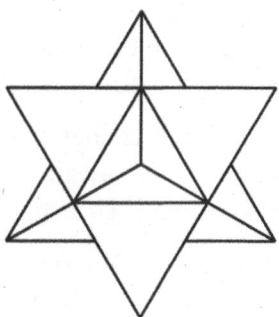

Our soul's evolution will bring us back to this harmonious full-spectrum rainbow of light.

The more soul work we do to heal our soul wounds and learn our soul lessons, the higher the light quotient we will have. Once the light body is activated, spiritual practices in unconditional love are necessary to elevate the light body to the rainbow body state. The rainbow body is the result of maintaining a constant frequency of unconditional love.

THE CHAKRAS

Chakra is a Sanskrit word meaning "wheel." Our aura field has seven layers powered by the chakras, the wheels of spiritual energy along our spine. These chakra energies are the powerhouses for each aura layer in our electromagnetic field. The chakra energy system originated from India's ancient Hindu philosophical texts, the Vedas, written between 1500 and 500 B.C.E. There are seven major chakras (energy centers) along our spine; six of them are within our body, with the crown chakra at the top of our crown. The seven major chakras are root chakra, sacral chakra, solar plexus chakra, heart chakra, throat chakra, third eye chakra, and crown chakra.

THE AURA COLOR WHEEL

1. ***Root chakra*** is at the base of our spine, and it powers the red aura layer. This aura layer is also called the etheric/physical body, because it governs our overall physical health as well as the etheric realm and subtle energy body relating to our ancestors, karma, and past lives.

2. ***Sacral chakra*** is a few inches below the navel. It powers the orange aura layer and governs our emotions, sexuality, fertility, and creativity. It's also called the emotional body.

3. ***Solar plexus chakra*** is a few inches below the sternum. It powers the yellow aura layer and governs our thoughts and self-identity. It's also called the mental body.

4. ***Heart chakra*** is in the center of our chest, and it's the home for our soul and inner guidance. It powers the green aura layer and is called the astral body because it's connected to the nonphysical realm of our body. Astral travel is a psychic ability we all possess described as an out-of-body experience—your soul is traveling somewhere else, witnessing your body lying below. It's also your soul's connection with other souls, the collective, and everything: the oneness realization.

5. ***Throat chakra*** is located in the throat and the front and back of the neck. It powers the blue aura layer and is an energetic record of what is going on in your physical body. It can be holographically projected, which means you can access it from anywhere in the Universe. It's also the blueprint of our truth, and that's why this aura layer is called the etheric template body. We strengthen or heal this aura layer by knowing who we are, expressing our truth, and taking soul-alignment actions toward our purpose.

6. ***Third eye chakra*** sits in the center of the forehead, above the eyebrows. It is the seat of our intuition. It powers the violet aura layer and is called the celestial body, because it is our connections to the stars, our soul families, and star families. It's beyond our physical body and a spiritual connection in the cosmos.

7. ***Crown chakra*** is right above our crown, and it powers the white aura layer. It's the totality of all the aura layers as a whole and your connection to your spirit team. This aura layer is called the ketheric template or causal body, because it holds all of your soul's past, present, and future memories. This layer is not included in the Aura Color Wheel system, because when you heal and strengthen all the other aura layers, this aura layer's vibrational frequency will increase to match the Divine. People radiate this aura color after they've healed their soul wounds and learned their soul lessons. When all the aura layers are strengthened and combined, their soul aura becomes mostly white. These are the souls who have awakened and led a conscious lifestyle to maintain their aura health.

Besides the seven major chakras, there are four more "higher chakras," which will activate once you've worked on your spiritual energy system for a consistent period. These "higher chakras" are higher in their vibrations but not necessarily in the position of our bodies. They are the Earth Star Chakra (6 to 12 inches below our feet), Gaia Gateway Chakra (12 inches or more below our feet), Soul Star Chakra (6 to 12 inches above our head), and Stella Gateway Chakra (12 inches or more above our head). The Earth Star Chakra and Gaia Gateway Chakra are our connection to Mother Earth. The Soul Star Chakra and Stella Gateway Chakra are our connection to Father Sky, heaven, or divine energy.

These higher chakras are the gateways to light. They will be activated after a consistent spiritual practice, so that we can have a direct experience with the divine matrix and the quantum field. These energies are not chakras that can become imbalanced; we can just be more connected or disconnected from them. The more soul work you've done, the more connected experiences you will have. These chakras are the gateways to Mother Earth's and Father Sky's energy in connection with our soul, so that we can understand our soul's purpose, integrate what we are experiencing, seed the light on Earth, and have more direction.

THE AURA COLOR WHEEL

Here is an illustration of the chakras and corresponding aura layers and colors:

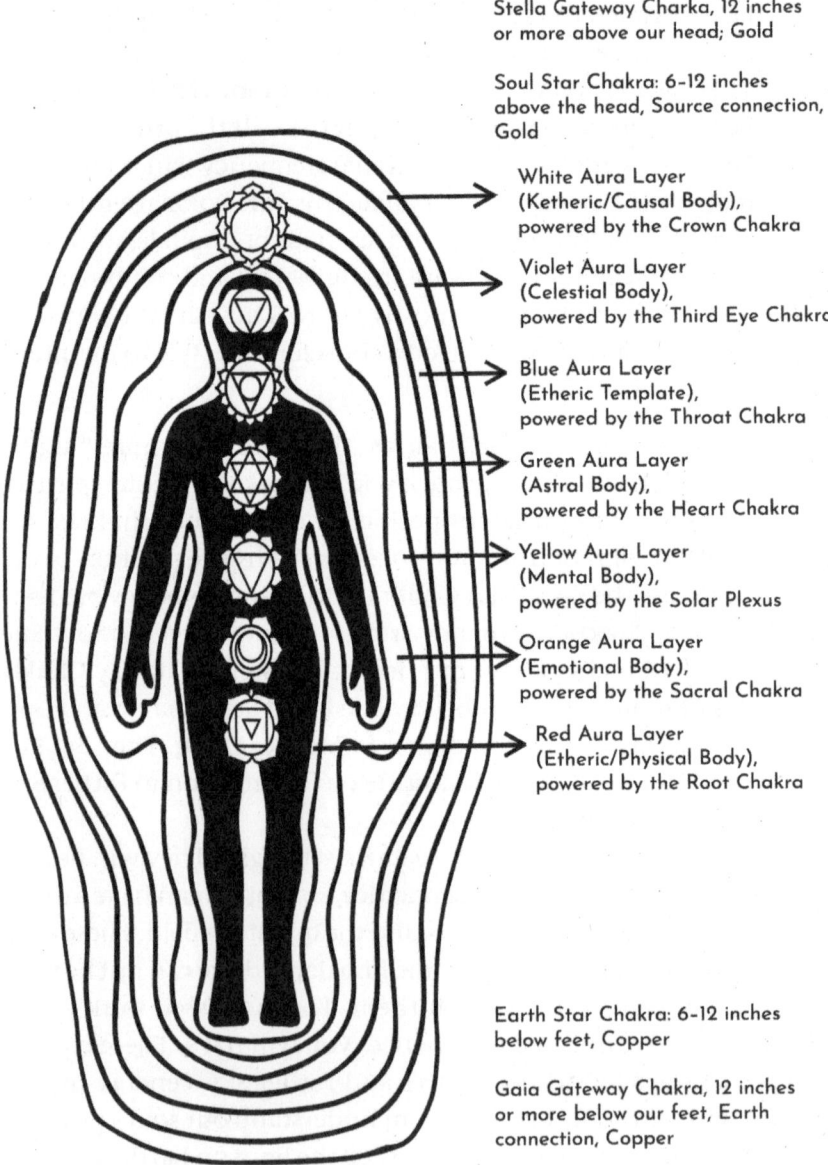

WHY AND HOW SPIRITUAL HEALING AND MANIFESTATION WORK

The image illustrates that our physical body is encompassed by our emotional body, which in turn is encompassed by our mental body. Collectively, these are all contained within the spiritual body associated with the higher chakras. This hierarchy explains how our mind has the capacity to heal our emotions, and together, our mind and emotions can facilitate physical healing. Positive affirmations play a crucial role by transforming negative mental patterns into positive thoughts, thereby improving our mood and overall physical well-being. This also explains why prayers and connections with the spirit realm, made through the outer layers of your auric field, can facilitate healing on mental, emotional, and physical layers. While many still refer to these experiences as miracles, they are simply the natural ways in which our auric field functions. In the next chapter we'll look more carefully at healing chakra imbalances.

When you view the aura layers from the inside out, it becomes clear that manifesting with Source energy starts from within. Gaining clarity about who you truly are and what you desire to create in alignment with your soul's purpose is essential (see spiritual meaning of the root chakra in Chapter 2). By embodying the emotions and mindset of the version of yourself who has already manifested your dreams, you naturally broadcast powerful energetic signals through the outer layers of your auric field to the Universe. This alignment invites the Universe to co-create the reality you wish to experience.

CHAPTER 2

YOUR GO-TO AURA LAYER HEALTH GUIDE

In this chapter, we'll focus on using the aura layers and chakras to help you self-diagnose and heal. I will provide characteristics and spiritual tools for each chakra and its corresponding aura layer so that you can discover and heal any imbalances. You may recognize yourself in some of the descriptions. For example, if you suffer from anxiety, your root chakra may be blocked. If you suffer from frequent colds, you may need to balance your heart chakra. It's good to have a basic understanding of each of your chakras, but it will be especially helpful once you know your Soul Aura Color and your corresponding soul wounds and soul lessons.

CHARACTERISTICS AND SPIRITUAL TOOLS FOR EACH CHAKRA/AURA LAYER

Based on more than a decade of study and working with energies, I've included a summary of location, characteristics, symptoms, and various holistic practices for each major chakra/aura layer. It's not all-inclusive, but it will help you obtain a good understanding of when each chakra (energy center) is in or out of balance. These recommendations and antidotes are not a substitution for medical diagnoses or treatments.

They are, however, a good addition to your treatment plan to heal from the root cause or at a soul level. The holistic energy medicine listed below for each chakra and aura layer is part of your spiritual toolbox to strengthen that energy center's soul gifts, heal the soul wounds, and learn the soul lessons.

When you become more self-aware, you can easily self-diagnose and use your intuition to "heal" certain areas of your life. For example, if you are attracted to certain colors, sounds, music, or smells, or feel good after you eat certain types of food or drink certain types of tea, it's because you either need that energy to heal your soul wound or to recharge that energy you radiate out using your soul gifts to be of service.

Please remember that *yoga* in Sanskrit means "to unite" with God or universal consciousness. Therefore, yoga poses are not simply poses but are designed to put your physical body into the optimal state to meditate so that you can commune with God—connect with your spirit team (see Chapter 18).

The chakra symbol is a sacred geometry that serves as a visual representation of the energy for each aura layer. You can meditate while gazing at it in and out of focus when you are working on a specific chakra or aura layer. You can also use these symbols as a crystal grid base to affirm your intention for working on a specific aura layer (see Crystal Healing in Chapter 17).

The Feng Shui directions can help when you're doing a certain aura layer's work (see Feng Shui in Chapter 15). For example, I would recommend you face the northeast direction when you're performing ancestral wound healing or trauma clearing work, because it's related to the red aura layer powered by the root chakra. I've often told my creative entrepreneur friends to face west to bring in the cosmic creative energy with them on their projects. It's related to the orange aura layer powered by the sacral chakra.

Solfeggio frequencies have been recognized as vibrational sounds since ancient times with the creation of sacred music, which is believed to promote healing. When you play sounds at the frequencies recommended for each chakra and aura layer, you can bring your chakras back into resonance with their natural state.

THE AURA COLOR WHEEL

There are nine types of spirit guides (see Chapter 18) whom you can connect with and call upon for assistance when you're doing spiritual work to heal or strengthen a certain aura layer or chakra. We sense their presence and receive messages from them through our psychic abilities (see Chapter 19). Based on the vibrational resonance of each aura layer or chakra, different types of spirit guides are easier to connect with than others. For example, if one of your aura layer strengths is the violet aura layer powered by the third eye chakra, you will have a stronger connection with angel spirit guides than deities, which resonate closer to the blue aura layer powered by the throat chakra. And your clairvoyance psychic ability might be stronger than your clairaudience psychic ability in receiving spirit messages.

The archangels corresponding to each aura layer are also great to call upon to assist you with soul-healing work. You will see recommended archangels to work with depending on your Soul Gift Archetype and information on connecting with your spirit team in Chapter 18. Here is a simple prayer you can say out loud or silently to invoke a specific archangel for guidance:

> "Dear Archangel _____, please come to assist me with healing/strengthening my _____ (aura layer) on this _____ (specific issue). I am open and surrender to your guidance. Please show me signs, symbols, and messages that are easy for me to understand. My heart is full of gratitude, thank you, thank you, thank you."

Root Chakra: Red Aura Layer

Symbol:

Location: Between the anus and genitals
Color: Red (wearing or visualizing shades of red in meditation strengthens this aura layer)
Mantra: Lam

Musical Key: C
Element: Earth
Sense: Smell
Psychic Abilities: Clairsalience, Physical Sympathy, Psychometry

Characteristics of the Red Aura Layer

- *Physically Governs:* legs, ankles, feet, skeleton, joints, muscles, the cell structure, the bowels (constipation or diarrhea), the prostate, the circulatory system, the groin area, sciatica, and the large intestine. If any physical dis-ease occurs in these areas, it means your red aura layer is out of balance.

- *Emotional:*
  —BALANCED: feeling of safety and security, awareness of opportunity and danger
  —OVERACTIVE: anger, aggression, frustration, paranoia, greed, control, hoarding
  —BLOCKED: depression and anxiety

- *Mental:* This layer reflects the sum of our karma (includes positive and negative patterns), past-life wounds and gifts, and ancestral wounds or gifts (in both your father's and your mother's bloodlines or in the collective—for example, if you are born Jewish, you not only have ancestral patterns passed down from your parents' bloodline but also the Jewish community as a collective influence). If any negative mental thoughts occur in these areas, it means your red aura layer is out of balance.

- *Spiritual:* This chakra develops when we are still in our mother's womb until about seven years old. It's like a computer chip encoded very early on in our lives. Therefore, it relates to who we are, what we are here to do, the lessons we need to learn, and what we need to heal in this lifetime. It also carries our ancestral traits or traumas if we have any. If you have any issues around these areas, you might have a soul wound in the red aura layer (see Spiritual Practices in the following section to heal or balance this aura layer).

THE AURA COLOR WHEEL

Holistic Energy Medicine for the Red Aura Layer

- *Crystals:*
  - —BLOCKED: red jasper, garnet, red calcite, hematoid quartz, red tiger's eye, zircon
  - —OVERACTIVE: amazonite, moss agate, snowflake obsidian, black obsidian, jet, hematite
  - —GENERAL BALANCE: carnelian, mookaite jasper, smoky quartz, petrified wood, black tourmaline, black moonstone, agate
- *Yoga Poses:* tree pose, forward bend, pigeon pose
- *Foods:* beets, red berries, radishes, peppers, kidney beans, root vegetables
- *Essential Oils:* rosewood, cinnamon, patchouli, myrrh
- *Herbs & Flowers:* hibiscus flower, red clover, hawthorn, raspberry leaf, ginger (except for Pitta Dosha)
- *Flower Essences:* ashwagandha, red poppy, horse chestnut flower, paper birch flower, teasel flower
- *Feng Shui Energy Direction:* northeast
- *Solfeggio Frequency:* 396 Hz
- *Archangels:* Ariel, Sandalphon
- *Spirit Guides:* ancestors
- *Spiritual Practices:* Ayurveda (Indian traditional diet and medicine according to your body type) and Feng Shui, because food and shelter are our basic needs, which relates to the root chakra; ancestral, karmic, and past-life trauma clearing; grounding, walking bare feet on earth, sand, or grass

Sacral Chakra: Orange Aura Layer

Symbol:

Location: A few inches below the navel
Color: Orange (wearing or visualizing shades of orange in meditation strengthens this aura layer)
Mantra: Vam
Musical Key: D
Element: Water
Sense: Taste
Psychic Abilities: Clairgustance, Clairsentience

Characteristics of the Orange Aura Layer

- *Physically Governs:* water within the body and relates to any issues with fluid retention and hydration, hormones, the reproductive system, the kidneys, fertility, the bladder, sciatica, and the lower back. This chakra is very sensitive to stress and moon cycles. If any physical dis-ease occurs in these areas, it means your orange aura layer is out of balance.

- *Emotional:*
  —BALANCED: creative, joyful, healthy relationships, self-regulation
  —OVERACTIVE: emotional swings, unhealthy relationships, indulgence, addiction
  —BLOCKED: apathetic, low libido, shame, guilt, poor body image

- *Mental:* This aura layer relates to desires in the form of affections, sex, approval, food or other oral stimulations like coffee or cigarettes, or an eating disorder, or any types of addiction. If any negative mental thoughts occur in these areas, it means your orange aura layer is out of balance.

THE AURA COLOR WHEEL

- *Spiritual:* This chakra develops when we are between 7 and 14 years old. Our inner child dwells in this aura layer. Our childhood living environment, both physical and cultural, plays an important role for this layer's development. Emotional or sexual abuse survivors often find the need to heal this aura layer. If you have any issues around these areas, you might have a soul wound in the orange aura layer (see Spiritual Practices in the following section to heal or balance this aura layer).

Holistic Energy Medicine for the Orange Aura Layer

- *Crystals:*
  —BLOCKED: tangerine quartz, amber, vanadinite, orange calcite, copper, Picasso jasper, sunstone, aragonite, pearl, carnelian
  —OVERACTIVE: chiastolite, blue apatite, amethyst
  —GENERAL BALANCE: moonstone, halite, sardonyx, Botswana agate

- *Yoga Poses:* sage twists, reverse warrior pose, bridge pose, reclined bound angle pose, goddess pose

- *Foods:* oranges, peaches, carrots, apricots, sweet potatoes, papaya, salmon

- *Essential Oils:* tangerine, orange, sandalwood, ylang-ylang, jasmine, neroli

- *Herbs & Flowers:* jasmine, geranium, orange blossom, bird of paradise, poppy

- *Flower Essences:* oriental poppy, calendula buttercup, bladderwort

- *Feng Shui Energy Directions:* west, southwest

- *Solfeggio Frequency:* 417 Hz

- *Archangels:* Gabriel, Raguel

- *Spirit Guides:* nature spirits and the fairy realm

- *Spiritual Practices:* seasonal living (Wheel of the Year, moon phases, days of the week energies), cultivating creative flow, mindful eating, emotional releasing, inner child healing, healthy relationships, and boundaries

Solar Plexus Chakra: Yellow Aura Layer

Symbol:

Location: A few inches below the sternum
Color: Yellow (wearing or visualizing shades of yellow in meditation strengthens this aura layer)
Mantra: Ram
Musical Key: E
Element: Fire
Sense: Sight
Psychic Abilities: Claircognizance

Characteristics of the Yellow Aura Layer

- *Physically Governs:* digestion, the liver, the spleen, the gallbladder, the abdomen, the stomach, the pancreas, the small intestine, metabolism, diabetes, the lower back, and the autonomic nervous system. If any physical dis-ease occurs in these areas, it means your yellow aura layer is out of balance.
- *Emotional:*
  —BALANCED: confident, motivated, strong identity, willpower, take action, ambitious
  —OVERACTIVE: anger, arrogant, manipulative, ego-driven, controlling
  —BLOCKED: powerless, lack of motivation, aimless, lack of self-identity, low self-esteem

- *Mental:* This energy center rules our thoughts, and it's vital for our mental health. It reflects our unique personality, personal power, confidence, and determination. Our first intuitive thought dwells in this aura layer, our mental body. Our basic intuitions, or gut feelings, also reside here. If any negative mental thoughts occur in these areas, it means your yellow aura layer is out of balance.
- *Spiritual:* This chakra develops when we are between 14 and 21 years old. This chakra forges our sense of identity, who we are as an individual. It also powers our self-worth and healthy self-esteem. It is the inner fire that motivates us to act on our goals for manifestation. If you have any issues around these areas, you might have a soul wound in the yellow aura layer (see Spiritual Practices in the following section to heal or balance this aura layer).

Holistic Energy Medicine for the Yellow Aura Layer

- *Crystals:*
  —BLOCKED: golden tiger's eye, imperial topaz, sulfur, heliodor, yellow jasper
  —OVERACTIVE: ametrine, blue calcite, tanzanite
  —GENERAL BALANCE: citrine, lemon (yellow) quartz, honey calcite

- *Yoga Poses:* sun salutations, warrior I, triangle, cobra, plank
- *Foods:* bananas, lemons, pineapples, mangos, corn, squash, turmeric, ginger (except for Pitta Dosha)
- *Essential Oils:* lemon, verbena, lemongrass, rosemary
- *Herbs & Flowers:* daffodil, marigold, sunflower, chrysanthemum, balsam fir
- *Flower Essences:* calendula, sunflower, buttercup flower, chamomile, dandelion, bladderwort, yellow iris, kabocha squash flower, golden rod flower

- *Feng Shui Energy Direction:* south
- *Solfeggio Frequency:* 528 Hz
- *Archangels:* Jophiel, Jeremiel
- *Spirit Guides:* animal spirits
- *Spiritual Practices:* self-discovery knowledge (Western and Vedic astrology, Feng Shui Birth Element and Kua Number, Numerology, Enneagram, Human Design, Gene Keys) and practices to cultivate healthy self-identity and boost confidence and conscious action and nonaction

Heart Chakra: Green Aura Layer

Symbol:

Location: Center of the chest
Color: Green (wearing or visualizing shades of green in meditation strengthens this aura layer)
Mantra: Yam
Musical Key: F
Element: Air
Sense: Touch
Psychic Abilities: Clairtangency, Clairsentience, Relational Sympathy

Characteristics of the Green Aura Layer

- *Physically Governs:* the heart, the chest and breasts, the lungs, asthma, pneumonia, the lymph glands, blood pressure and circulation, the upper back, shoulder problems, colds, influenza, fevers, ulcers, stress-related illnesses, signs of aging. If any physical dis-ease occurs in these areas, it means your green aura layer is out of balance.

- *Emotional:*
  - —BALANCED: compassion
  - —OVERACTIVE: jealousy, clingy, people pleaser
  - —BLOCKED: sadness, mistrust, emotional withdrawal or meltdown, difficulty with forgiveness
- *Mental:* This aura layer controls our ability to give and receive love and understand and empathize with others, without drawing in guilt or assuming too much responsibility. If any negative mental thoughts occur in these areas, it means your green aura layer is out of balance.
- *Spiritual:* This chakra develops when we are between 21 and 28 years old, when we're typically seeking love, a significant partnership, or marriage. The heart chakra marks our evolutionary leap into the first level of the four "higher" chakras—that is, the chakras that are less about human affairs, food, relationships, or promotion and more about our connection, our oneness, and our understanding of spiritual truths. It's a zone of compassion, forgiveness, generosity, and the process of grieving. It generates unconditional love. It's the seat of our soul and inner guidance. If you have any issues around these areas, you might have a soul wound in the green aura layer (see Spiritual Practices in the following section to heal or balance this aura layer).

Holistic Energy Medicine for the Green Aura Layer
- *Crystals:*
  - —BLOCKED: emerald, peridot, ruby, malachite, garnet
  - —OVERACTIVE: pink tourmaline, rhodochrosite, morganite, unakite, chrysoprase
  - —GENERAL BALANCE: rose quartz, green moss agate, jade, amazonite, aventurine, chrysocolla, rainbow fluorite

- *Yoga Poses:* cobra, warrior I with heart-opening, half-moon, supported fish pose
- *Foods:* lettuces, spinach, kale, mint, green pepper, celery, cucumber
- *Essential Oils:* rose, lotus, bergamot, eucalyptus, lemon balm
- *Herbs & Flowers:* rose, carnation, peony, cherry blossom, marjoram, helichrysum
- *Flower Essences:* lily magnolia, pink zinnia, rose, European columbine
- *Feng Shui Energy Directions:* southeast, east
- *Solfeggio Frequency:* 639 Hz
- *Archangels:* Raphael, Chamuel
- *Spirit Guides:* your soul, ascended masters
- *Spiritual Practices:* self-compassion and self-love, clearing limiting beliefs, Theta healing, shadow work

Throat Chakra: Blue Aura Layer

Symbol:

Location: Throat, front and back of the neck
Color: Light blue/turquoise (wearing or visualizing shades of blue in meditation strengthens this aura layer)
Mantra: Ham
Musical Key: G
Element: Ether
Sense: Hearing
Psychic Abilities: Clairaudience, Channeling, Trance Mediumship

THE AURA COLOR WHEEL

Characteristics of the Blue Aura Layer

- *Physically Governs:* the throat and speech organs, the thyroid gland, nose, sinuses, ears, tonsils, esophagus, eustachian tubes, teeth, gums, tongue, neck and shoulders, ear canals, and the mouth and jaw. If any physical dis-ease occurs in these areas, it means your blue aura layer is out of balance.

- *Emotional:*
  —BALANCED: communicative
  —OVERACTIVE: prone to outbursts, hyperactivity, ADHD
  —BLOCKED: shy, suppressed, speech impediments, sore throat, autism

- *Mental:* This aura layer is related to our creativity (closely working with our sacral chakra), self-expression, and communication—including body language and mental contact (telepathy) and listening as well as speaking, formulating, and expressing ideas—and developing ideals. Implicated on the autism spectrum when blocked, this layer of the aura also controls dreaming. If any negative mental thoughts occur in these areas, it means your blue aura layer is out of balance.

- *Spiritual:* This chakra is related to expressing our inner truth, authenticity, and sharing the teaching we each have to give. It develops between age 29 and 35. Communicating with spirits and the universal source is an important aspect of the throat chakra. Ideals, a sense of justice, sacred knowledge, and wisdom all come from this contact, whether conscious or not. Since this chakra relates to sound, sound healing and chanting are very useful to balance this chakra. If you have any issues around these areas, you might have a soul wound in the blue aura layer (see Spiritual Practices in the following section to heal or balance this aura layer).

Holistic Energy Medicine for the Blue Aura Layer

- *Crystals:*
  - —BLOCKED: sapphire, blue kyanite, azurite, aqua aura quartz
  - —OVERACTIVE: golden healer quartz, lemon quartz, yellow apatite
  - —GENERAL BALANCE: turquoise, blue lace agate, blue chalcedony, blue quartz, angelite, aquamarine, blue opal, larimar, lapis lazuli
- *Yoga Poses:* neck and shoulder roll, bow, lion's roar, fish pose
- *Foods:* blueberries, blue butterfly pea flower, blackberries, coconut water, raw honey, herbal tea
- *Essential Oils:* lavender, chamomile, peppermint, blue spruce, spearmint
- *Herbs & Flowers:* blue lotus, bluebells, morning glory, iris, coriander, cypress
- *Flower Essences:* blue cornflower, shooting star flower, purple iris, blue lotus
- *Feng Shui Energy Direction:* center
- *Solfeggio Frequency:* 741 Hz
- *Archangels:* Michael, Haniel
- *Spirit Guides:* deities, God/Goddess
- *Spiritual Practices:* chanting; sound healing (solfeggio frequencies and binaural beats); daily affirmations; mantras; conscious communication with the self, others, and the Divine; divination tools to communicate with the spirit: automatic writing, cartomancy, pendulum dowsing, muscle testing, rune casting, scrying

Third Eye Chakra: Violet Aura Layer

Symbol:

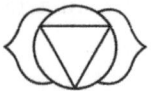

Location: Center of the forehead, above eyebrows
Color: Indigo/violet (wearing or visualizing shades of violet in meditation strengthens this aura layer)
Mantra: Sham
Musical Key: A
Element: Light
Sense: Sight
Psychic Abilities: Clairvoyance, Precognition

Characteristics of the Violet Aura Layer

- *Physically Governs:* the celestial body and the third eye chakra control the eyes, all mucus problems, headaches (including migraines), the pituitary gland, the pineal gland, the cerebellum, the forebrain, mental illness. If any physical dis-ease occurs in these areas, it means your violet aura layer is out of balance.

- *Emotional:*
  —BALANCED: intuitive
  —OVERACTIVE: lack of psychic abilities, nightmares, paranoia
  —BLOCKED: overanalyzing, dull memory

- *Mental:* When this chakra is blocked, negative ideas set in, and thoughts tumble aimlessly through our minds. This clogs up the creative paths, forming a fog in our minds that is difficult to see through. Our awareness drops and we lose touch with our senses. Intellectual and psychic abilities suffer, and we feel blocked to new ideas and stuck in an emotional and mental rut. This layer of the aura also controls dreaming. If any negative mental thoughts occur in these areas, it means your violet aura layer is out of balance.

- *Spiritual:* The third eye is the seat of our intuition and psychic abilities. It develops between the ages of 35 and 42. It acts as a receiver for a whole host of information flowing into our energy system. Most of the time this stream of data is processed subconsciously, rather like a program running in the background of a computer. As with a computer, in which we can bring a window to the front or open a new window, the third eye chakra can be brought forward to bring extrasensory information into our conscious mind. This promotes clarity, inspiration, and innovation. If you have any issues around these areas, you might have a soul wound in the violet aura layer (see Spiritual Practices in the following section to heal or balance this aura layer).

Holistic Energy Medicine for the Violet Aura Layer

- *Crystals:*
  - —BLOCKED: Herkimer diamond, labradorite, moldavite, pietersite, tanzanite, rutile, charoite, purple angelite
  - —OVERACTIVE: obsidian, shungite, black tourmaline
  - —GENERAL BALANCE: lapis lazuli, amethyst, prehnite, celestite

- *Yoga Poses:* downward dog, child pose, wide-legged forward fold

- *Foods:* eggplant, purple cabbage, purple kale

- *Essential Oils:* basil, frankincense, pine, thyme, clary sage

- *Herbs & Flowers:* gardenia, lily of the valley, wisteria, violet, palo santo

- *Flower Essences:* bull thistle, witch hazel flower, satin flower

- *Feng Shui Energy Direction:* north

- *Solfeggio Frequency:* 852 Hz

- *Archangels:* Uriel, Raziel, Zadkiel

- *Spirit Guides:* angels

- *Spiritual Practices:* develop intuition and psychic abilities: your five clair senses—channeling, precognition, astral travel, telepathy, seeing and sensing subtle energies

Crown Chakra: White Aura Layer

Symbol:

Location: Top of the head
Color: White (wearing or visualizing shades of white in meditation strengthens this aura layer)
Mantra: Om
Musical Key: B
Element: Thought (both individual and collective)
Psychic Abilities: Astral Travel, Prophecy

Characteristics of the White Aura Layer

- *Physically governs:* the skull, problems with scalp and hair growth, the autoimmune system, eczema, all neurological functions, the upper brain, the cerebral cortex, the cerebrum, and the central nervous system. It integrates the functions of the body, mind, and spirit. If any physical dis-ease occurs in these areas, it means your white aura layer is out of balance.

- *Emotional:*
  —BALANCED: connected, aligned
  —OVERACTIVE: ungrounded, ego-centered, greedy
  —BLOCKED: skeptical, isolated, hopeless

- *Mental:* When the crown chakra is out of balance, we feel unconnected. It can seem as if we are lost, wandering through life without purpose or direction. It can cause chronic fatigue (myalgic encephalomyelitis). If any negative mental thoughts occur in these areas, it means your white aura layer is out of balance.

- *Spiritual:* The crown chakra is your connection to all the energy in the Universe. It develops between the ages of 42 and 49. The Universe in this sense is God, Goddess, Universal Energy, the Tao, Krishna, Buddha, Christ, the Source, or whatever you want to call it. The name doesn't matter, but the connection does. It's our inspiration to go further, our guide providing the map of our life plan, and our light that shows us the way. This aura layer will be activated once your spiritual connection is initiated. (See Spiritual Practices in the following section to activate this aura layer.)

Holistic Energy Medicine for the White Aura Layer

- *Crystals:*
  —BLOCKED: spirit quartz, charoite, sugilite, rutilated quartz, labradorite, Herkimer diamond
  —OVERACTIVE: black tourmaline, smoky quartz
  —GENERAL BALANCE: clear quartz, amethyst, howlite, selenite
- *Yoga Poses:* shoulder stand, lotus pose, shavasana, tree pose
- *Foods:* detox and fasting (except for Pitta Dosha)
- *Essential Oils:* lavender, holy basil, lotus, water lily, sage
- *Herbs & Flowers:* lotus, water lily, cosmo, fig blossom, honeysuckle, mugwort
- *Flower Essences:* white morning glory flower, white yarrow flower, black locust
- *Feng Shui Energy Direction:* northwest
- *Solfeggio Frequency:* 963 Hz
- *Archangels:* Metatron, Azrael
- *Spirit Guides:* star beings
- *Spiritual Practices:* connect with your spirit team, star family, oneness consciousness

THE DIFFERENCE BETWEEN HEALING AND CURING

Before the end of this chapter, I want to distinguish between "healing" and "curing." A lot of modern medicine is symptom based. If you have a certain symptom, doctors will prescribe you a specific medicine to stop that symptom, so you feel better. This is curing, so you no longer have the symptom. Healing, on the other hand, targets the root cause—its definition is to bring someone back to the wholeness state, the natural homeostasis state of being. This is real soul healing, meaning that your soul is completely healed from this aspect and no longer needs to reincarnate and heal this aspect again.

One of my clients, Mary, was referred to me by her daughter after being diagnosed with stage one pancreatic cancer. She had just begun chemotherapy to try to shrink or slow the growth of the cancer, a physical manifestation of a severe yellow aura layer wound. After taking the Soul Aura Color quiz, we discovered her Soul Aura Color was Magenta with an Artist Soul Gift Archetype, and her soul wound was indeed in the solar plexus chakra.

Using the questions in the guided journal (see Chapter 13), Mary reflected on her life and realized she was happiest when doodling during her childhood. However, due to her parents' expectations and the responsibilities of raising three children, she chose a stable career as an accountant. I encouraged her to start doodling again, reconnecting with her creative joy.

For her physical symptoms, we adopted an Ayurvedic approach (Chapter 14), starting with a Pitta balancing diet. Ayurveda is my go-to for any physical manifestation of a soul wound. Recognizing pancreatic cancer as inflammation (overactive) in the solar plexus chakra, I recommended drinking elixirs made from ametrine, blue calcite, and tanzanite crystals (Chapter 17) and sleeping facing her personal Feng Shui (Chapter 15) health direction. A custom crystal grid, intended to heal her yellow aura soul wound, was hung facing her bed. She practiced the yoga poses recommended for the yellow aura layer and listened to yellow aura layer guided meditations with solfeggio frequency music.

We explored her Western and Vedic astrology birth charts, Numerology, Feng Shui Birth Element and Kua Number, Enneagram, Human

Design, and Gene Keys, helping her understand her soul's purpose and cultivate a new, empowered self-identity. She realized she was more than just a mom and daughter—she was a soul full of creativity and beauty.

During our angelic channeling sessions, we connected with Archangel Jophiel as one of her main spirit guides (see Chapter 18), associated with the yellow aura layer and the Artist Soul Gift Archetype. Mary recalled feeling Jophiel's presence while doodling and was encouraged to make conscious choices aligning with her soul.

After about six months of in-depth spiritual healing, Mary returned to the hospital for a scan and was found to be completely cancer-free. This is the power of soul healing. While I do not claim to cure cancer, this experience demonstrates the profound impact of addressing soul wounds for those willing to do the deep work.

THE UNIVERSAL LAW OF POLARITY: YIN & YANG

The antidote for an overactive chakra or aura layer is its complementary color in the color wheel. Just like all creations have both Yin and Yang polarity, chakras also work in pairs. The third eye chakra vision is brought into manifestation through the solar plexus chakra's motivated action. They are violet and yellow, complementary colors on the color wheel. Our throat chakra's personal truth and ideas are expressed by the sacral chakra's creativity. They are blue and orange, another complementary pair of colors on the color wheel. Our loving and forgiving heart chakra energy is channeled through the safety and security in our home and body from the root chakra. They are green and red, complementary colors on the color wheel.

Your root chakra mainly governs your general health and vitality, your sacral chakra governs your relationships, and your solar plexus chakra governs manifestations of money and power. The higher chakras give insights, inspiration, and meanings to the lower chakras' manifestations. If you are a musician or sound healer, you know that the vibrational frequencies/sounds from these chakra pairs are harmonious because they work closely with each other. In addition, if you find your physical symptoms are manifested on the left side of your body, it's related to the Yin element, your mother line, or your Mother Earth connection. If the physical symptoms are on the right side of your body, it's related to the Yang element, your father line, or your Father Sky connection.

The Yin and Yang pattern also occurs in the Aura Color Wheel system. In most stable couples and long-term relationships, the Soul Aura Colors of the couple are generally complementary to each other, although it doesn't have to be directly across the color wheel. For example, I know a couple where the wife's Soul Aura Color is Aqua, while the husband's is Crimson. My Soul Aura Color is Tangerine, and my husband's is Sapphire. We've been married for 14 years now. Some couples have Soul Aura Colors in the same color spectrum, like warm colors or cool colors. In terms of friendships, some long-term friendships show similar Soul Aura Colors or Soul Gift Archetypes, which we'll explore in the next chapter. These are the types of friends you vibe with and have fun with. Other friendships exhibit complementary Soul Aura Color patterns, and they are often the ones you turn to for consolation.

Now that you have a basic understanding of the auras and chakras, in the following chapters, I will introduce you to the Aura Color Wheel self-discovery system, which is based on the chakras and the aura layers powered by them. You will learn how to identify your Soul Gift Archetype and Soul Aura Color.

CHAPTER 3

THE AURA COLOR WHEEL AND THE NINE SOUL GIFT ARCHETYPES

As we mentioned in Chapter 1, there are three types of auras: mood, personality, and soul. The Aura Color Wheel focuses on the more permanent Soul Aura Color. There are three components to your Soul Aura Color: your soul gifts, one major soul wound, and three soul lessons. Your soul gift aura layers are the strongest aura colors from birth. You gained these strengths from your past lives. Your soul wound is what you are here to heal, and your soul needs to learn your soul lessons to transcend this lifetime. If you fail to heal your soul wound and learn your soul lessons, your soul will remain in the incarnation cycle until you've mastered them all.

There are six aura layers powered by the six major chakras along our spine in our physical bodies. Two of them are our soul gifts. Based on my healing work and aura color studies, I've discovered that an individual's Soul Gift Archetype is a combination of two aura layers: one aura layer powered by the lower three chakras (root, sacral, or solar plexus), and one aura layer powered by the higher three chakras (heart, throat, or third eye), which intuitively coincides with most energy-healing modalities. The higher three chakras give insights, inspiration, and meanings to the manifestation work of the lower three chakras, which ground the higher thoughts in the physical. One of the other four aura layers is our major soul wound. The other three aura layers are the soul lessons we need to learn in this lifetime.

There are nine universal Soul Gift Archetypes, each carrying its own unique purpose and power. Remember, no single archetype is more advanced than the others. The goal of your soul's evolution is to work through all of your aura layers, whether you transition into a new Soul Gift Archetype or remain in the same archetype but with a different Soul Aura Color. Each shift or continuation brings new lessons and opportunities for growth.

The aura layer powered by the crown chakra is not included in the Aura Color Wheel. Its predominant aura color is white. People radiate this aura color after they've healed their soul wounds and learned their soul lessons. When all the aura layers become their strengths, their aura color becomes mostly white. These are the souls who have awakened and led a conscious lifestyle to maintain their aura health.

In this chapter I'll delve more deeply into the dynamic nature of your Soul Aura Color, soul wounds, and soul lessons. I'll also explain the nine Soul Gift Archetypes, and you'll learn how to identify which archetype you are.

YOUR SOUL AURA IS DYNAMIC

One important note about the Aura Color Wheel is that your soul aura is dynamic. This means that even if you enter this life with your soul gifts, if you don't practice these skills or use them for service, the colors of strong aura layers will fade. The same is true of your soul wound and soul lessons. Once you've healed or learned one of your soul lessons, your Soul Aura Color composition will add one or more colors as your strength, but if you don't continue healing or acting on the lesson you've learned, that aura layer will fade as well. Continued spiritual practices are crucial.

Having strong aura layers as your soul gifts doesn't mean the chakras that power your soul gift aura layers will never become imbalanced. On the contrary, if you don't use your soul gift aura layers to be of service—it doesn't have to be a job; it can be your serious hobby or helping family or friends—your aura layers will become blocked. Just as ascended master Jesus once said, "If you bring forth what is within you, what you bring forth will save you. If you do not bring forth what is within you, what you do not bring forth will destroy you."[1] For example, one of my clients developed breast cancer because she didn't use her strong green aura layer to be of service, and she was born with a Healer Soul Gift Archetype. If you keep on utilizing and working on these aura layers, they remain your core strength throughout this lifetime when you maintain a natural state of balance. On the contrary, if you overuse the energy of your strong aura layers, you will need to recharge it with the holistic medicine recommended in Chapter 2. For example, my husband is a Visionary Soul Gift Archetype with strong yellow and violet aura layers. He has the tendency to over supervise. Guess what his favorite fruits are? Bananas, pineapples, and mangos. What do they have in common? They are all yellow food to recharge the yellow aura layer.

Even though you were born with a certain Soul Gift Archetype, as you heal your soul wound and learn your soul lessons, your soul aura will gain another aura layer color of strength, thus changing the color composition and allowing you to combine your strong aura layers to change into another Soul Gift Archetype. For example, if you were born with strong yellow and violet aura colors, you are a Visionary Soul Gift Archetype. You have a soul wound in the orange aura color, which is powered by the sacral chakra. As you continue your healing work, the orange aura will add to your current yellow and violet aura layers as your strength. If you combine orange and violet aura layers as your self-expression, you become the Artist Soul Gift Archetype. (You don't combine the orange and yellow aura layers because Soul Gift Archetypes consist of one aura layer powered by the lower three chakras and one aura layer powered by the higher three chakras.) However, when your soul is going through another major upgrade to a higher frequency, this aura layer might require more work to remain a strength as your Soul Aura Color composition.

Healing your soul wound and learning your soul lessons doesn't happen linearly. They can occur simultaneously or separately. Sometimes beginning a focus area doesn't mean you'll complete it first.

For example, even if your soul chooses to heal your soul wound first, and then learn one of your soul lessons, the lesson might complete to a satisfactory level before the soul wound. Then the soul lesson aura layer will become your aura strength first.

When you have healed your soul wound, learned your soul lessons, and maintained your spiritual practices for your aura health, you will possess all colors of the rainbow aura. When you add all colors together, it becomes white, the color of your crown chakra. You open your divine connection to channel the source light, becoming one omnipresent, radiant light. You can then choose to use any combination of your aura layers in a specific time and space. In other words, you can basically manifest anything. You instantaneously become one with the universal creative force with infinite possibilities. This is what people describe as the ascended master's halo (the golden aura around enlightened people) when they have achieved enlightenment.

Even before reaching enlightenment, when your soul has sufficiently healed and learned its lessons, you gain the freedom to adopt any Soul Gift Archetype or even embody multiple Soul Gift Archetypes simultaneously. As this transformation occurs, your Soul Aura Color will gradually shift toward white, indicating a radiant state. In this state, your electromagnetic auric field becomes highly attractive, drawing in all things of high vibrational quality into your life, such as opportunities and synchronicities. This effect is why such individuals are often considered "lucky," as they seem to manifest positive outcomes quickly.

For those of you just beginning your spiritual soul discovery journey, focus on your current state when taking the Soul Gift Archetype and Soul Aura Color quizzes. Use the results as insight into what aura layer might need healing or balancing. The second journaling prompt in Chapter 13 helps you identify your current Soul Gift Archetype and when you are transitioning into a different Soul Gift Archetype or Soul Aura Color. If you're further along in your spiritual journey, you might notice that some quiz answers resonate with your past self, while others align with who you're becoming. This is a sign of your soul aura's evolution, potentially reflecting both your past and future Soul Aura Colors. As I've mentioned before, your aura colors form a spectrum, shimmering like water reflections. You may embody one, two, three, or even more Soul Aura Colors simultaneously.

Your original state, possibly from a previous time in your life, reveals the Soul Gift Archetype you were born with. You will recognize and resonate with your birth Soul Gift Archetype through self-reflection, meditation, journaling, discernment, and solitude—what I like to call "dating your soul." The first journaling prompt in Chapter 13 helps you identify your birth Soul Gift Archetype and how it's related to your current Soul Gift Archetype. The more you nurture this relationship with your soul, the clearer your soul gifts become. These gifts hold the key to understanding why you are here: to use them in service, experiencing abundance and fulfillment in return.

For instance, I knew I was born with the Artist Soul Gift Archetype. As a child, nothing made me happier than coloring and creating special gifts for my friends and family. This theme repeated throughout my life, and I often considered becoming a professional artist. However, societal and parental pressures led me in a different direction. Although the Artist Soul Gift Archetype was dominant for much of my life, I have since evolved into the Teacher and Entrepreneur Soul Gift Archetypes. Yet, my original Artist Archetype still deeply influences the kind of teacher and entrepreneur I've become—a creative one with an artistic flair. Similarly, if you were born with a Healer Soul Gift Archetype and evolved into a Visionary Archetype, your healing and compassionate nature would naturally carry into your visionary leadership.

SOUL WOUNDS AND LESSONS

We all have one major soul wound to heal during this lifetime. The soul wound symptoms can be physical, mental, emotional, or spiritual. For example, when I was a kid, I had chronic nosebleeds and frequent bouts of strep throat. I knew I had to heal my blue aura layer powered by the throat chakra. Interestingly, my favorite color as a child was light blue. My soul knew I needed that color energy to heal. When I started to work with angels later during my spiritual path, I realized both my guardian angel and main archangel, Haniel, radiate light blue rays—they have been with me assisting my healing since childhood.

THE AURA COLOR WHEEL

If you heal your soul wound, it can become one of your biggest gifts in this lifetime. After I'd healed and integrated my blue aura layer soul wound, I became a channeler of the spirit realm, which requires strong throat charka energy.

Soul wounds are deeper wounds we carry from our past lives, ancestral traumas, or karmic patterns. Sometimes they are collective wounds we need to clear up from our ancestral line or traumas that have accumulated from many lifetimes, which might take longer and deeper spiritual work to heal. They typically show up in one, two, or all levels of your consciousness: symptoms that are physical, emotional, mental, and spiritual, and that require spiritual healing at a soul level rather than symptom-based healing. For example, my client Miranda had a soul wound in her red aura layer powered by the root chakra. Her mother, raised in scarcity as a child of first-generation immigrants to the U.S., experienced infidelity in her marriage. These experiences made her a protective mother who wanted to keep Miranda sheltered, particularly from men, whom she viewed negatively. Growing up, Miranda struggled to meet her mother's high expectations, finding it almost impossible. She found herself following in her mother's footsteps, unmarried and pregnant at age 19. Unfortunately, she ended up in a verbally and physically abusive relationship like her mother's. At 22, Miranda decided to end the relationship, separate from her mother's influence, and become independent. Despite facing condemnation from the community church, she focused on raising her first son. Her deep soul wound was a collective wound deeply rooted in her mother's ancestral line.

During a soul-healing session, my client Sherry opened up to me that she had been sexually abused by her older brother and verbally abused by her younger brother when she was young. She had been suffering emotionally all her life and, now in her 60s, needed help to release this pain. I asked her to take the Soul Aura Color quiz and her result was turquoise, indicating a soul wound in the orange aura layer powered by the sacral chakra. Remember in the last chapter, when we discussed that sacral chakra governs sexuality?

Fortunately, Sherry's Soul Gift Archetype is Healer, making her spiritually inclined with a well-developed violet aura layer powered

The Aura Color Wheel and the Nine Soul Gift Archetypes

by the third eye chakra. Therefore, my primary healing modalities for her were angelic channeling and crystal healing, as she could sense the crystal energy and her spirit team's presence. Her spirit team guided her toward love and forgiveness, essential for healing this wound at a soul level.

After 10 private healing sessions, Sherry decided to forgive her brothers. Her strong heart chakra's green aura energy enabled her to conquer this challenge. Remarkably, the day after our final session, her younger brother called and apologized for his past actions, even though they hadn't spoken in over a decade. Although her older brother had already passed away, both Sherry and I felt his presence and his apology. From that moment on, Sherry felt a significant emotional release, as if a heavy stone had been lifted from her chest.

Soul lessons are not as deep as soul wounds. They tend to be repeated negative patterns (either mental or behavioral) that need to be consciously changed, lessons that we need to learn in this lifetime to transcend the incarnation cycle. One of my students, Tina, struggled with finding clear direction in life and often hesitated to make decisions. As we explored the issue further, we realized she was learning her violet aura layer soul lesson, which involves trusting her intuition for guidance. We focused on developing her psychic abilities and connecting with her spirit team during meditation. After completing the Flowing with Your Rainbow Course in three months, Tina became highly intuitive and gained the clarity she previously lacked. It all began with her willingness to open up, learn, and do the work. During our last coaching call, we chuckled at the idea that she had become an intuitive wizard—no need to suffer from indecision or lack of clarity in the next lifetime.

When transitioning between different Soul Gift Archetypes and their corresponding Soul Aura Colors or remaining the same Soul Gift Archetype but in a different Soul Aura Color, you may find that your soul wounds and lessons are interchangeable. During the transition, you can view your soul wound as the most pressing issue you need to heal or work on right now. Based on the symptoms described in the previous chapter, you can intuitively know which aura layer it is. In the next section, I will share my personal journey to illustrate this process. I was born with a Tangerine Soul Aura Color, reflecting the Artist Soul Gift Archetype, with a blue aura layer as my soul wound. As I worked through healing my blue aura layer, restoring it to a balanced state, it transformed into a strength. Similarly, my yellow aura layer, which initially presented as a soul lesson, also evolved. By integrating the blue and yellow aura layers, I transitioned into the Entrepreneur Soul Gift Archetype, with a Lime Soul Aura Color. At this stage, the red aura layer emerged as my new soul wound, indicating the area I needed to heal and balance most. This is why I encourage you to take the Soul Aura Color quiz periodically, especially if you sense you're actively learning soul lessons or healing soul wounds, to see how your aura may have changed.

When you embody multiple Soul Gift Archetypes, you may notice that certain aura layers, which are strengths in one archetype, can present as soul wounds in another. This interaction between archetypes reflects the dynamic nature of our soul aura.

For example, I now embody three Soul Gift Archetypes:

- *Artist* (Tangerine Soul Aura Color) with strong orange and violet aura layers, soul wound in the blue layer
- *Entrepreneur* (Lime Soul Aura Color) with strong yellow and blue layers, soul wound in the red layer
- *Teacher* (Lilac Soul Aura Color) with strong red and blue layers, soul wound in the orange layer

This may seem contradictory at first. For instance, my orange aura layer is a strength in the Artist Archetype, yet it becomes a soul wound in the Teacher Archetype. Similarly, the red aura layer, which is a wound in the Entrepreneur Archetype, becomes a strength in the Teacher Archetype.

When working across multiple archetypes, it's essential to see your aura as a unified field rather than isolated layers. The purpose of our soul's evolution is to harmonize all aura layers, ultimately becoming a "rainbow" that radiates white light. From this holistic view, I can see that my primary focus for growth lies in my blue, red, and orange layers.

The Aura Color Wheel and the Nine Soul Gift Archetypes

Since my blue aura layer is now sufficiently healed and balanced, it allows me to embody the Entrepreneur and Teacher Archetypes alongside the Artist Archetype. Therefore, I understand that my next step in spiritual growth is to further develop my red and orange layers. Although my orange aura layer is naturally strong within the Artist Archetype, this next stage can be seen as an upgrade—refining and expanding the qualities of these layers as I evolve.

Your soul is consistently working toward healing when opportunity presents itself, whether you're aware of it or not. If you're aware and choose to work on it, you're in alignment with your soul's mission, and healing is easier and faster. However, if you're unaware when situations present themselves as opportunities for healing work and don't take any actions toward it, the Universe will provide similar situations until you make a change to resolve it. And if you keep ignoring it or suppressing it, that soul wound will be manifest in extreme forms like cancer, psychiatric emergencies, or psychic attacks. For each of the Soul Aura Colors, I offer guidance on beneficial tools for healing that specific soul wound or soul lessons. These include practices like Ayurveda, Feng Shui, living with nature's cycles, crystal healing, and connecting with your spirit team. These spiritual tools can be found in Part III of the book.

The more inner work you do to heal your soul wound and learn your soul lessons, the higher your light quotient: the amount of energy that your light body can absorb, carry, emit, and embody, which helps sustain multiple Soul Gift Archetypes simultaneously. You will reach a state of infinite possibilities. When your soul has healed its deep wound and learned its lessons while maintaining this health for a stable period, you will radiate pure white light, a combination of all your aura layers.

HOW DO WE KNOW WE HEALED A SOUL WOUND OR LEARNED A SOUL LESSON?

I want to emphasize the importance of Chapter 2, which serves as your go-to aura health guide—think of it as a checkup list for your energy, much like a regular doctor's visit but for your spiritual well-being. The

THE AURA COLOR WHEEL

more familiar you become with your aura layers, the better you can intuitively sense which layer needs healing and which layer is healed to a satisfactory degree now because you are back to balance.

Depending on whether the symptoms manifest physically, emotionally, mentally, or spiritually, you can identify the specific aura layer where a wound needs healing or a lesson needs to be learned. Once you've healed a wound or learned a lesson, the challenges related to that aura layer will diminish or disappear. For example, if you've been dealing with digestive issues (physical symptom), you might find these issues improve or resolve altogether as a result of healing a yellow aura soul wound or integrating a lesson related to self-worth (emotional, mental, or spiritual level).

When a major soul wound heals or a soul lesson is fully integrated, it often leads to a cascade of releases—physical, emotional, mental, and spiritual. Bodily inflammation is gone. You experience a profound sense of freedom and lightness, feeling renewed and ready to take inspired action again.

I'd like to share a personal experience of when I learned and integrated a soul lesson from my red aura layer. I hope this can help you identify when your soul wound is healed or lesson is learned. During the final editing phase of this book, I underwent a significant shift in understanding my red aura layer soul lesson. (You'll read more about my Soul Aura Color evolution journey at the end of this chapter.) I had long been aware that I needed to heal ancestral trauma from my maternal line. I received repeated messages from my spirit team to forgive and release my mother, but my human side resisted. My breaking point came during the launch of a spiritual course, which had fewer sign-ups than I had hoped. I knew the course was valuable and was eager to share it, yet the low engagement triggered an automatic negative thought: "Why doesn't anyone want what I have to offer?"

During a coaching session, my business coach at the time mirrored my thoughts back to me: "Helen expects a certain number of people to sign up for her course; X number signed up, and she equates this to no one wanting her work." Hearing this reflected back sounds almost ridiculous. My coach asked about the strongest emotion present and the thoughts feeding it. I realized my frustration stemmed from the belief that "no one wants my life's work," which made me feel unworthy. But my value isn't tied to how many people sign up for my course! My automatic negative thoughts had taken over, pushing me into autopilot mode.

At that moment, it became clear that these feelings were rooted in childhood memories. Growing up in China in the 1980s, where women were undervalued, I was constantly driven to prove my worth. A painful memory resurfaced later that night: When I was seven, my mom told me that our family was kicked out of my paternal grandparents' house because I was born a girl, not a boy. Throughout my life, I worked extra hard to outperform my male cousins—to get the best grades, run faster, jump higher, grow taller, do everything better—yet nothing was ever good enough for my mother. Because if I got an A in school, she would ask me, "Why isn't it an A+?" It wasn't until my early 20s that my mother revealed the real reason we were expelled from my grandparents' house: it was because of something she had said about my grandmother, which made my grandmother angry at my mother, not because of my gender. This revelation both angered and confused me; my mother had no idea how much pain her narrative had caused me.

I realized my frustration was a symptom of an overactive red aura layer (root chakra), accompanied by physical issues like bowel problems (either constipation or diarrhea). Mentally, the automatic all-or-nothing negative thought is from my mom. The beliefs that I must work hard, constantly do something to get ahead, and have a winning result to prove that I am worthy or valuable, rather than celebrating incremental achievements, are passed down generationally in women in Asian countries. This is an ancestral trauma in the red aura layer that is affecting the yellow aura layer of self-worth and my personal power to manifest the goals I want to achieve for my business.

To heal, I dedicated days to process and integrate this self-realization. I drank the detoxing and cleansing crystal elixir for the red aura layer, created an ancestral healing crystal grid, and took a self-love crystal bath (see Chapter 17). I did an ancestral trauma release ceremony: I listed all the thoughts, behaviors, and patterns that no longer serve me, which belong to my mother line and the collective energy I was associated with, and burned that piece of paper. Then I used the inner light meditation facing northeast for spiritual growth (see Chapters 13 and 15) and called all my energy fragments that were leaking my personal power in the past back into my personal auric field. I know that when I am one with Spirit, I am inherently worthy. I don't need to prove anything to be valuable. I celebrate every small victory and even the setbacks on my journey, recognizing both as acts of courage. I have learned to be patient with my growth, releasing my attachment to outcomes and embracing the beauty of uncertainty. My spirit team continues to send me countless signs—numbers, symbols, license plates, songs, tea bag messages—all reassuring me that I am on the right path!

This process brought me a profound sense of freedom. I no longer operate from a place of fear and have released the physical symptoms I was experiencing. Most important, I have forgiven my mother and released that deep-seated pain. I now see her actions were shaped by her own circumstances and cultural upbringing and have so much compassion for her. This healing journey marked a significant upgrade for my green aura layer (heart chakra). Whether my mother changes or not is irrelevant; I have not only healed my red aura layer but also made peace with the past.

This experience taught me that my ambition to share my work and help more people required a soul upgrade. By learning my red aura layer soul lesson, which also asserts my self-worth and personal power, thus upgrading my yellow aura layer, I now can embody the Teacher Soul Gift Archetype (a combination of red and blue aura layers) to better serve as a spiritual teacher and entrepreneur (yellow and blue aura layers), attracting greater success, abundance, and fulfillment. I also intuitively picked up that the Healer Soul Gift Archetype is rising in me because of my green aura layer upgrade, if my soul chooses to embody it as well. That's why I am a "spiritual" entrepreneur, because of the Healer Archetype's empathic and intuitive nature.

Interestingly, I also rebranded my business into a triad harmony of colors: Lilac (a Teacher Soul Gift Archetype Soul Aura Color), Lime (an Entrepreneur Soul Gift Archetype Soul Aura Color), and Tangerine (my original born Soul Aura Color of an Artist Soul Gift Archetype).

The Aura Color Wheel and the Nine Soul Gift Archetypes

As you can see, learning one aura layer soul lesson can also trigger or upgrade another aura layer soul lesson as well, especially when your soul is ready to increase its light quotient for you to hold the higher energy to sustain multiple Soul Gift Archetypes.

An intriguing shift can occur when you're transitioning into a new Soul Gift Archetype, especially as you begin to embody more than one archetype. You may notice that your original strong aura layer(s) require additional attention to facilitate a soul upgrade. For instance, after I completed the soul lessons of my red aura layer and elevated my yellow aura layer, transitioning into both the Teacher and Entrepreneur Soul Gift Archetypes, I realized my inner child, located in the orange aura layer, still needed deeper healing, because my mother line ancestral healing brought up lots of intense negative emotions that I needed to process. These emotions are stored in my orange aura layer, and they are related to the high expectations and verbal and emotional abuse from my mother. As you can see, each aura layer is interconnected. When a deeply rooted wound or lesson is being addressed, it can trigger healing across all aura layers, clearing away old negative energy and amplifying your soul's light.

To bring this home, I attended a conference hosted by my business coach, James, and his fiancée, Jenni, a few months later. During a Toltec recapitulation meditation guided by Jenni, painful memories surfaced once again. However, at the end of the meditation, I experienced something profound: a vision of a little girl running toward me. I gently told her, "You can rest now. Go play!" It was clear that my inner child needed this moment of release and healing.

The following day, after returning home, my daughter handed me a drawing of a bunny with a note that said, "A bunny can be a bunny, and you can be you." We have a pet bunny at home. My daughter had no knowledge of what I had experienced at the conference. At that moment, I realized a generational trauma had been healed and stopped right there. The synchronicity was profound.

This is the power of soul healing. We are all deeply interconnected at a soul level, and when you heal your own soul, you also contribute to the healing of those connected to you. The journey of soul healing unfolds in unexpected ways—it cannot be planned. You might not attend an event thinking you will have a transformative experience, yet the opportunity for growth arises when you are ready and aware of what you are working on. It is an ongoing journey, but with time, you become more attuned and skilled at it, experiencing deeper and deeper healing along the way.

Please remember that your soul wound healing and soul lesson learning process is not linear. It is more of an upward spiral like our chakra energies. You might heal a soul wound and return to a balanced state or evolve into a new Soul Gift Archetype based on your current light quotient. When it's time for your soul to have another upgrade to increase your light quotient so that you can attract even bigger fulfillment, success, abundance, joy, love, and so on, your soul will need to work on the same aura layer again, but this time you might sustain a longer and larger amount of light quotient. The story I shared here also serves as an example of my soul's upgrade to sustain three Soul Gift Archetypes and Soul Aura Colors simultaneously. This happened after I'd written my personal Soul Aura Color Evolution Journey in the last section of this chapter.

YOU CAN ALSO REMAIN IN A SOUL GIFT ARCHETYPE

Even if you heal your soul wound and learn your soul lessons, you can choose to remain in your Soul Gift Archetype instead of becoming a different archetype. My client Kimberly chose this path.

Kimberly remembered a joyful childhood experience of feeding and caring for her Christmas gift, a baby doll, on her father's lap. She always knew in her heart that she wanted to be a mother when she grew up. It was a deeply rooted knowing within her from as far back as she could remember. However, she was "touched inappropriately" when she was six or seven years old. She told her mother about it, but her mother remained silent and pretended nothing had happened. Kimberly buried this so deep that she wasn't open to discussing it until much later. During her teenage years, she had a bleeding issue, and she heard a doctor tell her mother that she would never be able to get pregnant, which made her feel sad. It was a misdiagnosis, which she

The Aura Color Wheel and the Nine Soul Gift Archetypes

found out years later. She knew deep within her that she was supposed to be a mother. Kimberly was born a Healer Soul Gift Archetype with a Turquoise Soul Aura Color. Her soul wound is in the orange aura layer powered by the sacral chakra.

She married her high school sweetheart and has been married for 39 years and has two children and five grandchildren. Her mother divorced her father because he had an affair, and she always talked negatively about him, but Kimberly chose to let go of these negative narratives in her own family. She remembered having to move into a new house and neighborhood for her children's school, which made her feel insecure. It took her a while to settle into her new home. These events in her life helped her learn the red aura layer soul lesson.

A big trigger for her soul's growth was her father's death, because they were very close. She began to see angel numbers and felt her father's spirit. Although she grew up Protestant, she has become open to all forms of spirituality and took classes to actively seek her soul's purpose. She has learned her violet aura soul lesson. This event also made her open up about her childhood sexual abuse, which was buried, unheard, and unseen. This helped her heal the orange aura layer soul wound. Her Soul Aura Color changed into Yellow (remaining the Healer Soul Gift Archetype, indicating the next pressing aura layer to heal for her is the blue aura layer powered by the throat chakra). Later, she had a discussion with her mom in a very loving and caring way. By speaking her truth, she has not only healed her blue aura layer soul wound, but also learned her blue aura layer soul lesson and is healing her orange aura layer soul wound. Remember, these two aura layers work closely together.

With this soul upgrade, I can see her inner light shine through her smile and how she talks about her life. She is radiant, attracting opportunities and synchronicities she never thought of before. She was even invited to be photographed as a model for a Goddess oracle deck! She is fully embodying her Healer Soul Gift Archetype. Although she hasn't changed into other Soul Gift Archetypes, she didn't resist healing her soul wound and learning her soul lessons when life presented her with opportunities. And she continues using her soul gift's green and yellow aura layers in her daily life raising her grandchildren and taking care of her family. She is now remaining open and receptive to spirit guidance. I can't wait to see how her beautiful soul light unfolds into that brilliant light being we all are!

THE AURA COLOR WHEEL

Color vision in humans is based on the additive color theory. This theory states that all perceivable colors can be made by mixing different amounts of red, green, and blue light (RGB), the primary colors of the additive color system. Because aura colors are fundamentally light mixing instead of color mixing, the additive color wheel is used here. The main difference between the additive and subtractive color wheels is how colors are mixed. In the additive color wheel, used for light, combining red and green light produces yellow. In the subtractive color wheel, used for painting, the primary colors are red, yellow, and blue. Yellow is a primary color and not a mix of others. When mixing red and green in the subtractive color model, the result is typically brown or a muddy color.

The Aura Color Wheel consists of 9 Soul Gift Archetypes and 36 Soul Aura Colors. The 36 Soul Aura Colors are based on a 12-color additive color wheel with two tints (adding more light) of each color. The color tints are based on luminance, the amount of light in a color. The colors closer to the center have more luminance than the true hue of the colors on the outer rim of the color wheel. Aura color is a spectrum, not one static color, with CMYK codes associated with each color. The CMYK color model is a subtractive color model used in color printing, and the abbreviation refers to the four ink plates used: cyan, magenta, yellow, and key. Your Soul Aura Color is a spectrum of colors that shift like water reflections. It's not a static color. Therefore, the Soul Aura Color is based on general color vocabulary for familiarity. I added numbers for easy reference and identification purposes; number 1 doesn't mean a better or more evolved soul than number 36. Each Soul Aura Color is produced by adding the two strong aura layers from the Soul Gift Archetype and subtracting the soul wound aura layer color from the composition. For example:

The Aura Color Wheel and the Nine Soul Gift Archetypes

Jade Soul Aura Color

= Yellow + Green (Healer Soul Gift Archetype) − Red (soul wound)

= Red + Green (Red and Green mix Yellow) + Green − Red

= An aura field that is mostly green, with some yellow, but no red

= Jade (a shade of yellow green)

THE AURA COLOR WHEEL

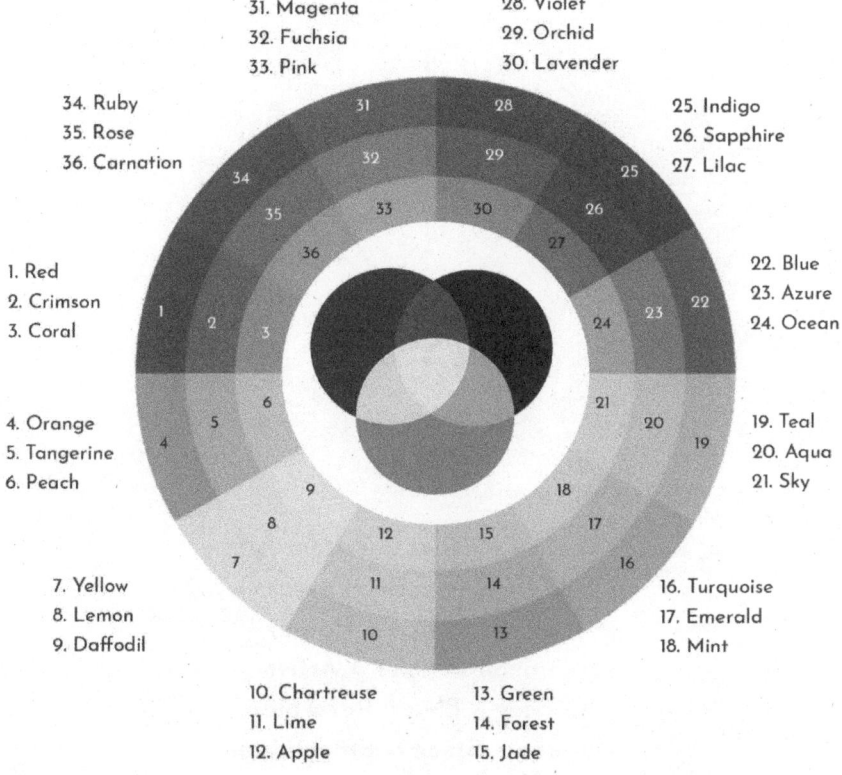

31. Magenta
32. Fuchsia
33. Pink

28. Violet
29. Orchid
30. Lavender

34. Ruby
35. Rose
36. Carnation

25. Indigo
26. Sapphire
27. Lilac

1. Red
2. Crimson
3. Coral

22. Blue
23. Azure
24. Ocean

4. Orange
5. Tangerine
6. Peach

19. Teal
20. Aqua
21. Sky

7. Yellow
8. Lemon
9. Daffodil

16. Turquoise
17. Emerald
18. Mint

10. Chartreuse
11. Lime
12. Apple

13. Green
14. Forest
15. Jade

Please visit www.helencreatesbeauty.com/pages/auracolorwheelbook for a full-color version.

THE AURA COLOR WHEEL

9 Soul Gift Archetypes

Your Soul Gift Archetype =
1 Aura Layer powered by the lower three chakras +
1 Aura Layer powered by the higher three chakras

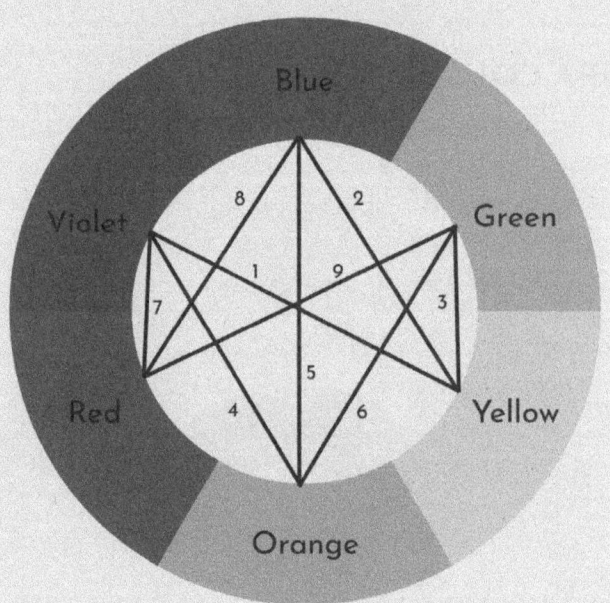

Yellow + Violet = **Visionary**
Yellow + Blue = **Entrepreneur**
Yellow + Green = **Healer**
Orange + Violet = **Artist**
Orange + Blue = **Reformer**
Orange + Green = **Entertainer**
Red + Violet = **Researcher**
Red + Blue = **Teacher**
Red + Green = **Warrior**

The Aura Color Wheel and the Nine Soul Gift Archetypes

QUIZ: FIND YOUR SOUL GIFT ARCHETYPE

Are you ready to discover your Soul Gift Archetype? For each question, please select the option that best describes you based on your current state. I highly recommend you pick an answer intuitively—don't overthink it! If you have a few questions or really can't choose an answer, please leave it blank. If you have more than one selection that applies, please select all of them. Have fun!

1. **What is your favorite color combination? (Think about your clothing, accessories, or art that you like.)**
    a. Yellow + Violet
    b. Yellow + Blue
    c. Yellow + Green
    d. Orange + Violet
    e. Orange + Blue
    f. Orange + Green
    g. Red + Violet
    h. Red + Blue
    i. Red + Green

2. **You're happiest when you're:**
    a. Leading a group to achieve your vision
    b. Building your own business empire based on your ideas
    c. Helping others to heal their wounds
    d. Creating a one-of-a-kind masterpiece of art
    e. Working for social changes to make the world a better place
    f. Performing and entertaining a crowd
    g. Researching the subjects that interest you
    h. Teaching others what you've mastered
    i. Fighting for justice and human rights

3. **Your friends and family often compliment you on:**
    a. Your vision and leadership skills
    b. Your entrepreneurial spirit
    c. Your caring and loving nature
    d. Your artistic and creative talents
    e. Your innovative ideas that move others to make changes
    f. Your fun characteristics that make people happy

g. Your deep understanding of any subject matter you put your heart into
   h. Your ability to communicate complicated concepts simply
   i. Your courage to fight for a compelling cause

4. **What is your favorite thing to do in your spare time?**
   a. Share new ideas and have deep conversations with a group of friends
   b. Be an explorer and create your own adventure
   c. Volunteer at a local animal shelter, orphanage, senior home, or garden center
   d. Do anything creative—make a piece of art, write poems, compose music, cook a new dish, or simply dance under the moon
   e. Participate in a meaningful social change or an environmental group you care about
   f. Hang out with your friends and put on a good show
   g. Participate in anything intellectual—a chess game, learning a new language, attending a lecture, etc.
   h. Read, learn something new, or write a book
   i. Do something active—outdoor sports, camping, etc.

5. **When you go out on weekends, you like to:**
   a. Hang out with like-minded friends and share your growth journey
   b. Travel and explore different foods, cultures, and people
   c. Be in nature and absorb its energy
   d. Explore galleries, museums, or gardens to be inspired
   e. Visit history museums or historical sites
   f. See a show, a play, or some kind of performance
   g. Spend time in your garage studio, making something new or testing out your ideas
   h. Learn something new that interests you
   i. Have a workout, go to a yoga class, or train in an endurance sport

6. **Look at yourself through the eyes of others. What do you see?**
    a. A solid, courageous person
    b. An independent person
    c. A loving soul
    d. A creative individual
    e. A passionate social advocate
    f. Someone full of imagination
    g. An expert in anything you put your mind to
    h. A good and supportive friend
    i. A high-energy, active friend

7. **What is your favorite type of music?**
    a. Symphony, or something spacey or futuristic
    b. Powerful, classic rock
    c. Soulful, singer-songwriter genre
    d. Something jazzy
    e. Broadway, movie musical
    f. Intriguing or engaging, something eclectic
    g. Refreshing, alternative rock
    h. Classical music, opera
    i. Energetic, dance, hip-hop, big band

8. **The colors you like to decorate your home with are:**
    a. Blue or purple
    b. Yellow and cheerful or turquoise like the ocean
    c. Relaxing green or lots of plants
    d. Eclectic, changing things up occasionally with different color themes each season
    e. Dark blue or indigo
    f. Bright and happy colors like yellow, chartreuse, and fuchsia
    g. Sky blue or deep red or violet
    h. Soft and pastel, pink, lavender, lilac
    i. Red, rust, orange

THE AURA COLOR WHEEL

9. Your view of the world is generally:
   a. It's in chaos and to live well we must act with energy and direction.
   b. Life is about diving in deep and discovering what we can.
   c. It is a spiritually informed place, whether we see it daily or not.
   d. We are all here to create using our unique talents, making the world a more beautiful place.
   e. We are all in this together, so let's help each other grow and survive.
   f. It's a fun place to be, and there are a multitude of ways to enjoy life.
   g. There's much more to the world than meets our eyes, and you hope to learn more about it.
   h. You think about the world around your and want to help others grow.
   i. We are here to get our heart pumping and our lungs full of air through activities that make us feel alive.

10. If asked in an interview, you'd say "I am":
   a. Future-directed and visionary
   b. Focused and self-directed
   c. Kind and considerate
   d. Creative and instinctive
   e. Tenacious and motivated
   f. Optimistic and connecting
   g. A curious thinker and researcher
   h. Sympathetic and communicative
   i. Full of energy and direction

Please mark down how many of each selection you have:

   a. _____   f. _____
   b. _____   g. _____
   c. _____   h. _____
   d. _____   i. _____
   e. _____

The Aura Color Wheel and the Nine Soul Gift Archetypes

If you have two or more equal selections, it can mean one of the following:

1. You have these two or more Soul Gift Archetypes in you.
2. You are shifting from one Soul Gift Archetype into another (or others).
3. Some of the Soul Gift Archetypes represent your past self, and some of the Soul Gift Archetypes are your present self.

This means you could have two or more Soul Aura Colors. Please take all the quizzes in the Soul Gift Archetypes you identify with. When you have multiple Soul Aura Colors, it typically shows up clairvoyantly as two or more gradient aura colors mixed together. However, once you finish the transition, only one Soul Aura Color will remain.

- If you chose mostly A answers, your Soul Gift Archetype is *Visionary*.
- If you chose mostly B answers, your Soul Gift Archetype is *Entrepreneur*.
- If you chose mostly C answers, your Soul Gift Archetype is *Healer*.
- If you chose mostly D answers, your Soul Gift Archetype is *Artist*.
- If you chose mostly E answers, your Soul Gift Archetype is *Reformer*.
- If you chose mostly F answers, your Soul Gift Archetype is *Entertainer*.
- If you chose mostly G answers, your Soul Gift Archetype is *Researcher*.
- If you chose mostly H answers, your Soul Gift Archetype is *Teacher*.
- If you chose mostly I answers, your Soul Gift Archetype is *Warrior*.

THE NINE SOUL GIFT ARCHETYPES

Soul Gift Archetype	Aura Layer Strength	Soul Gifts
1. Visionary	Yellow + Violet	Visionaries possess intuitive, clairvoyant abilities and often form new ideas or paradigms in their mind's eye. They are born with a strong yellow aura layer powered by the solar plexus chakra and violet aura layer powered by the third eye chakra. Because of their innate claircognizance ability, they can make decisions on the spot. They are generally confident leaders.
2. Entrepreneur	Yellow + Blue	Entrepreneurs are problem solvers and natural leaders. They are born with a strong yellow aura layer powered by the solar plexus chakra and blue aura layer powered by the throat chakra. They can lead a team of like-minded people to build something from their visions. They are a strong manifester on planet Earth.
3. Healer	Yellow + Green	Healers are compassionate and intuitive beings concerned with the well-being of humanity. They are born with a powerful green aura layer powered by the heart chakra and yellow aura layer powered by the solar plexus chakra. They combine ancient healing techniques with new ones to offer a unique blend of medicine to the world.

The Aura Color Wheel and the Nine Soul Gift Archetypes

Soul Gift Archetype	Aura Layer Strength	Soul Gifts
4. Artist	Orange + Violet	Artists are the channelers of the Divine and beauty creators of the planet. They are born with a strong orange aura layer powered by the sacral chakra and violet aura layer powered by the third eye chakra. They channel their strong emotions through their artistic endeavors, and they have extremely vivid creative visions.
5. Reformer	Orange + Blue	Reformers are the catalysts of change in society. They are born with a strong orange aura layer powered by the sacral chakra and blue aura layer powered by the throat chakra, and are naturally passionate public speakers. They move groups through motivational speeches for social changes and a better world.
6. Entertainer	Orange + Green	Entertainers are fun people to be around. They are genuine, fun-loving beings who are born with a strong orange aura layer powered by the sacral chakra and green aura layer powered by the heart chakra. They like to channel their strong emotions by performing for a crowd. Entertainers aren't just performers; event organizers, teachers, and public speakers can be fun and engaging entertainers too.

THE AURA COLOR WHEEL

Soul Gift Archetype	Aura Layer Strength	Soul Gifts
7. Researcher	Red + Violet	Researchers can channel their vision through grounded daily research to move the current knowledge base forward. They are born with a strong red aura layer powered by the root chakra and violet aura layer powered by the third eye chakra. They are generally self-disciplined and love to read and explore new ideas. Continued learning is crucial for them.
8. Teacher	Red + Blue	Teachers see the goodness in people and believe everyone should have an equal chance through education. They are born with a strong red aura layer powered by the root chakra and blue aura layer powered by the throat chakra. They are generally calm and grounded and are great communicators within their specialties. They are encouraging and great motivators for transformation.
9. Warrior	Red + Green	Warriors are physically strong, natural athletes. They are born with a strong red aura layer powered by the root chakra and green aura layer powered by the heart chakra. Because of their physical strength and a strong sense of righteousness, they make great police officers, firefighters, and paramedics. They are willing to stand up for their loved ones.

SOUL GIFT ARCHETYPE CHARACTERISTICS

The nine Soul Gift Archetypes can be categorized into three groups with the aura layers powered by the lower three chakras and aura layers powered by the higher three chakras as shown in the chart below.

AURA LAYER	Violet	Blue	Green	MOTIVATORS
Yellow	Visionary	Entrepreneur	Healer	VISION
Orange	Artist	Reformer	Entertainer	PASSION
Red	Researcher	Teacher	Warrior	ACTION
ARCHETYPE	CREATORS	DIRECTORS	MANIFESTERS	

People with violet as one of the soul gift aura layers tend to be the creators. They are the Visionaries, Artists, and Researchers. If life is an orchestra, they are the composers. People with blue as one of their soul gift aura layers are the directors. Entrepreneurs, Reformers, and Teachers—the catalysts and enzymes for change and transformation—comprise this group. In an orchestra, they are the conductors. People with green as one of their soul gift aura layers are the manifesters. They are the Healers, Entertainers, and Warriors, who bring visions to the physical realm. They are the musicians in the orchestra, performing the music written by the creators and conducted by the directors.

The motivator for people with a yellow soul gift aura layer is vision. These are the Visionaries, Healers, and Entrepreneurs. They generally hold a higher vision and achieve fulfillment by working on their visions. People with an orange soul gift aura layer are motivated by passion. They have strong emotional senses and a zest for life that they want to share. They are the Artists, Reformers, and Entertainers. They fulfill their soul mission by sharing their creative talents with the world. People with a red soul gift aura layer are driven by action. They are the Researchers, Teachers, and Warriors. They are self-disciplined and take daily action to fulfill their soul's mission.

Please note that we all have more than one Soul Gift Archetype within us. We can even say we possess all of them to varying degrees. Your current, predominant Soul Gift Archetype may be your natural born gifts (acquired from past lives), the soul wound you've healed, the soul lessons you've learned in this lifetime, or a combination of them.

THE AURA COLOR WHEEL

YOUR SOUL AURA COLOR

Your Soul Gift Archetype will help you determine your Soul Aura Color. You can find the chapter that corresponds to your archetype, and within that chapter you will take a quiz to identify your Soul Aura Color. The following chart will provide you with an overview of the soul wound aura layer and the aura layers associated with the soul lessons for the 36 Soul Aura Colors in the Aura Color Wheel.

Many people find that their favorite color aligns with their Soul Aura Color, because it represents the energy they naturally radiate. You may often notice yourself drawn to clothing or accessories in your Soul Aura Color. Interestingly, half of the respondents to the Soul Aura Color Quiz also express a fondness for the color of their soul wound aura layer, recognizing it as the energy they need to heal. The other half, however, tend to dislike their soul wound aura layer color, which often indicates they are still struggling to work through their soul wound.

If your soul wound aura layer is red, orange, or yellow, you tend to have trouble manifesting earthly goals and possessions, and your soul work in this lifetime is to break karmic patterns. This means that you are making your good karma in this lifetime.

If your soul wound aura layer is green, blue, or violet, you will find that you are a good manifester. Your soul work in this lifetime is to transcend your ego and live your divine purpose—this will bring out your fullest potential. This means that you are reaping your good karma from your past lives in this lifetime.

The Aura Color Wheel and the Nine Soul Gift Archetypes

SOUL AURA COLORS AND THEIR SOUL GIFTS, WOUNDS, AND LESSONS

Soul Gift Archetype	Soul Aura Color	Soul Wound Aura Layer	Soul Lessons Aura Layers
Visionary Violet + Yellow	14. Forest	Red	Orange, Green, Blue
	26. Sapphire	Orange	Red, Green, Blue
	28. Violet	Green	Red, Orange, Blue
	09. Daffodil	Blue	Red, Orange, Green
Entrepreneur Blue + Yellow	11. Lime	Red	Orange, Green, Violet
	20. Aqua	Orange	Red, Green, Violet
	19. Teal	Green	Red, Orange, Violet
	18. Mint	Violet	Red, Orange, Green
Healer Green + Yellow	15. Jade	Red	Orange, Blue, Violet
	16. Turquoise	Orange	Red, Blue, Violet
	07. Yellow	Blue	Red, Orange, Violet
	17. Emerald	Violet	Red, Orange, Blue
Artist Violet + Orange	12. Apple	Red	Yellow, Green, Blue
	31. Magenta	Yellow	Red, Green, Blue
	35. Rose	Green	Red, Yellow, Blue
	05. Tangerine	Blue	Red, Yellow, Green
Reformer Blue + Orange	21. Sky	Red	Yellow, Green, Violet
	25. Indigo	Yellow	Red, Green, Violet
	23. Azure	Green	Red, Yellow, Violet
	13. Green	Violet	Red, Yellow, Green
Entertainer Green + Orange	10. Chartreuse	Red	Yellow, Blue, Violet
	32. Fuchsia	Yellow	Red, Blue, Violet
	06. Peach	Blue	Red, Yellow, Violet
	08. Lemon	Violet	Red, Yellow, Blue
Researcher Violet + Red	29. Orchid	Orange	Yellow, Green, Blue
	24. Ocean	Yellow	Orange, Green, Blue
	34. Ruby	Green	Orange, Yellow, Blue
	36. Carnation	Blue	Orange, Yellow, Green

THE AURA COLOR WHEEL

Soul Gift Archetype	Soul Aura Color	Soul Wound Aura Layer	Soul Lessons Aura Layers
Teacher Blue + Red	22. Blue	Orange	Yellow, Green, Violet
	27. Lilac	Yellow	Orange, Green, Violet
	30. Lavender	Green	Orange, Yellow, Violet
	33. Pink	Violet	Orange, Yellow, Green
Warrior Green + Red	02. Crimson	Orange	Yellow, Blue, Violet
	01. Red	Yellow	Orange, Blue, Violet
	04. Orange	Blue	Orange, Yellow, Violet
	03. Coral	Violet	Orange, Yellow, Blue

MY SOUL AURA COLOR EVOLUTION

I was born with the Artist Soul Gift Archetype and a Tangerine Soul Aura Color. I have strong orange and violet aura layers and the blue aura layer is my deep soul wound. I was born and raised in China, where speaking up—especially as a girl—was not encouraged. Luckily, my father adored me just as I am. I was born in the early 1980s, and at that time most Chinese families preferred boys over girls. My father's unconditional love and acceptance really helped me cultivate healthy self-esteem and heal my soul wound of struggling to speak my truth as a woman in a male-dominant culture.

As I was healing my soul wound, my blue aura layer grew stronger. Combining my orange aura layer strength with my blue aura layer, I became a Reformer. I had a strong sense of righteousness and was ready to stand up for my friends at school. I was often the leader of the pack and helped the weak. At this stage of my life, my Soul Aura Color was predominately Sky. It was also my favorite color at the time.

My father's love and encouragement as well as his hardworking mentality brought me significant yellow energy. Both helped me learn my yellow aura layer soul lesson and cultivate healthy self-esteem. I'm also an avid student of all kinds of spiritual, self-discovery tools. In fact, I'm so intrigued by the self-discovery journey that I studied psychology as an undergraduate with a deep desire to understand the self.

The Aura Color Wheel and the Nine Soul Gift Archetypes

At this stage of my life, my yellow aura layer became my strength. My soul could choose to combine my yellow aura layer with my violet aura layer to become a Visionary, or my yellow aura layer with my blue aura layer to become an Entrepreneur. My soul chose the latter. My entrepreneurial spirit began in college, with fundraising and organizing all kinds of events for our school's student council. I became motivated to advance my studies in the U.S. with a full fellowship until I founded my first interior design business. During this period of my life, my Soul Aura Color was mainly Lime.

During my Ph.D. studies, I met my husband. I was madly in love, and green was my favorite color at the time. My heart was opening, and my soul was ready to learn its green aura layer soul lesson. We got married after one year of dating. Two families merged, and I began taking care of my stepson, who was two. Then came our daughter, my greatest teacher of unconditional love. At this stage of my life, my green aura layer became my strength. My soul could choose to combine my green aura layer with my orange aura layer and become an Entertainer or combine my green aura layer with my yellow aura layer and become a Healer. My soul chose the latter. I began my crystal healing certificate program, refreshed my Ayurveda studies, and then went on to study Theta healing and angelic channeling. My Soul Aura Color was Jade at the time.

The hardest soul lesson for me was in the red aura layer, where I needed to heal my ancestral wounds. My father passed away when I was 19. I'm an only child, and my mom moved in with my family when my daughter was born. I was sent to the psychiatric ER because of her sarcastic, passive-aggressive behavior toward me, which had occurred since I was a child. It took me a while to fully understand that this was emotional abuse, and I spent about five years healing this wound. But my soul knew I was ready for it. At this point, I consciously chose not to pass this down to my daughter. The pain had to stop in me and from me. It worked. My mom still lives with us and is difficult, but I have changed. As I was at the last editing stage of the book, my soul received another upgrade of learning and integration of my red aura layer soul lesson. Please refer to the story in the earlier section—How Do We Know We Healed a Soul Wound or Learned a Soul Lesson?—in this chapter.

THE AURA COLOR WHEEL

At this point in my life, I can combine my red aura layer (now a strength in my aura composition) with my violet aura layer and blue aura layer to become a Researcher and Teacher. I have become an art and spiritual teacher. My soul knows that it is time to birth this book.

I use my personal Soul Aura Color journey to illustrate how dynamic this Aura Color Wheel is. Although your Soul Aura Color is the most permanent of the three aura colors, it's not static. Unlike the zodiac signs, in which you only have one sun sign, your Soul Aura Color changes depending on where you are on your soul-healing and soul-learning journey.

Although orange and violet are my soul gift aura layers, I still encounter difficulties where they are concerned. My family and culture don't support me in any field of art because of the starving artist cliché. I participated in one art competition and didn't win, which made me think I had no talent. This blocked my orange aura layer's creative flow for a long time, until I found it again and reclaimed myself as an artist.

Growing up in the Chinese elementary school system, we were taught to believe there was no God or any type of spirit. This was the correct answer in a multiple-choice exam. My soul knew it was wrong when I first meditated during my yoga teacher training. Something bigger was there with me, holding me the entire time! I was home. That's when I reclaimed my violet aura layer power.

The more I practice spiritual tools like living with the seasons and moon cycles, the more my orange aura layer creativity flows with ease. The more I develop my psychic abilities and connect with angels and spirit guides, the more my violet aura layer shines through, sending me inspirations and insights for my painting visions and guiding me toward what my clients and students need for their healing journey.

Please note that there might not be a finish line for your soul wound or soul lessons in this lifetime. You may heal your soul wound to a certain degree, but it can come back in a later stage of life if the wound is not fully healed. You will need to work on it some more.

Now, are you ready to find out your Soul Aura Color?

PART II

FINDING YOUR SOUL AURA COLOR

CHAPTER 4

VISIONARY ARCHETYPE

If your Soul Gift Archetype is Visionary, you have a strong yellow aura layer powered by the solar plexus chakra and violet aura layer powered by the third eye chakra. These two aura layers are intertwined, fostering intuitive vision and mental clarity in action, which naturally shapes the essence of Visionary Archetype leaders. The main difference among the Soul Aura Colors is their soul wound and soul lessons. Archangel Metatron and Archangel Michael are the great angels to call upon to assist you to fully embody your Visionary soul gifts. Trust and use your innate clairvoyance and claircognizance psychic abilities to receive spirit guidance.

VISIONARY SOUL AURA COLOR QUIZ

For each question, please select the option that best describes you based on your current state. I highly recommend you pick an answer intuitively—don't overthink it. If you have questions or really can't choose an answer, please leave it blank. If you have more than one selection that applies, please select all of them. Remember, auras are a spectrum of colors, not one static color. These questions are channeled to approximate your Soul Aura Color. Have fun!

THE AURA COLOR WHEEL

1. **In which area of life do you experience the most difficulties?**
    a. Family relationships or ancestral traumas
    b. Regulating emotions
    c. Being vulnerable, giving and receiving love
    d. Speaking my truth without being self-conscious or worrying about what other people think of me

2. **Where do you feel discomfort or illness most often?**
    a. Legs, feet, knees, bone structure
    b. Hormones, reproductive system, lower back
    c. Heart, chest, breast, asthma, blood pressure
    d. Throat, nose, ears, teeth, neck, mouth, jaw

3. **Which circumstances cause the most discomfort?**
    a. Fitting in with my family, feeling out of place
    b. Sharing or relating with other people's emotions or being too emotional
    c. Having intimate relationships
    d. Expressing myself with clarity in public

4. **What are you most afraid of feeling?**
    a. Lack of safety and security
    b. Guilt and shame
    c. Jealousy, desire to please others, sadness
    d. Shyness, being suppressed or speaking too much, ADHD

5. **What are you missing that prevents you from living life to the fullest?**
    a. A sense of being grounded and centered
    b. Creativity and spontaneity
    c. Vulnerability and forgiveness
    d. Truthful communications

6. Which emotional blocks do you feel most often?

  a. Anxiety or depression
  b. Sadness, isolation, or emotional eating
  c. Jealousy, or fear of inadequacies
  d. Nervousness, unease, or lingering emotional trauma

7. Which issues do you frequently encounter?

  a. Insecurity, doubt, low self-worth
  b. Inability to say no, guilt
  c. Lack of hope or faith
  d. Inability to relax, the need to always be doing something

8. Which superpower would change your life?

  a. The power to stay present and bring spiritual knowledge into daily actions
  b. The power to find calm and peace in everyday life
  c. The power of connection and harmony with my loved ones and community
  d. The power to communicate with the Divine and Higher Spirit

9. If you could change one thing about yourself, what would it be?

  a. I want to have the courage to move forward in life: change career, accept new adventures and opportunities, etc.
  b. I want to feel inspired, creative, decisive, and flowing with life.
  c. I want to have an intimate connection with my significant other and a loving relationship with myself.
  d. I want to possess strong leadership skills to move society forward according to my ideals.

THE AURA COLOR WHEEL

10. Does your birthday fall in any of the following groups of timing? If not, just leave this blank.

   a. July 26, 1943, 6:42 P.M. – November 17, 1944, 11:23 P.M.
March 23, 1945, 10:50 P.M. – July 22, 1945, 12:31 P.M.
February 8, 1951, 8:26 P.M. – June 18, 1951, 9:13 A.M.
November 8, 1951, 11:22 P.M. – January 27, 1955, 11:28 A.M.
September 3, 1993, 1:32 P.M. – September 9, 1995, 10:28 A.M.
December 11, 2001, 6:04 P.M. – February 21, 2005, 12:33 P.M.
July 31, 2005, 11:48 P.M. – December 5, 2005, 8:03 P.M.

   b. May 28, 1938, 8:39 A.M. – September 29, 1940, 11:44 P.M.
December 27, 1940, 12:59 A.M. – June 16, 1941, 2:34 P.M.
May 28, 1977, 2:05 P.M. – June 21, 1983, 8:19 A.M.
November 29, 1983, 8:19 A.M. – April 10, 1984, 11:19 P.M.
June 21, 1988, 5:40 A.M. – July 21, 1991, 11:54 A.M.
June 19, 2026, 5:17 P.M. – September 17, 2026, 9:54 P.M.

   c. November 27, 1944, 11:23 P.M. – March 23, 1945, 10:50 P.M.
July 22, 1945, 12:31 P.M. – November 10, 1946, 2:14 A.M.
March 26, 1960, 8:39 P.M. – August 19, 1960, 2:31 A.M.
January 20, 1961, 8:50 P.M. – April 1, 1968, 2:08 A.M.
October 18, 1968, 6:36 P.M. – January 30, 1969, 3:12 P.M.
September 9, 1995, 10:28 P.M. – December 29. 1996, 6:16 P.M.
April 4, 1997, 11:50 A.M. – September 2, 1997, 11:24 P.M.
April 20, 2010, 2:28 A.M. – July 20, 2010, 5:46 P.M.
February 8, 2011, 2:55 P.M. – April 17, 2018, 4:09 A.M.
September 25, 2018, 8:12 P.M. – February 18, 2019, 4:07 A.M.

   d. January 27, 1955, 11:28 A.M. – March 26, 1960, 8:39 A.M.
August 19, 1960, 2:31 A.M. – January 20, 1961, 8:50 P.M.
June 21, 1983, 9:54 A.M. – November 29, 1983, 8:19 A.M.
April 10, 1984, 11:19 P.M. – June 21, 1988, 5:40 A.M.
February 21, 2005, 12:33 P.M. – July 31, 2005, 11:48 P.M.
December 5, 2005, 8:03 P.M. – April 20, 2010, 2:28 P.M.
July 20, 2010, 5:46 A.M. – February 8, 2011, 2:55 P.M.
July 19, 2033, 9:35 A.M. – October 23, 2033, 6:21 P.M.
May 5, 2034, 5:50 P.M. – July 22, 2038, 1:49 A.M.

Visionary Archetype

Please mark down how many of each selection you have:
a. _____   c. _____
b. _____   d. _____

- If you chose mostly A answers, your aura color is 14: *Forest*.
- If you chose mostly B answers, your aura color is 26: *Sapphire*.
- If you chose mostly C answers, your aura color is 28: *Violet*.
- If you chose mostly D answers, your aura color is 08: *Daffodil*.

If you have two or more equal selections, it can mean one of the following:

1. You have two or more aura colors in your auric field. Please read the descriptions and intuitively pick which one resonates with you the most to work with now.
2. You are in transition from one aura color to another within the same Soul Gift Archetype. This happens when you heal a certain aura layer soul wound and are now working on another aura layer soul wound or soul lesson. Remember, soul wounds are just deeper soul lessons.

FOREST AURA COLOR SOULS

If your Soul Aura Color is Forest, you have long-term visions. You have a higher perspective and larger scope of life. Working on your long-term goals with consistent actions brings you fulfillment. You're also a guide for those who seek perspective and clarity in their dreams. Wearing forest-colored clothing or accessories and decorating your home or office space with forest colors accentuate your soul gifts. Working with crystals like golden labradorite, Herkimer diamond, and tremolite strengthens your soul gifts.

Your deep soul wound is the red aura layer powered by the root chakra. You tend to have long-term physical issues, or family issues from either the paternal or maternal lineage. Sometimes you feel lack of belonging, security, and safety. Learning to incorporate some

THE AURA COLOR WHEEL

Ayurveda and Feng Shui practices into your home and life would be beneficial to you. Clearing and healing ancestral, karmic, and past-life wounds are some of your soul's missions in this lifetime. Wearing clothing or accessories in shades of red helps bring in this color energy while you are healing your soul wound. Carnelian, black tourmaline, and elestial quartz are great crystal companions for your soul-healing journey.

Your main soul lessons are the orange, green, and blue aura layers, powered by the sacral, heart, and throat chakras. Learning to regulate your emotions, opening your heart to give and receive love, and communicating your truth authentically is your soul's journey in this lifetime. You will encounter different situations at various times of your life where these themes reoccur. This is a signal from the Universe that the timing is right for your soul to learn that lesson. If you miss the signal the first time, this soul lesson theme will reoccur until you finally learn the lesson. Learning how to honor your body, live with nature's cycles, heal your inner child, and rewrite your limiting beliefs are powerful practices that can help you navigate through life's challenges.

If your soul chooses to work on your red aura layer soul wound first, once you have healed your soul wound, the red aura layer will become one of your strengths in your Soul Aura Color composition. Because aura layers work in pairs, with one layer from the higher three chakras and one layer from the lower three chakras, at this point your soul can choose to combine your red and violet aura layers so that you can become a Researcher Soul Gift Archetype to bring forth new ideas and a paradigm that helps the evolution of planet Earth.

Once you have learned your orange aura layer soul lesson, you can blend your violet and orange aura layers and shape-shift into an Artist. When you learn your green aura layer soul lesson, you can combine it with your yellow aura strength to become a Healer or your red aura strength to become a Warrior. The same is true of your blue aura layer soul lesson. Once you've learned it, your blue aura layer can be a strength, and you can mix it with your yellow aura strength to become an Entrepreneur or your red aura strength to become a Teacher.

Visionary Archetype

SAPPHIRE AURA COLOR SOULS

If your Soul Aura Color is Sapphire, you are the leader of the pack. You have a sharp mind and are quick to take decisive action. Building a like-minded team to create something out of your vision brings you fulfillment. Wearing sapphire-colored clothing or accessories and decorating your home or office space with sapphire colors accentuate your soul gifts. Working with crystals like sapphire, Libyan desert glass, yellow fluorite, and astrophyllite strengthens your soul gifts.

Your deep soul wound is the orange aura layer powered by the sacral chakra. Regulating your emotions is challenging for you, and it was especially difficult when you were a child. The feeling of shame or guilt sometimes blocks your vision. Establishing a healthy relationship and boundaries for yourself and others is crucial to your well-being. Childhood trauma healing helps heal your deep soul wound. Sometimes you feel frustrated that your goals aren't achieved at the time you want them to be. Learning to live with nature's seasonal cycles and to surrender to divine timing is your soul's mission in this lifetime. Wearing clothing or accessories in shades of orange helps bring in the color energy while you are healing your soul wound. Watermelon tourmaline and rainbow moonstone are great energy companions for your soul-healing journey.

Your main soul lessons are the red, green, and blue aura layers, powered by the root, heart, and throat chakras. Learning to take good care of your body; clearing and healing ancestral, karmic, and past-life wounds; opening up your heart to give and receive love; and communicating your truth authentically is your soul's journey in this lifetime. Cultivating a healthy lifestyle based on your Ayurvedic body type, healing your inner child, and rewriting your limiting beliefs are powerful practices that can help you navigate through life's challenges.

If your soul chooses to work on your orange aura layer soul wound first, once you have healed your soul wound, the orange aura layer will become one of your strengths in your Soul Aura Color composition. Because aura layers work in pairs, with one layer from the higher three chakras and one layer from the lower three chakras, at this point your soul can choose to combine your orange and violet aura layers so that you can become an Artist Soul Gift Archetype who uses creativity to channel your visions.

Once you have learned your red aura layer soul lesson, you can blend your violet and red aura layers and shape-shift into a Researcher. When you learn your green aura soul lesson, you can combine it with your yellow aura strength to become a Healer or your orange aura strength to become an Entertainer. The same is true of your blue aura layer soul lesson. Once you've learned it, your blue aura layer can be your strength, and you can mix it with your yellow aura strength to become an Entrepreneur or your orange aura strength to become a Reformer.

VIOLET AURA COLOR SOULS

If your Soul Aura Color is Violet, you possess powerful visions and are likely clairvoyant. If you can tap into this innate intuition, you will see the future clearly. You can become a powerful manifester using this visualization skill. Wearing violet-colored clothing or accessories and decorating your home or office space with violet colors accentuate your soul gifts. Working with crystals like charoite, golden tiger's eye, and cat's eye strengthens your soul gifts.

Your deep soul wound is the green aura layer powered by the heart chakra. Trusting and surrendering to the Divine is difficult for you, and it was especially challenging when you were a child. Learning to be less self-critical and more compassionate toward yourself and others is crucial to your soul-healing journey. You have a perfectionist tendency; since your vision is so clear, you want everyone else to follow it. Practicing self-love and healing your inner child are wonderful spiritual tools for your soul. Wearing clothing or accessories in shades of green helps bring in the color energy while you are healing your soul wound. Variscite, green opal, and kunzite are great energy companions for your soul-healing journey.

Your major soul lessons in this lifetime are the red, orange, and blue aura layers, powered by the root, sacral, and throat chakras. Healing your physical body, learning to trust and surrender your control, regulating your emotions, and speaking your truth authentically are

Visionary Archetype

some of the themes of your soul lessons. Learning and integrating the knowledge of Feng Shui and Ayurveda and leaning in to seasonal living with the moon phases and the Wheel of the Year will make you more grounded and process your deep emotions. Practicing daily affirmations and clearing your ancestral, karmic, and past-life wounds and limiting beliefs will unlock your visionary potential.

If your soul chooses to work on your green aura layer soul wound first, once you have healed your soul wound, the green aura layer will become one of your strengths in your Soul Aura Color composition. Because aura layers work in pairs, with one layer from the higher three chakras and one layer from the lower three chakras, at this point your soul can choose to combine the green and yellow aura layers so that you can become a Healer Soul Gift Archetype who can integrate your own healing journey into healing others with similar difficulties.

Once you have learned your red aura layer soul lesson, you can blend your red and violet aura layers and shape-shift into a Researcher or your red and green aura layers to transform into a Warrior. When you learn your orange aura layer soul lesson, you can combine it with your violet aura strength to become an Artist or your green aura strength to become an Entertainer. The same is true of your blue aura layer soul lesson. Once you've learned it, your blue aura layer can be a strength, and you can mix it with your yellow aura strength to become an Entrepreneur.

DAFFODIL AURA COLOR SOULS

If your Soul Aura Color is Daffodil, you are filled with joy and light. You are the happy visionary who brings positivity and change to this planet. Your light and joy are contagious. Being the light in the midst of darkness and guiding others to see the light brings you fulfillment. Wearing daffodil-colored clothing or accessories and decorating your home or office space with daffodil colors accentuate your soul gifts. Working with crystals like feldspar, celestine, and purple angelite strengthens your soul gifts.

Your deepest soul wound is the blue aura layer powered by the throat chakra. Speaking up for yourself is challenging, and it was especially difficult when you were a child. You tend to be socially conscious and chose conformity over conflict at an early age. As your soul grows, you begin to take a rebellious approach to social norms. When you find the balance between the two, your soul matures. You understand that you are light, you don't have to do anything, and your presence is enough. You may have physical illnesses related to the throat chakra, such as strep throat, serious allergies, or sinus issues. Practicing daily affirmations, sound baths, and clearing any ancestral and past-life limiting beliefs are important spiritual practices for your soul. Wearing clothing or accessories in shades of blue helps bring in the color energy while you are healing your soul wound. Blue opal and quantum quattro are great crystal companions for your soul-healing journey.

Your major soul lessons for this lifetime are your red, orange, and green aura layers, powered by the root, sacral, and heart chakras. Since your natural born light quotient (the amount of energy that your light body can absorb, carry, emit, and embody as mentioned in Chapter 1) is high, you tend to forget to ground yourself in the physical. Tending to your physical body, nurturing your body with a seasonal Ayurvedic diet, finding a physical exercise that appeals to you, and spending time in nature are beneficial for you. Daily emotional releases and returning to your center grounds you. Learning to be less critical of yourself and others is another important soul lesson you need to learn. Practicing self-compassion and tending to your inner child is wonderful medicine for your soul.

If your soul chooses to work on your blue aura layer soul wound first, once you have healed your soul wound, the blue aura layer will become one of your strengths in your Soul Aura Color composition. Because aura layers work in pairs, with one layer from the higher three chakras and one layer from the lower three chakras, at this point your soul can choose to combine the blue and yellow aura layers so that you can become an Entrepreneur Soul Gift Archetype.

Once you have learned your red aura soul lesson, you can blend your violet and red aura layers and shape-shift into a Researcher or your red and blue aura layers to transform into a Teacher. When you learn your orange aura layer soul lesson, you can combine it with your violet aura strength to become an Artist or your blue aura strength to become a Reformer. The same is true of your green aura layer soul lesson. Once you've learned it, your green aura layer can be a strength, and you can mix it with your yellow aura strength to become a powerful Healer.

VISIONARY EVOLUTION PATHS

The diagrams on the following pages show the four possible starting points and different paths for your Soul Gift Archetype evolution journey. You can choose to work on your soul wound first or learn one of the three soul lessons. As your soul grows, more aura layers will become your strength. When your soul works on healing soul wounds or learning soul lessons and these aspects are completed to a satisfactory degree, free will can be exercised to combine aura layer strengths to embody different Soul Gift Archetypes. Of course, you can also choose to remain the Soul Gift Archetype you were born with but just have more light quotient in your Soul Aura Color composition, thus magnetizing high vibrational opportunities in your life and manifesting faster.

THE AURA COLOR WHEEL

Visionary Soul Gift Archetype Evolution Path 1

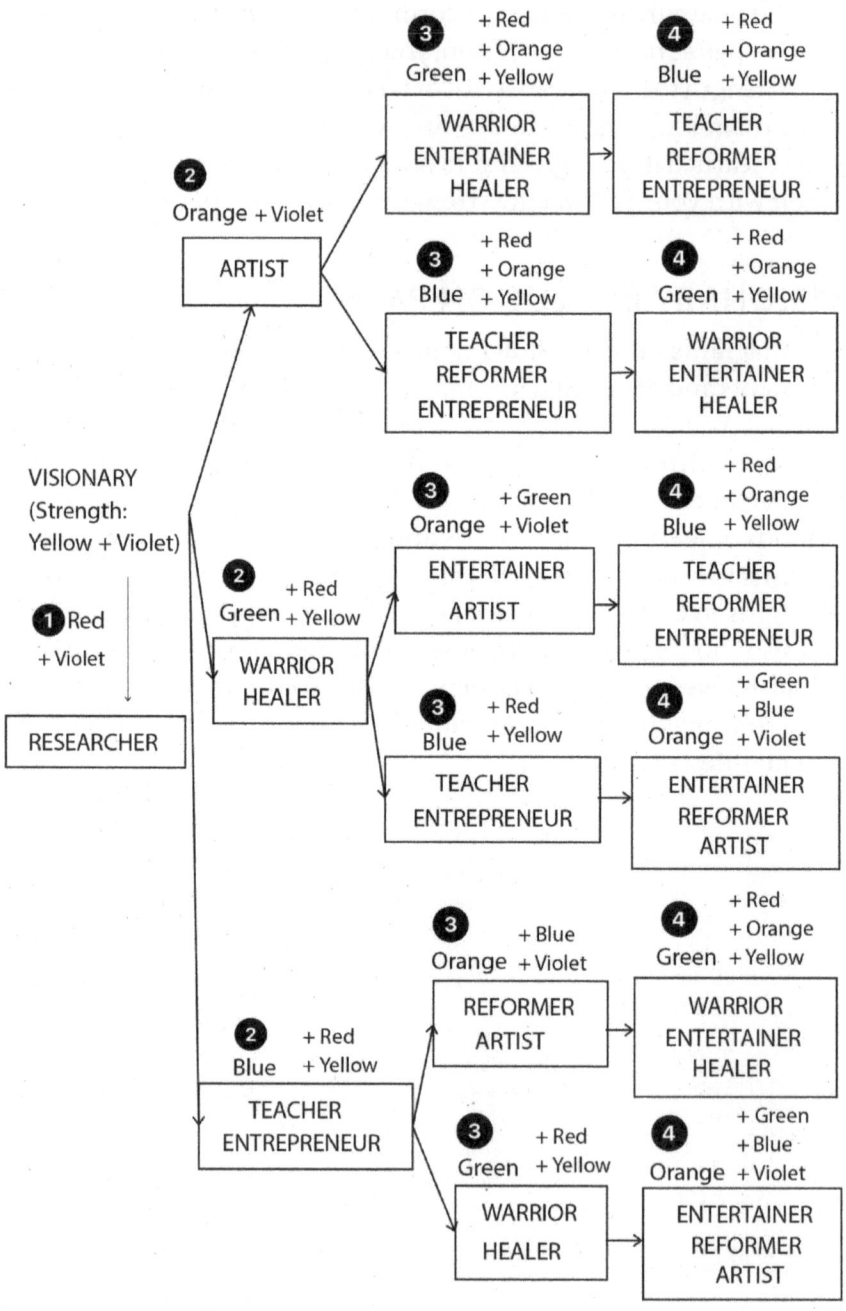

Visionary Archetype

Visionary Soul Gift Archetype Evolution Path 2

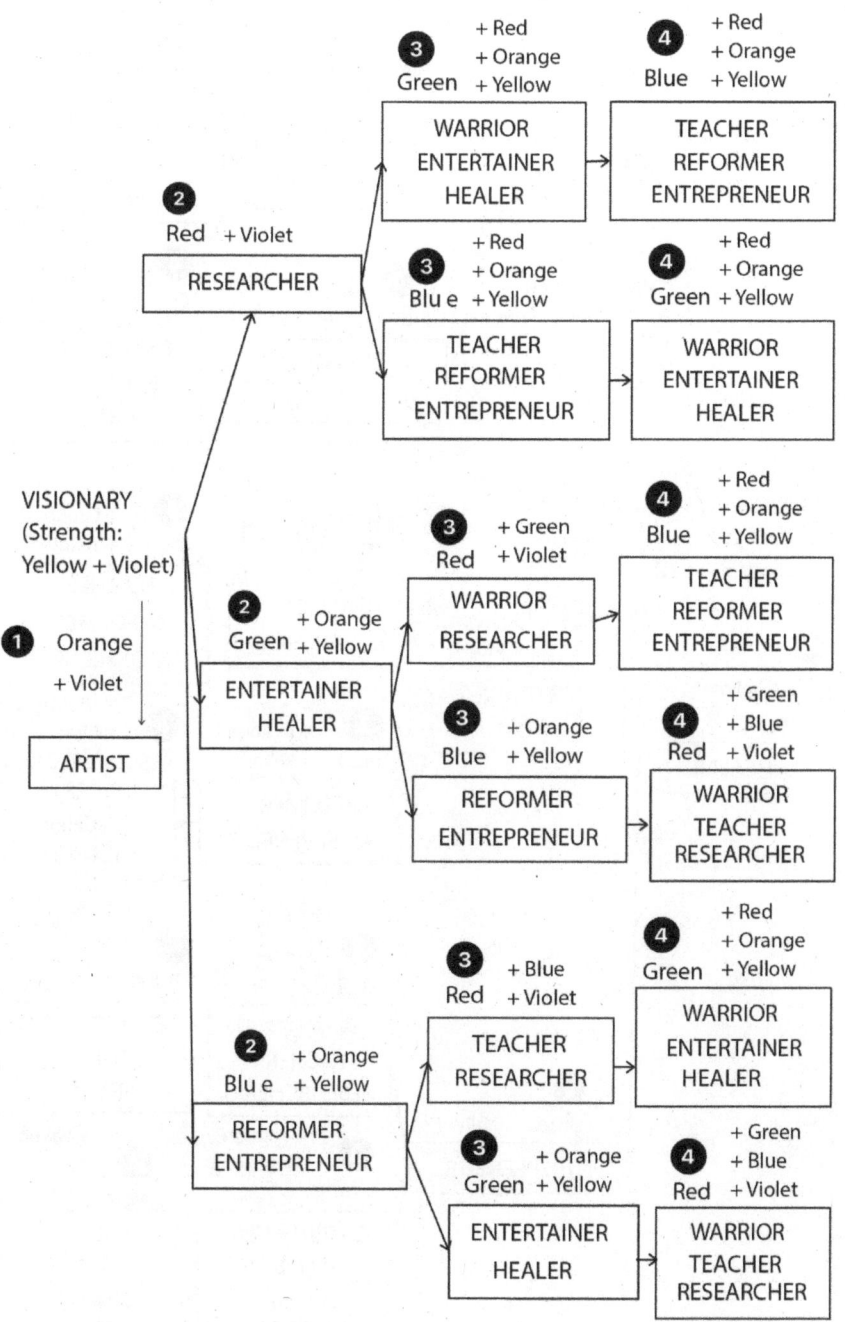

THE AURA COLOR WHEEL

Visionary Soul Gift Archetype Evolution Path 3

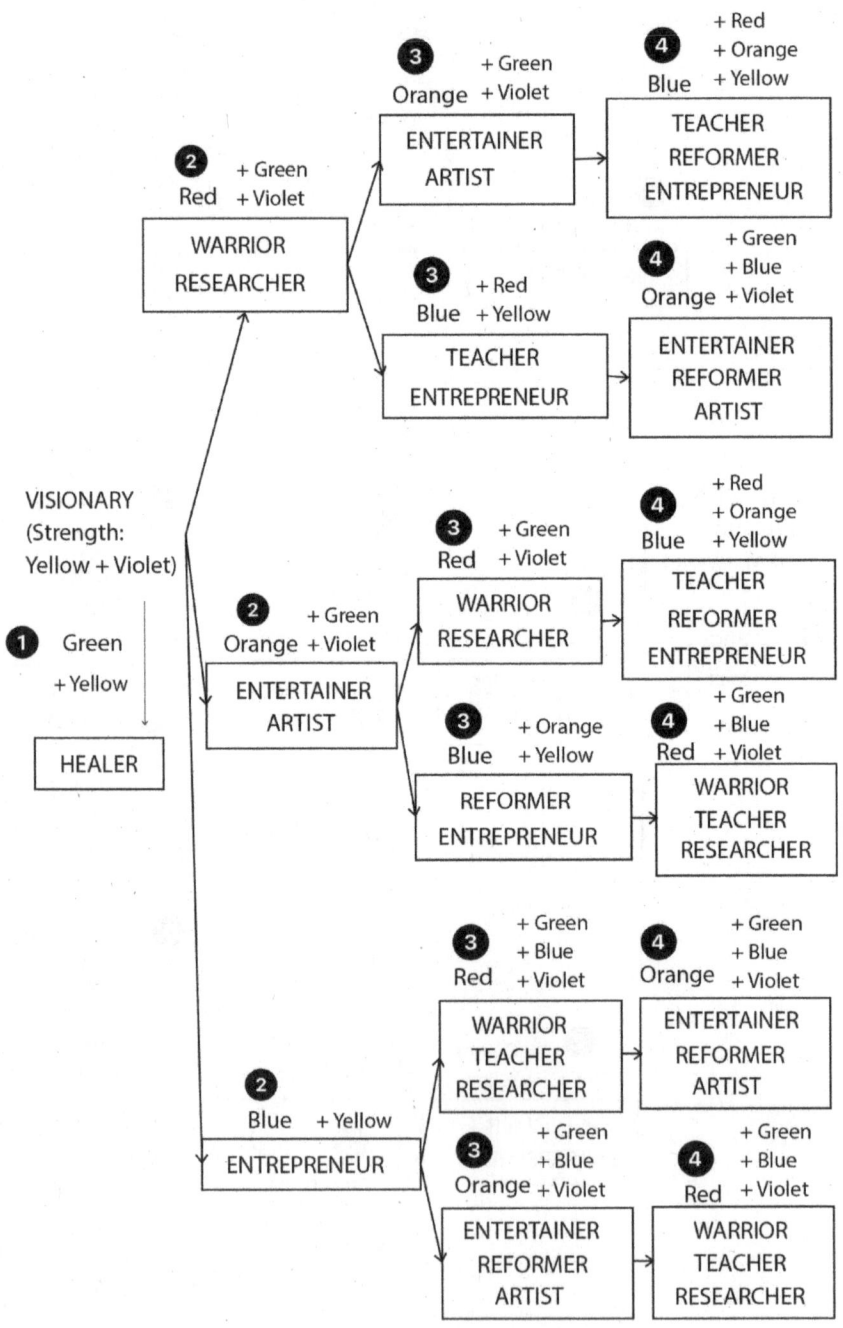

Visionary Archetype

Visionary Soul Gift Archetype Evolution Path 4

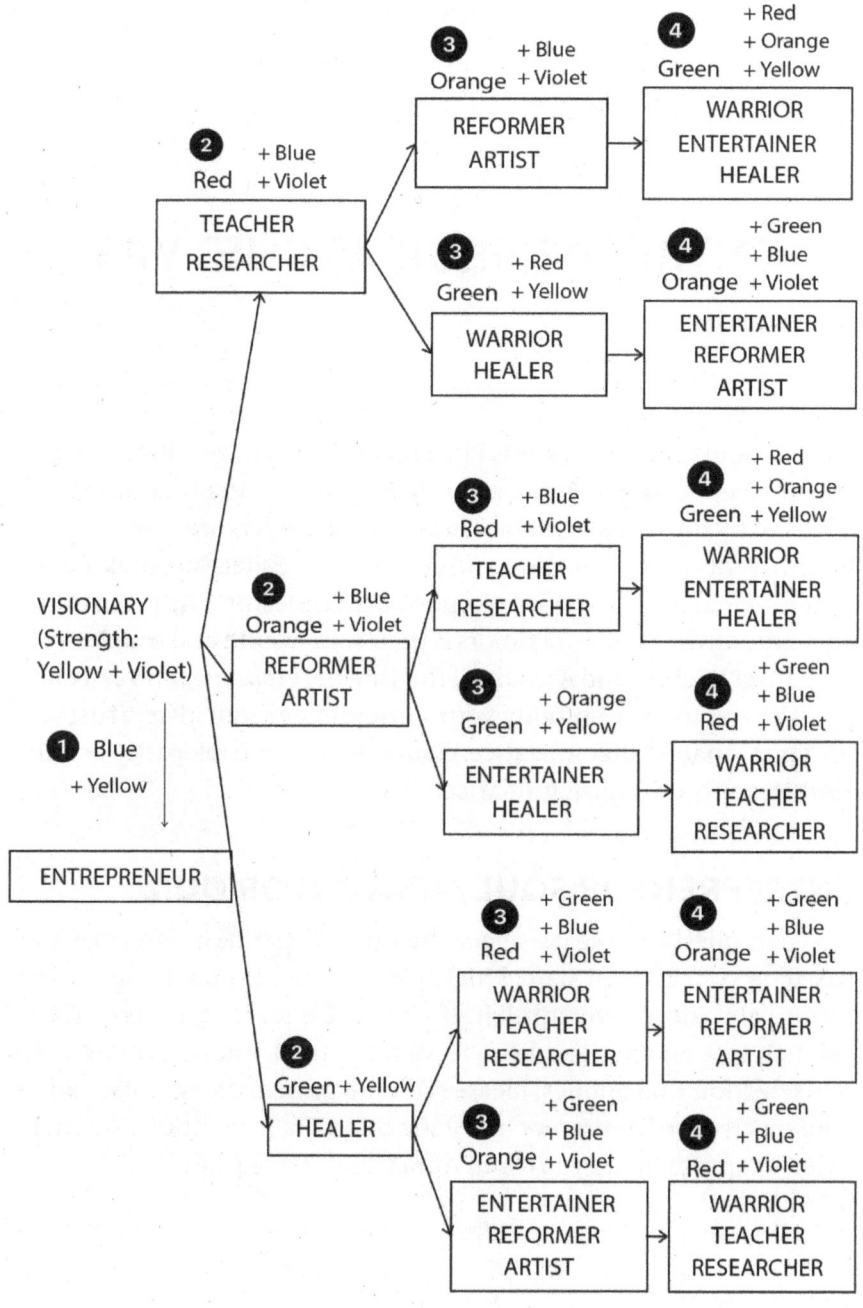

CHAPTER 5

ENTREPRENEUR ARCHETYPE

If your Soul Gift Archetype is Entrepreneur, you have a strong yellow aura layer powered by the solar plexus chakra and blue aura layer powered by the throat chakra. These two aura layers are deeply linked to confident communication and empowered leadership, making the Entrepreneur Archetype an exceptional manifestor. The main difference among the Soul Aura Colors is their soul wound and soul lessons. Archangel Michael and Archangel Ariel are the great angels to call upon to assist you to fully embody your Entrepreneur soul gifts. Trust and use your innate claircognizance, clairaudience, and telepathy psychic abilities to receive spirit guidance.

ENTREPRENEUR SOUL AURA COLOR QUIZ

For each question, please select the option that best describes you based on your current state. I highly recommend you pick an answer intuitively—don't overthink it. If you have a few questions or really can't choose an answer, please leave it blank. If you have more than one selection that applies, please select all of them. Remember, auras are a spectrum of colors, not one static color. These questions are channeled to approximate your Soul Aura Color. Have fun!

Entrepreneur Archetype

1. In which area of life do you experience the most difficulties?
   a. Family relationships or ancestral traumas
   b. Regulating emotions
   c. Being vulnerable, giving and receiving love
   d. Planning and visualizing the future

2. Where do you feel discomfort or illness most often?
   a. Legs, feet, bone structure
   b. Hormones, reproductive system, lower back
   c. Heart, chest, breast, asthma, blood pressure
   d. Sinuses, headaches, scalp, hair, autoimmune diseases, skin

3. Which circumstances cause the most discomfort?
   a. Fitting in with my family, feeling out of place
   b. Sharing emotions, being too emotional, empathizing with others
   c. Having intimate relationships
   d. Sensing other people's energy

4. What are you most afraid of feeling?
   a. Lack of safety and security
   b. Guilt and shame
   c. Jealousy, desire to please others, sadness
   d. Paranoia or bad feelings about the future

5. What are you missing that prevents you from living life to the fullest?
   a. A sense of being grounded and centered
   b. Creativity and spontaneity
   c. Vulnerability and forgiveness
   d. Intuition and psychic abilities

6. Which emotional blocks do you feel most often?
    a. Anxiety or depression
    b. Sadness, isolation, or emotional eating
    c. Jealousy, or fear of inadequacies
    d. Lack of intuition or inspiration

7. Which issues do you frequently encounter?
    a. Insecurity, doubt, low self-worth
    b. Inability to say no, guilt
    c. Lack of hope or faith
    d. Mental fog, feeling stuck or in a rut

8. Which superpower would change your life?
    a. The power to stay present and bring spiritual knowledge into daily actions
    b. The power to find calm and peace in everyday life
    c. The power of connection and harmony with my loved ones and community
    d. The power to gain vision, clarity, inspiration, and innovation

9. If you could change one thing about yourself, what would it be?
    a. I want to have the courage to move forward in life: career, new adventures and opportunities, etc.
    b. I want to feel inspired, creative, decisive, and flowing with life.
    c. I want to have an intimate connection with my significant other and a loving relationship with myself.
    d. I want to be open to insights and intuitive guidance from the Divine to better understand myself.

Entrepreneur Archetype

10. Does your birthday fall in any of the following groups of timing? If not, just leave this blank.

    a. July 26, 1943, 6:42 P.M. – November 17, 1944, 11:23 P.M.
       March 23, 1945, 10:50 P.M. – July 22, 1945, 12:31 P.M.
       February 8, 1951, 8:26 P.M. – June 18, 1951, 9:13 A.M.
       November 8, 1951, 11:22 P.M. – January 27, 1955, 11:28 A.M.
       September 3, 1993, 1:32 P.M. – September 9, 1995, 10:28 A.M.
       December 11, 2001, 6:04 P.M. – February 21, 2005, 12:33 P.M.
       July 31, 2005, 11:48 P.M. – December 5, 2005, 8:03 P.M.

    b. May 28, 1938, 8:39 A.M. – September 29, 1940, 11:44 P.M.
       December 27, 1940, 12:59 A.M. – June 16, 1941, 2:34 P.M.
       May 28, 1977, 2:05 P.M. – June 21, 1983, 8:19 A.M.
       November 29, 1983, 8:19 A.M. – April 10, 1984, 11:19 P.M.
       June 21, 1988, 5:40 A.M. – July 21, 1991, 11:54 A.M.
       June 19, 2026, 5:17 P.M. – September 17, 2026, 9:54 P.M.
       April 14, 2027, 10:56 P.M. – July 19, 2033, 9:35 A.M.

    c. November 27, 1944, 11:23 P.M. – March 23, 1945, 10:50 P.M.
       July 22, 1945, 12:31 P.M. – November 10, 1946, 2:14 A.M.
       March 26, 1960, 8:39 P.M. – August 19, 1960, 2:31 A.M.
       January 20, 1961, 8:50 P.M. – April 1, 1968, 2:08 A.M.
       October 18, 1968, 6:36 P.M. – January 30, 1969, 3:12 P.M.
       September 9, 1995, 10:28 P.M. – December 29. 1996, 6:16 P.M.
       April 4, 1997, 11:50 A.M. – September 2, 1997, 11:24 P.M.
       April 20, 2010, 2:28 A.M. – July 20, 2010, 5:46 P.M.
       February 8, 2011, 2:55 P.M. – April 17, 2018, 4:09 A.M.
       September 25, 2018, 8:12 P.M. – February 18, 2019, 4:07 A.M.

    d. November 10, 1946, 2:14 P.M. – February 8, 1951, 8:26 P.M.
       January 18, 1951, 9:13 A.M. – November 8, 1951, 11:22 P.M.
       December 29, 1996, 6:16 A.M. – April 4, 1997, 11:50 A.M.
       September 2, 1997, 11:24 P.M. – December 11, 2001, 6:04 P.M.

Please mark down how many of each selection you have:

    a. _____   c. _____
    b. _____   d. _____

THE AURA COLOR WHEEL

- If you chose mostly A answers, your aura color is 11: *Lime*.
- If you chose mostly B answers, your aura color is 20: *Aqua*.
- If you chose mostly C answers, your aura color is 19: *Teal*.
- If you chose mostly D answers, your aura color is 18: *Mint*.

If you have two or more equal selections, it can mean one of the following:

1. You have two or more aura colors in your auric field. Please read the descriptions and intuitively pick which one resonates with you the most to work with now.
2. You are in transition from one aura color to another within the same Soul Gift Archetype. This happens when you heal a certain aura layer soul wound and are now working on another aura layer soul wound or soul lesson. Remember, soul wounds are just deeper soul lessons.

LIME AURA COLOR SOULS

If your Soul Aura Color is Lime, you are creative and bold in all forms of self-expression. You like to think outside the box for solutions, and you may have your own business to fulfill your creative ideas. You act on your goals and motivate other like-minded souls to work with you. Abundance is your birthright when you embody your personal power and become a super manifester. Wearing lime-colored clothing or accessories and decorating your home or office space with lime colors accentuate your soul gifts. Working with crystals like amazonite, citrine, and blue onyx strengthens your soul gifts.

Your deep soul wound is the red aura layer powered by the root chakra. When you were a child, relationships with your parents or other family members were difficult. Sometimes you lack a sense of belonging, security, and safety. You feel safer in the bubble of imagination, rather than the reality of the world. Healing ancestral, karmic, and past-life wounds is your spiritual medicine for the soul. Learning and practicing Feng Shui and Ayurveda are beneficial to your healing.

Wearing clothing or accessories in shades of red helps bring in the color energy while you are healing your soul wound. Mookite jasper and dragon bloodstone are great crystal companions for your soul-healing journey.

Your major soul lessons are the orange, green, and violet aura layers. Learning how to release any sense of shame or guilt, nurturing self-compassion and tending to your inner child, and embracing your shadow self through shadow work are great spiritual tools for learning your soul lessons. Honing your intuition and psychic abilities through regular spiritual practice will elevate your entrepreneurial skills to the next level. You will know you've achieved progress when you are guided and take conscious actions in alignment with your soul.

If your soul chooses to work on your red aura layer soul wound first, once you have healed your soul wound, the red aura layer will become one of your strengths in your Soul Aura Color composition. Because aura layers work in pairs, with one layer from the higher three chakras and one layer from the lower three chakras, at this point your soul can choose to combine the red and blue aura layers so that you can become a Teacher Soul Gift Archetype.

Once you have learned your orange aura layer soul lesson, you can blend your blue and orange aura layers and shape-shift into a Reformer to move society forward. When you learn your green aura layer soul lesson, you can combine it with your yellow aura strength to become a powerful Healer or your red aura strength to become a Warrior. The same is true of your violet aura layer soul lesson. Once you've learned it, your violet aura layer can be a strength, and you can mix it with your yellow aura strength to become a Visionary or your red aura strength to become a Researcher.

AQUA AURA COLOR SOULS

If your Soul Aura Color is Aqua, you are a brave risk-taker. In entrepreneurial ventures, you like to go with the flow. You take actions toward your goals and have the mantra of learning by doing. You are not afraid of the new and unknown and often think on your feet. Wearing aqua-colored clothing or accessories and decorating your home or office space with aqua colors accentuate your soul gifts. Working with crystals like aquamarine, blue jade, and ametrine will strengthen your soul gifts.

Your deep soul wound is the orange aura layer powered by the sacral chakra. You sometimes have emotional outbursts, and regulating your emotions is challenging. Feelings of shame or guilt can sometimes block your vision. Establishing a healthy relationship and boundaries with yourself and others is crucial to your well-being. Childhood trauma healing will be beneficial for you. Sometimes, you may feel frustrated when your goals aren't achieved at the time you want them to be. Learning to live with nature's seasonal cycles and surrendering to divine timing is your soul's mission for this lifetime. Wearing clothing or accessories in shades of orange helps bring in the color energy while you are healing your soul wound. White jade and cinnabar are great energy companions to heal your soul wound.

Your main soul lessons are the red, green, and violet aura layers. Learning to take good care of your body; clearing and healing ancestral, karmic, and past-life wounds; opening up your heart to give and receive love; and developing your intuition and vision is your soul's journey for this lifetime. These themes will reoccur in different situations at various times of your life. This is a signal from the Universe that it is your soul's timing to learn that lesson. If you miss the signal the first time, the soul lesson will reoccur until you finally take notice and resolve it. Learning how to honor your body, clearing your ancestral and karmic wounds, healing your inner child, and rewriting your limiting beliefs are powerful practices that can help you navigate through life's challenges.

If your soul chooses to work on your orange aura layer soul wound first, once you have healed your soul wound, the orange aura layer will become one of your strengths in your Soul Aura Color composition. Because aura layers work in pairs, with one layer from the higher three chakras and one layer from the lower three chakras, at this point your soul can choose to combine the orange and blue aura layers so that you can become a Reformer Soul Gift Archetype.

Once you have learned your red aura layer soul lesson, you can blend your blue and red aura layers and shape-shift into a Teacher.

When you learn your green aura layer soul lesson, you can combine it with your yellow aura strength to become a Healer or your orange aura strength to become an Entertainer. The same is true of your violet aura layer soul lesson. Once you've learned it, your violet aura layer can be a strength, and you can mix it with your yellow aura strength to become a Visionary or your orange aura strength to become an Artist.

TEAL AURA COLOR SOULS

If your Soul Aura Color is Teal, you are a charismatic entrepreneur and probably an analytical thinker. You are typically the expert in your field, where your words carry weight, and you have good business instincts. You motivate others to work collaboratively to achieve goals. Wearing teal-colored clothing or accessories and decorating your home or office space with teal colors accentuate your soul gifts. Working with crystals like sodalite, blue tiger's eye, and rutilated quartz strengthens your soul gifts.

Your deep soul wound is the green aura powered by your heart chakra. Being vulnerable and open to heart-to-heart relationships is challenging for you. Learning to let go of your high standards and be less self-critical and more compassionate toward yourself and others is crucial to your soul-healing journey. Practicing self-love and compassion and healing your inner child are wonderful spiritual tools for your soul. Wearing clothing or accessories in shades of green helps bring in the color energy while you are healing your soul wound. Rose quartz, emerald, and rainforest rhyolite are great energy companions for your soul-healing journey.

Your major soul lessons are the red, orange, and violet aura layers. Healing your physical body, learning to trust and surrender control, regulating emotions, and speaking your truth authentically are some of the themes of your soul lessons. Integrating the knowledge of Feng Shui and Ayurveda and leaning in to seasonal living with the moon phases and the Wheel of the Year will make you more grounded and help you process your deep emotions. Clearing your ancestral, karmic, and past-life wounds, embracing your shadow self through shadow work, and developing your intuition and psychic abilities through a daily spiritual practice like meditation will unlock your full potential as an entrepreneur.

If your soul chooses to work on your green aura layer soul wound first, once you have healed your soul wound, the green aura layer will become one of your strengths in your Soul Aura Color composition. Because aura layers work in pairs, with one layer from the higher three chakras and one layer from the lower three chakras, at this point your soul can choose to combine the green and yellow aura layers so that you can become a Healer Soul Gift Archetype.

Once you have learned your red aura layer soul lesson, you can blend your red and green aura layers and shape-shift into a Warrior or your red and blue aura layers to transform into a Teacher. When you learn your orange aura layer soul lesson, you can combine it with your blue aura strength to become a Reformer or your green aura strength to become an Entertainer. The same is true of your violet aura soul lesson. Once you've learned it, your violet aura layer can be a strength, and you can mix it with your yellow aura strength to become a Visionary.

MINT AURA COLOR SOULS

If your Soul Aura Color is Mint, you are a practical Entrepreneur on this planet. You are down-to-earth and take practical actions to achieve your goals. Because you are driven to solve problems with practicality, innovative solutions are born from your brilliant mind. People trust you and are often amazed by the organizational skills that make you ideally suited for entrepreneurial ventures. Wearing mint-colored clothing or accessories and decorating your home or office space with mint colors accentuate your soul gifts. Working with crystals like green aventurine, bumblebee jasper, and blue tourmaline strengthens your soul gifts.

Your deep soul wound is the violet aura layer powered by the third eye chakra. You tended to have nightmares or experienced paranoia as a child. Having a clear vision or tapping into your intuition can be challenging. However, thanks to your powerful yellow aura layer powered by the solar plexus chakra, you trust your gut feelings as you manifest entrepreneurship. Studying spiritual wisdom of the true self or your soul's purpose (Western and Vedic astrology, Chinese Zodiac, Feng Shui Birth Element and Kua Number, Human Design, Enneagram, Gene Keys, Numerology, or simply a daily meditation practice) is helpful for you to understand your soul. Embracing your shadow self through shadow work and past-life regression work are crucial tools to release fear, develop intuition and psychic abilities, and receive spirit guidance. Wearing clothing or accessories in shades of violet helps bring in the color energy while you are healing your soul wound. Amethyst and clear quartz are great crystal companions for your soul-healing journey.

Your major soul lessons in this lifetime are your red, orange, and green aura layers. Tending to your physical body, nurturing your body with a seasonal Ayurvedic diet, finding physical exercise that agrees with you, and spending time in nature are beneficial for you. Daily emotional releases and returning to your center ground you. Adding some creative fun in your life relaxes you. Learning to be less critical of yourself and others is another important soul lesson you need to learn. Practicing self-compassion and tending to your inner child are wonderful medicine for your soul.

If your soul chooses to work on your violet aura layer soul wound first, once you have healed your soul wound, the violet aura layer will become one of your strengths in your Soul Aura Color composition. Because aura layers work in pairs, with one layer from the higher three chakras and one layer from the lower three chakras, at this point your soul can choose to combine the yellow and violet aura layers so that you can become a Visionary Soul Gift Archetype.

Once you have learned your red aura layer soul lesson, you can blend your blue and red aura layers and shape-shift into a Teacher, or blend your violet and red aura layers to transform into a Researcher. When you learn your orange aura layer soul lesson, you can combine it with your blue aura strength to become a Reformer or your violet aura strength to become an Artist. The same is true of your green aura layer soul lesson. Once you've learned it, your green aura layer can be a strength, and you can mix it with your yellow aura strength to become a powerful Healer.

ENTREPRENEUR EVOLUTION PATHS

The following diagrams show the four possible starting points and different paths for your Soul Gift Archetype evolution journey. You can choose to work on your soul wound first or learn one of the three soul lessons. As your soul grows, more aura layers will become your strength. When your soul works on healing soul wounds or learning soul lessons, and these aspects are completed to a satisfactory degree, free will can be exercised to combine aura layer strengths to embody different Soul Gift Archetypes. Of course, you can also choose to remain the Soul Gift Archetype you were born with but just have more light quotient in your Soul Aura Color composition, thus magnetizing high vibrational opportunities in your life and manifesting faster.

Entrepreneur Archetype

Entrepreneur Soul Gift Archetype Evolution Path 1

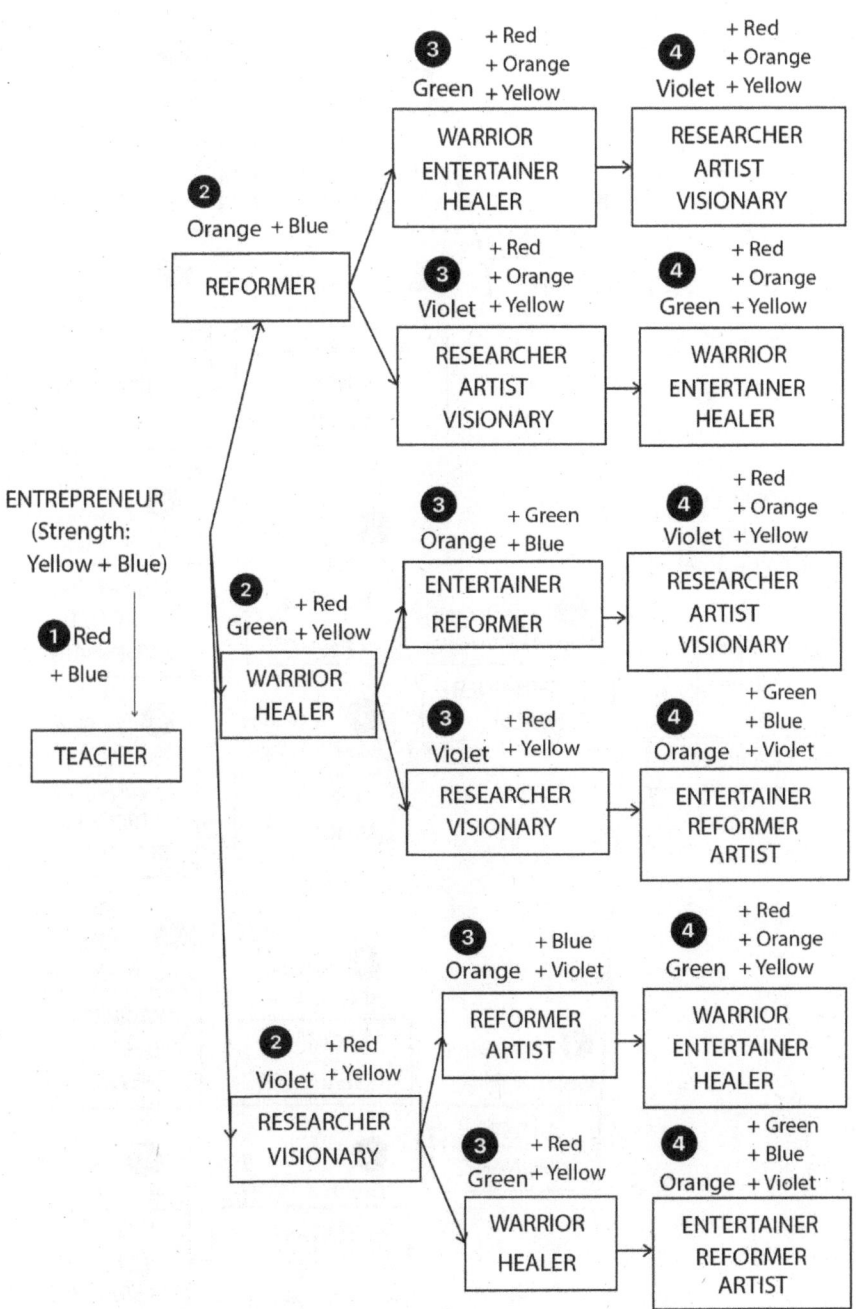

THE AURA COLOR WHEEL

Entrepreneur Soul Gift Archetype Evolution Path 2

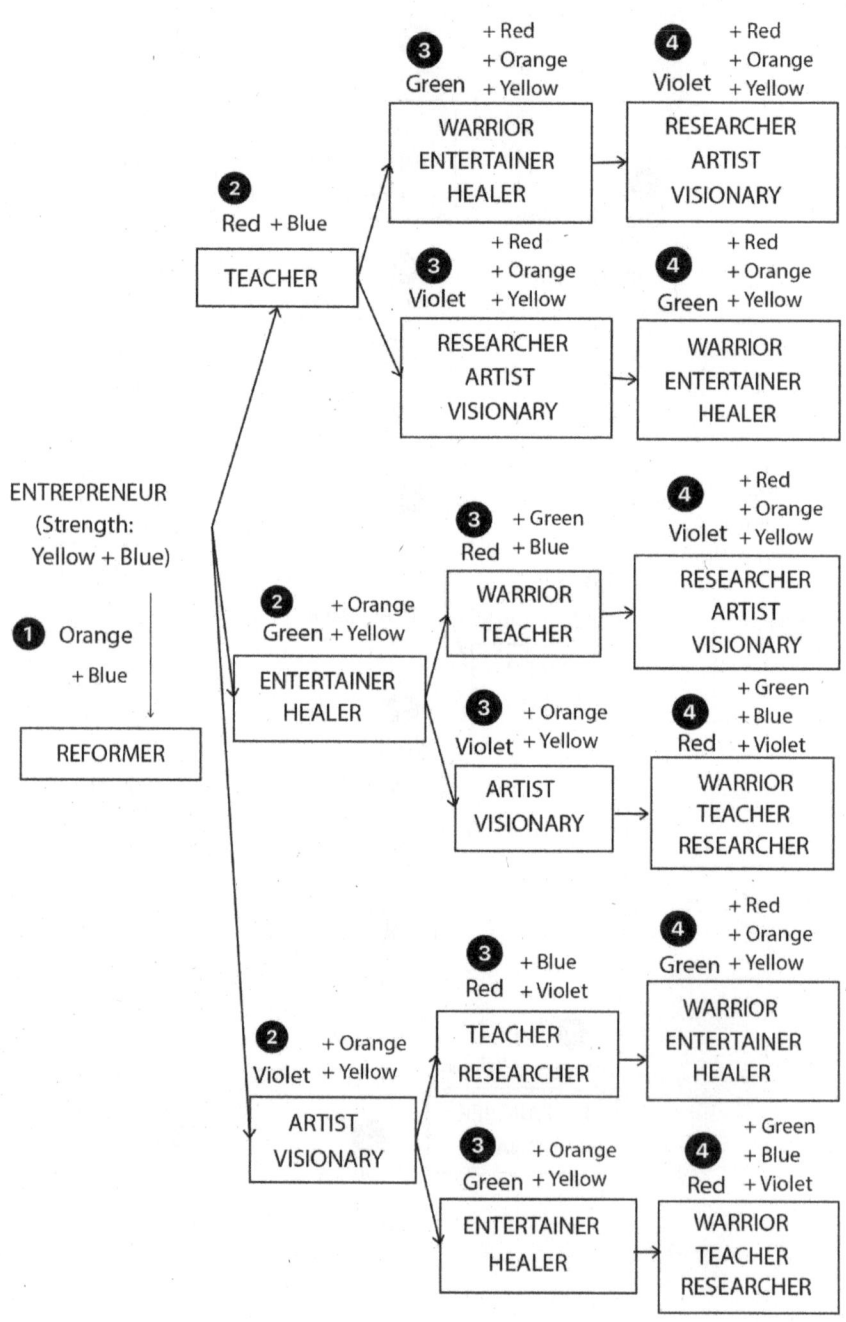

Entrepreneur Soul Gift Archetype Evolution Path 3

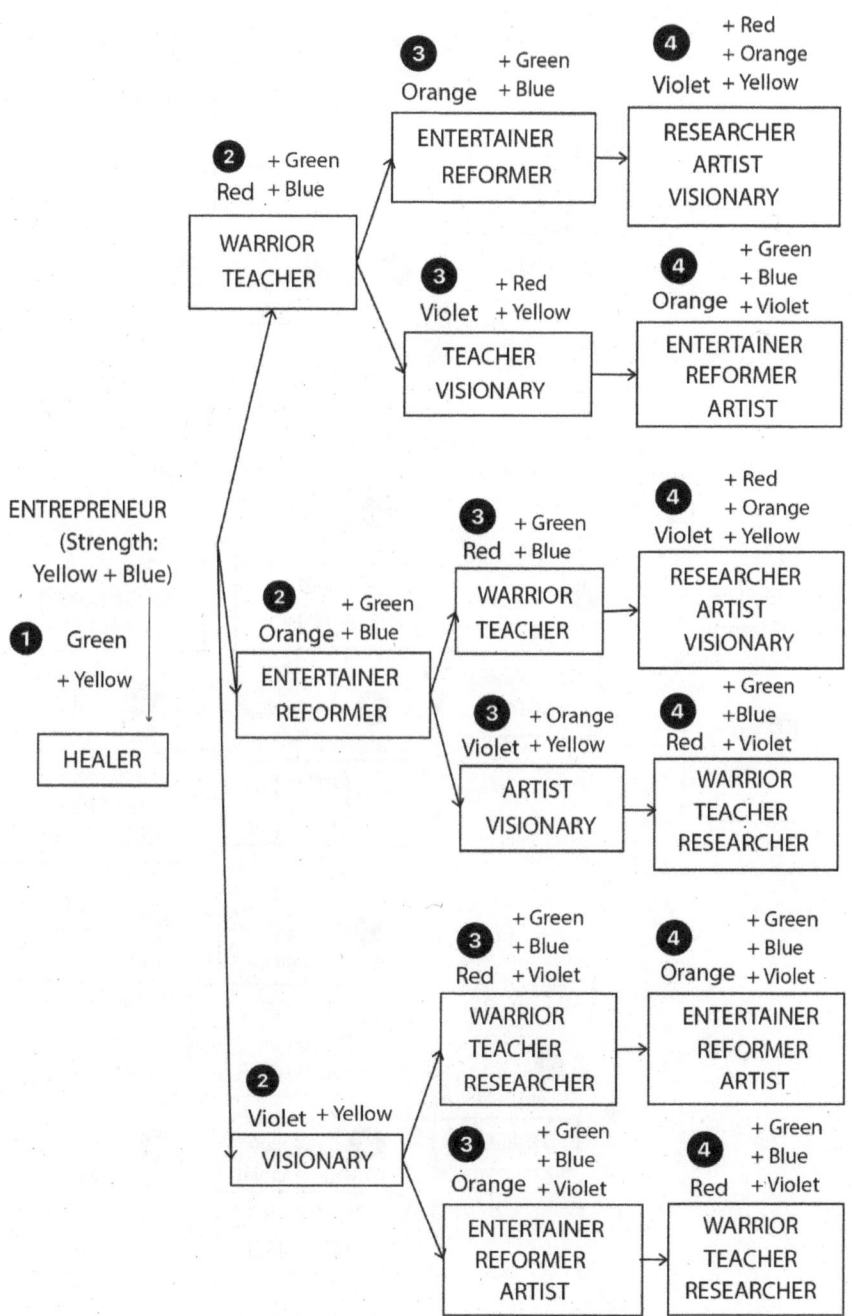

THE AURA COLOR WHEEL

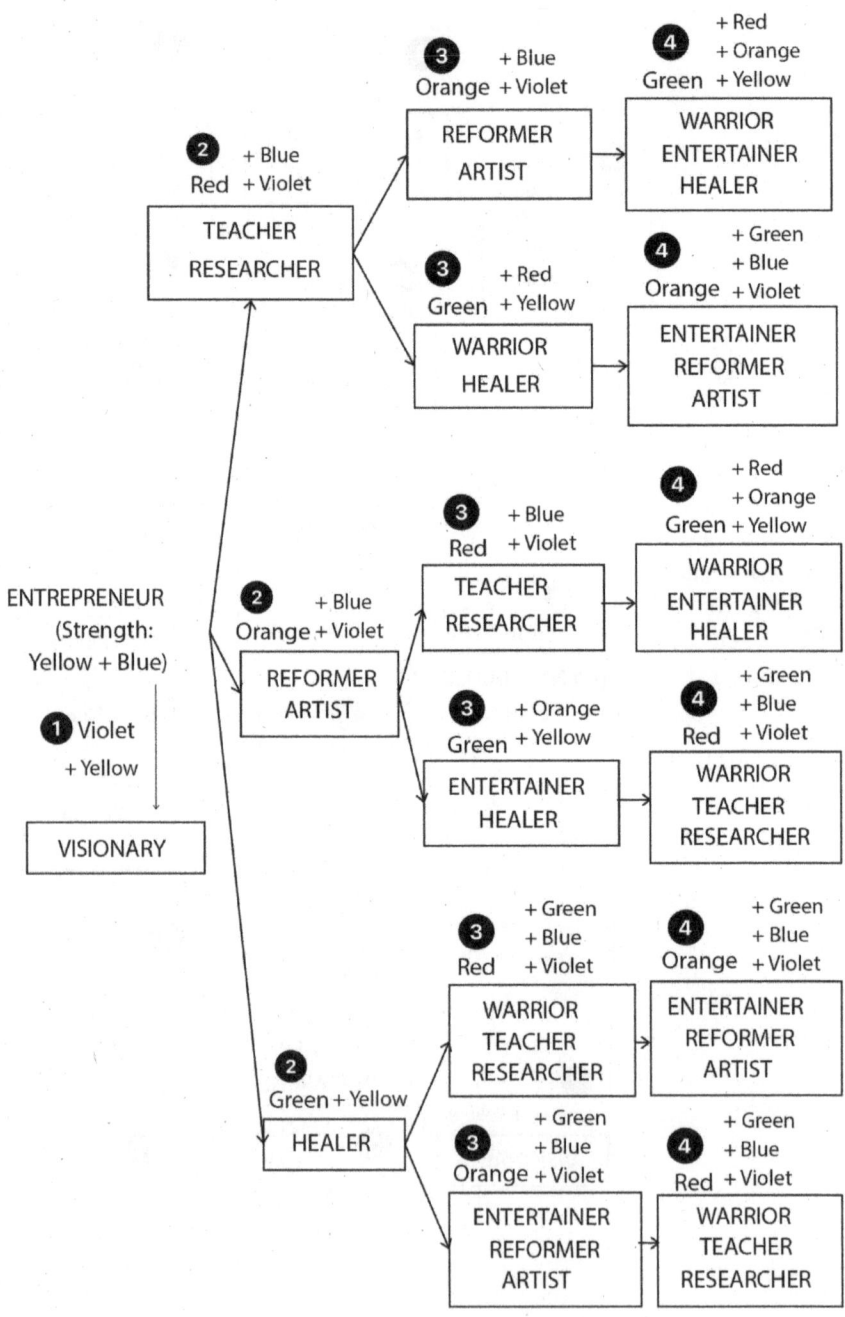

CHAPTER 6

HEALER ARCHETYPE

If your Soul Gift Archetype is Healer, you have a strong yellow aura layer powered by the solar plexus chakra and green aura layer powered by the heart chakra. These two aura layers are deeply connected to the heart center, fostering compassionate, authentic living. As a result, the Healer Archetype is naturally intuitive and deeply empathic. The main difference among Soul Aura Colors is their soul wound and soul lessons. Archangel Raphael and Archangel Chamuel are the great angels to call upon to assist you to fully embody your Healer soul gifts. Trust and use your innate claircognizance, clairtangency, clairsentience, and relational sympathy psychic abilities to receive spirit guidance.

HEALER SOUL AURA COLOR QUIZ

For each question, please select the option that best describes you based on your current state. I highly recommend you pick an answer intuitively—don't overthink it. If you have a few questions or really can't choose an answer, please leave it blank. If you have more than one selection that applies, please select all of them. Remember, auras are a spectrum of colors, not one static color. These questions are channeled to approximate your Soul Aura Color. Have fun!

THE AURA COLOR WHEEL

1. **In which area of life do you experience the most difficulties?**
   a. Family relationships or ancestral traumas
   b. Regulating emotions
   c. Speaking my truth without being self-conscious or worrying about what others think of me
   d. Planning and visualizing the future

2. **Where do you feel discomfort or illness most often?**
   a. Legs, feet, bone structure
   b. Hormones, reproductive system, lower back
   c. Throat, nose, ears, teeth, neck, mouth, jaw
   d. Sinuses, headaches, scalp, hair, autoimmune diseases, skin

3. **Which circumstances cause the most discomfort?**
   a. Fitting in with my family, feeling out of place
   b. Sharing emotions, being too emotional, empathizing with others
   c. Expressing myself clearly in public
   d. Sensing other people's energy

4. **What are you most afraid of feeling?**
   a. Lack of safety and security
   b. Guilt and shame
   c. Shyness, suppressing communication or talking too much, ADHD
   d. Paranoia or bad feelings about the future

5. **What are you missing that prevents you from living life to the fullest?**
   a. A sense of being grounded and centered
   b. Creativity and spontaneity
   c. Truthful communication
   d. Intuition and psychic abilities

Healer Archetype

6. Which emotional blocks do you feel most often?
   a. Anxiety or depression
   b. Sadness, isolation, or emotional eating
   c. Nervousness, unease, or lingering trauma
   d. Lack of intuition or inspiration

7. Which issues do you frequently encounter?
   a. Insecurity, doubt, low self-worth
   b. Inability to say no, guilt
   c. Inability to relax, a need to always be doing something
   d. Mental fog, feeling stuck or in a rut

8. Which superpower would change your life?
   a. The power to stay present and bring spiritual knowledge into daily actions
   b. The power to find calm and peace in everyday life
   c. The power to communicate with the Divine and spirits
   d. The power to gain vision, clarity, inspiration, and innovation

9. If you could change one thing about yourself, what would it be?
   a. I want to have the courage to move forward in life: career, new adventures and opportunities, etc.
   b. I want to feel inspired, creative, decisive, and flowing with life.
   c. I want to possess strong leadership skills to move society forward according to my ideals.
   d. I want to be open to insights and intuitive guidance from the Divine to better understand myself.

THE AURA COLOR WHEEL

10. Does your birthday fall in any of the following groups of timing? If not, just leave this blank.

   a. July 26, 1943, 6:42 P.M. – November 17, 1944, 11:23 P.M.
   March 23, 1945, 10:50 P.M. – July 22, 1945, 12:31 P.M.
   February 8, 1951, 8:26 P.M. – June 18, 1951, 9:13 A.M.
   November 8, 1951, 11:22 P.M. – January 27, 1955, 11:28 A.M.
   September 3, 1993, 1:32 P.M. – September 9, 1995, 10:28 A.M.
   December 11, 2001, 6:04 P.M. – February 21, 2005, 12:33 P.M.
   July 31, 2005, 11:48 P.M. – December 5, 2005, 8:03 P.M.

   b. May 28, 1938, 8:39 A.M. – September 29, 1940, 11:44 P.M.
   December 27, 1940, 12:59 A.M. – June 16, 1941, 2:34 P.M.
   May 28, 1977, 2:05 P.M. – June 21, 1983, 8:19 A.M.
   November 29, 1983, 8:19 A.M. – April 10, 1984, 11:19 P.M.
   June 21, 1988, 5:40 A.M. – July 21, 1991, 11:54 A.M.
   June 19, 2026, 5:17 P.M. – September 17, 2026, 9:54 P.M.
   April 14, 2027, 10:56 P.M. – July 19, 2033, 9:35 A.M.

   c. January 27, 1955, 11:28 A.M. – March 26, 1960, 8:39 A.M.
   August 19, 1960, 2:31 A.M. – January 20, 1961, 8:50 P.M.
   June 21, 1983, 9:54 A.M. – November 29, 1983, 8:19 A.M.
   April 10, 1984, 11:19 P.M. – June 21, 1988, 5:40 A.M.
   February 21, 2005, 12:33 P.M. – July 31, 2005, 11:48 P.M.
   December 5, 2005, 8:03 P.M. – April 20, 2010, 2:28 P.M.
   July 20, 2010, 5:46 A.M. – February 8, 2011, 2:55 P.M.
   July 19, 2033, 9:35 A.M. – October 23, 2033, 6:21 P.M.
   May 5, 2034, 5:50 P.M. – July 22, 2038, 1:49 A.M.

   d. November 10, 1946, 2:14 P.M. – February 8, 1951, 8:26 P.M.
   January 18, 1951, 9:13 A.M. – November 8, 1951, 11:22 P.M.
   December 29, 1996, 6:16 A.M. – April 4, 1997, 11:50 A.M.
   September 2, 1997, 11:24 P.M. – December 11, 2001, 6:04 P.M.

Please mark down how many of each selection you have:

   a. _____   c. _____
   b. _____   d. _____

Healer Archetype

- If you chose mostly A answers, your aura color is 15: *Jade*.
- If you chose mostly B answers, your aura color is 16: *Turquoise*.
- If you chose mostly C answers, your aura color is 7: *Yellow*.
- If you chose mostly D answers, your aura color is 8: *Emerald*.

If you have two or more equal selections, it can mean one of the following:

1. You have two or more aura colors in your auric field. Please read the descriptions and intuitively pick which one resonates with you the most to work with now.
2. You are in transition from one aura color to another within the same Soul Gift Archetype. This happens when you heal a certain aura layer soul wound and are now working on another aura layer soul wound or soul lesson. Remember, soul wounds are just deeper soul lessons.

JADE AURA COLOR SOULS

If your Soul Aura Color is Jade, you are compassionate and loving. In other lifetimes, some of you were Starseeds living on other planets and in other galaxies. Sometimes you lack a feeling of belonging and experience a longing for home. Your Healer soul gift becomes powerful when you remember and integrate your multidimensional nature, bringing that cosmic medicine to Mother Earth. Trusting your heart and your gut feelings are your soul's guidance on your path. Wearing jade-colored clothing or accessories and decorating your home or office spaces with jade colors accentuate your soul gifts. Working with crystals like jade, healerite (lemon jade), lemurian quartz, and golden healer quartz strengthens your soul gifts.

Your deep soul wound is the red aura layer powered by the root chakra. You tend to struggle with long-term, physical issues, or family issues from either the paternal or maternal lineage, especially when you were a child. Sometimes you feel a lack of security and safety. Learning to incorporate some Ayurveda and Feng Shui practices into your home and life would be extremely beneficial. Clearing and healing ancestral, karmic, and past-life wounds are important soul missions. Wearing clothing or accessories in shades of red helps bring in the color energy while you are healing your soul wound. Lodolite (garden quartz), brecciated jasper, and nuummite are great crystal companions for your soul-healing journey.

Your main soul lessons are the orange, blue, and violet aura layers powered by the sacral, throat, and third eye chakras. Identifying, processing, and facing your emotions are the best ways to transmute them. Some of you might struggle with relationships, whether an intimate relationship, a friendship, or with a family member. Learning to set healthy boundaries is important. Practicing daily affirmations, working through limiting beliefs, and embracing your shadow self are great spiritual practices for your soul. Forming a daily meditation or spiritual practice to connect with your spirit team for guidance will nourish your soul.

If your soul chooses to work on your red aura layer soul wound first, once you have healed your soul wound, the red aura layer will become one of your strengths in your Soul Aura Color composition. Because aura layers work in pairs, with one layer from the higher three chakras and one layer from the lower three chakras, at this point your soul can choose to combine the red and green aura layers so that you can become a Warrior Soul Gift Archetype.

Once you have learned your orange aura layer soul lesson, you can blend your green and orange aura layers and shape-shift into an Entertainer. When you learn your blue aura layer soul lesson, you can combine it with your yellow aura strength to become an Entrepreneur, or with your red aura strength to become a Teacher. The same is true of your violet aura layer soul lesson. Once you've learned it, your violet aura layer can be a strength, and you can mix it with your yellow aura strength to become a Visionary or your red aura strength to become a Researcher.

TURQUOISE AURA COLOR SOULS

If your Soul Aura Color is Turquoise, you are an "old soul" of planet Earth, and you have incarnated here across many lifetimes. You are the original shamans, medicine men and women, doulas, and healing witches of all kinds. You are drawn to holistic and alternative medicine modalities and may practice one of the traditional medicines like Chinese herbal medicine, Ayurveda, Reiki, acupuncture, sound healing, crystal healing, shamanism, and so on. Perhaps you are a psychotherapist or hypnotherapist in the modern world. Wearing turquoise-colored clothing or accessories and decorating your home or office space with turquoise colors accentuate your soul gifts. Working with crystals like turquoise, ammonite, seraphinite, and llanite (que sera) strengthens your soul gifts.

Your deep soul wound is the orange aura layer powered by the sacral chakra. A sensitive, highly empathetic, and emotional soul, you feel others' feelings and wounds. You tend to have health issues related to your hormonal system. If you are a female, you may have PMS or difficult menstrual cycles. Working with moonstones (all varieties) and peach selenite and leaning in to your body's natural rhythm, living with the seasons, moon cycles, and the Wheel of the Year are all beneficial practices for you. Use your soul gifts to heal your soul wound. Reclaiming your divine feminine power and healing others with similar difficulties is one of your soul's missions in this lifetime. Wearing clothing or accessories in shades of orange helps bring in the color energy while you are healing your soul wound.

Your main soul lessons are the red, blue, and violet aura layers powered by the root, throat, and third eye chakras. As a powerful mystic, you may have some past-life prosecution memories haunting you in this life. Clearing out past-life, ancestral, and karmic wounds are great healing tools. Affirming your personal power, being authentically you, and learning to trust your intuition while developing your psychic abilities are some of the soul lessons you are here to learn.

If your soul chooses to work on your orange aura layer soul wound first, once you have healed your soul wound, the orange aura layer will become one of your strengths in your Soul Aura Color composition.

Because aura layers work in pairs, with one layer from the higher three chakras and one layer from the lower three chakras, at this point your soul can choose to combine the orange and green aura layers so that you can become an Entertainer Soul Gift Archetype.

Once you have learned your red aura soul lesson, you can blend your green and red aura layers and shape-shift into a fierce Warrior. When you learn your blue aura layer soul lesson, you can combine it with your yellow aura strength to become an Entrepreneur, or with your orange aura strength to become a Reformer. The same is true of your violet aura soul lesson. Once you've learned it, your violet aura layer can be a strength, and you can mix it with your yellow aura strength to become a Visionary or your orange aura strength to become an Artist.

YELLOW AURA COLOR SOULS

If your Soul Aura Color is Yellow, you are a positive, modern healer on planet Earth. You may be a doctor, nurse, dietitian, nutritionist, esthetician, or work in the medical, health, or wellness fields. You are compassionate and care about the well-being of others. You are also ambitious and hardworking. Wearing yellow-colored clothing or accessories and decorating your home or office space with yellow colors accentuate your soul gifts. Working with crystals like rainbow fluorite, hydrogrossular garnet, and scepter quartz strengthens your soul gifts.

Your deep soul wound is the blue aura layer powered by the throat chakra. You tend to have physical issues related to your thyroid gland, sinuses, neck, and shoulders. Communicating your truth authentically is challenging for you. Daily affirmations, sound baths, and mantra meditations are helpful spiritual healing tools. Wearing clothing or accessories in shades of blue helps bring in the color energy while you are healing your soul wound. Blue apatite and tanzanite are great crystal companions for your soul-healing journey.

Your main soul lessons are the red, orange, and violet aura layers powered by the root, sacral, and third eye chakras. You are ambitious and work hard toward your goals. Daily grounding and body nourishment are crucial to you. The practice of Feng Shui and Ayurveda are beneficial to fulfill your soul gifts. Processing deeply buried emotions, embracing your shadow self, and learning to prioritize your intuition are some of your soul lessons for this lifetime. Cultivating a daily spiritual practice like meditation and connecting with your spirit team help balance your life.

If your soul chooses to work on your blue aura layer soul wound first, once you have healed your soul wound, the blue aura layer will become one of your strengths in your Soul Aura Color composition. Because aura layers work in pairs, with one layer from the higher three chakras and one layer from the lower three chakras, at this point your soul can choose to combine your blue and yellow aura layers so that you can become an Entrepreneur Soul Gift Archetype.

Once you have learned your red aura layer soul lesson, you can blend your red and green aura layers and shape-shift into a Warrior or your red and blue aura layers to transform into a Teacher. When you learn your orange aura layer soul lesson, you can combine it with your green aura strength to become an Entertainer or your blue aura strength to become a Reformer. The same is true of your violet aura layer soul lesson. Once you've learned it, your violet aura layer can be a strength, and you can mix it with your yellow aura strength to become a powerful Visionary.

EMERALD AURA COLOR SOULS

If your Soul Aura Color is Emerald, you are a powerful heart healer, a highly sensitive soul who is deeply empathetic. Your healing gifts apply not only to humans but also to animals and plants. You may be an animal lover or plant parent, and the world is a warmer place because of you. You have deep connections with Mother Earth and are drawn to plant-based diets and medicine. Wearing emerald-colored clothing or accessories and decorating your home or office space with emerald accentuate your soul gifts. Working with crystals like emerald, moss agate, fuchsite, and optical calcite strengthens your soul gifts.

Your deep soul wound is the violet aura layer powered by the third eye chakra. You had nightmares or experienced paranoia as a child. Having a clear vision or tapping into your intuition can be challenging. Studying spiritual wisdom of the true self or your soul's purpose

THE AURA COLOR WHEEL

(Western and Vedic astrology, Chinese Zodiac, Feng Shui Birth Element and Kua Number, Human Design, Enneagram, Gene Keys, Numerology, or simply a daily meditation practice) is helpful for you to understand your soul. Embracing your shadow self through shadow work and past-life regression work are crucial tools to release fear, find divine connections, and trust spiritual guidance. Wearing clothing or accessories in shades of violet helps bring in the color energy while you are healing your soul wound. Prehnite and apophyllite are great crystal companions for your soul-healing journey.

Your main soul lessons are the red, orange, and blue aura layers powered by the root, sacral, and throat chakras. You are often busy taking care of others, but taking time for self-care is important. Nurturing your physical body, regulating your emotions, and speaking your truth authentically are some of your soul lessons. Learning and integrating the knowledge of Feng Shui and Ayurveda and leaning in to seasonal living with the moon phases and the Wheel of the Year will make you more grounded and able to process your deep emotions more easily. Clearing limiting beliefs about yourself and setting healthy boundaries are beneficial practices.

If your soul chooses to work on your violet aura layer soul wound first, once you have healed your soul wound, the violet aura layer will become one of your strengths in your Soul Aura Color composition. Because aura layers work in pairs, with one layer from the higher three chakras and one layer from the lower three chakras, at this point your soul can choose to combine your violet and yellow aura layers so that you can become a Visionary Soul Gift Archetype.

Once you have learned your red aura layer soul lesson, you can blend your green and red aura layers and shape-shift into a fierce Warrior or your violet and red aura layers to transform into a Researcher. When you learn your orange aura layer soul lesson, you can combine it with your green aura strength to become an Entertainer or your violet aura strength to become an Artist. The same is true of your blue aura layer soul lesson. Once you've learned it, your blue aura layer can be a strength, and you can mix it with your yellow aura strength to become an Entrepreneur.

HEALER EVOLUTION PATHS

The following diagrams show the four possible starting points and different paths for your Soul Gift Archetype evolution journey. You can choose to work on your soul wound first or learn one of the three soul lessons. As your soul grows, more aura layers will become your strength. When your soul works on healing soul wounds or learning soul lessons and these aspects are completed to a satisfactory degree, free will can be exercised to combine aura layer strengths to embody different Soul Gift Archetypes. Of course, you can also choose to remain the Soul Gift Archetype you were born with but just have more light quotient in your Soul Aura Color composition, thus magnetizing high vibrational opportunities in your life and manifesting faster.

THE AURA COLOR WHEEL

Healer Soul Gift Archetype Evolution Path 1

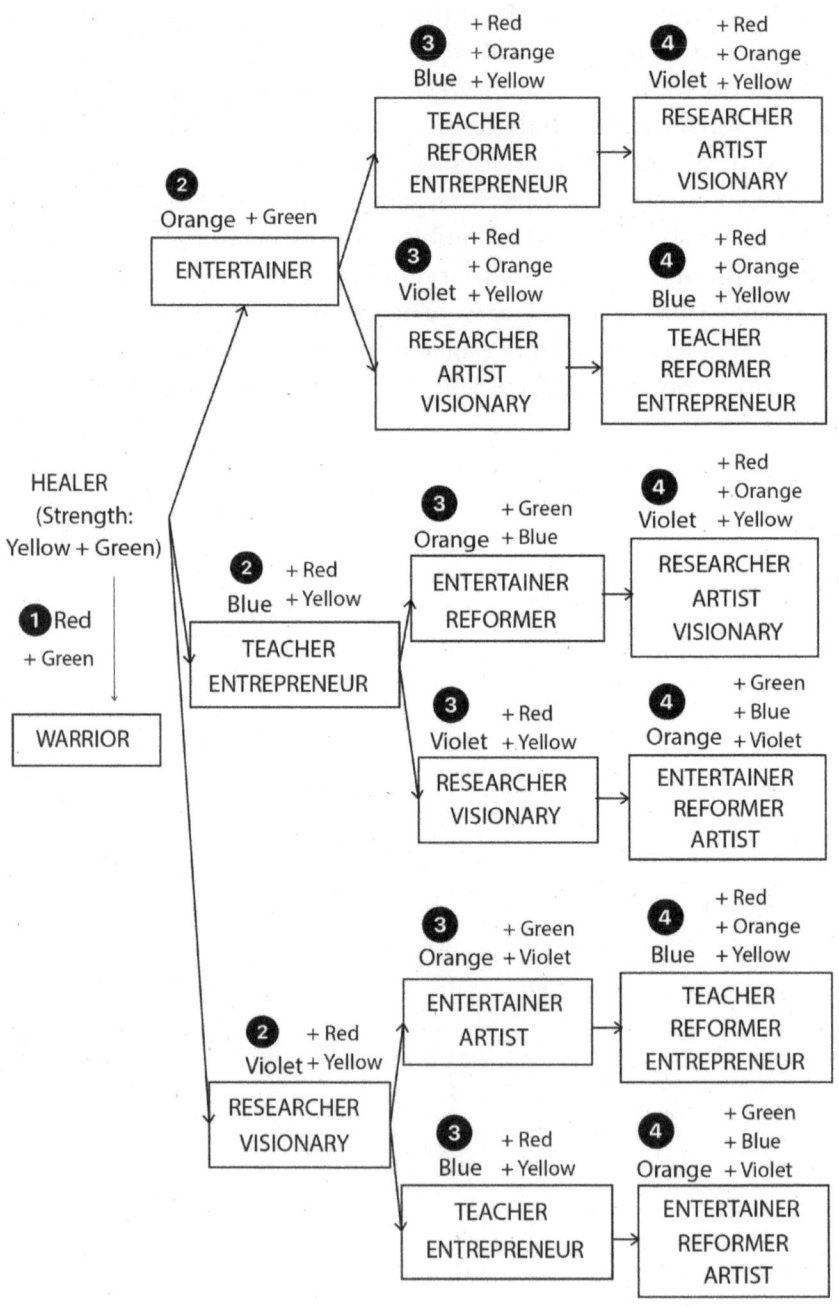

Healer Archetype

Healer Soul Gift Archetype Evolution Path 2

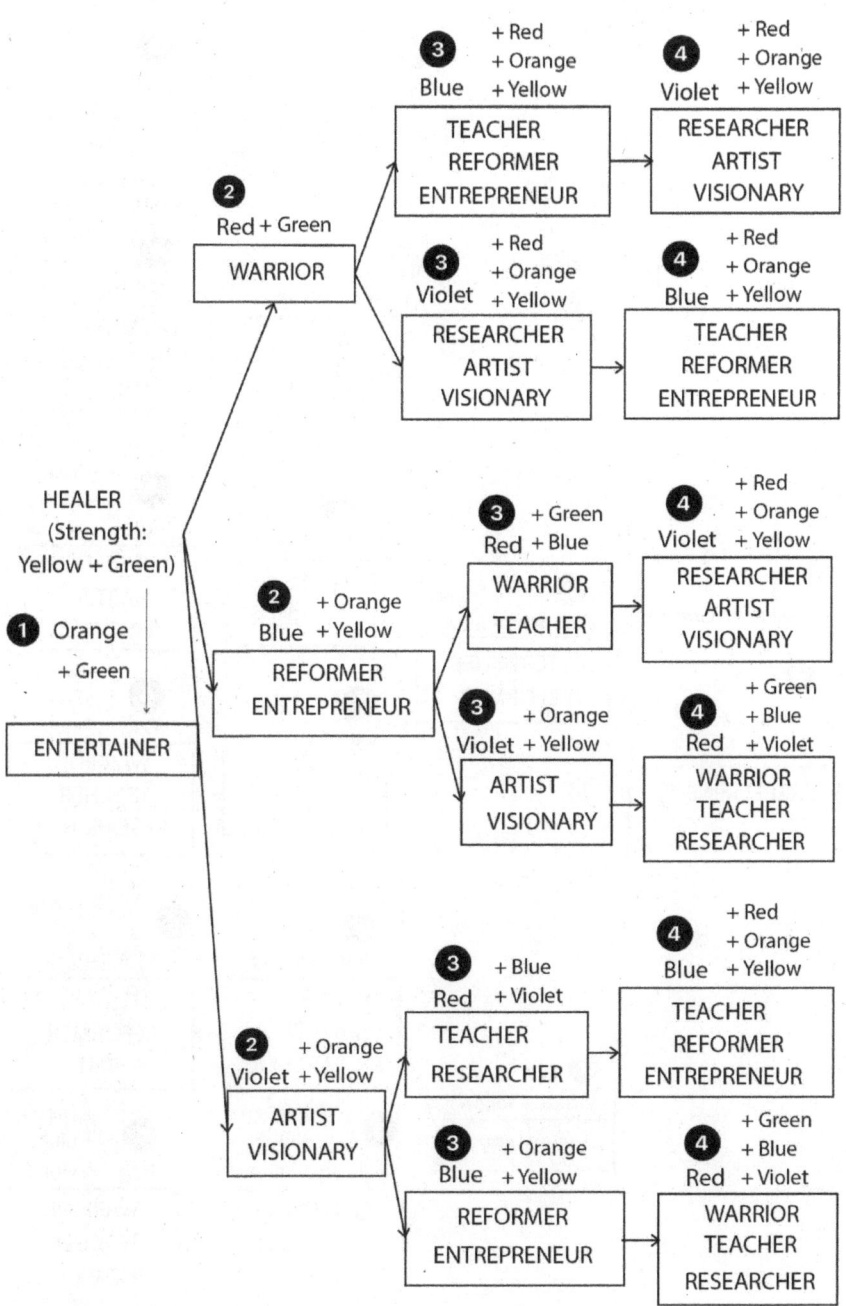

THE AURA COLOR WHEEL

Healer Soul Gift Archetype Evolution Path 3

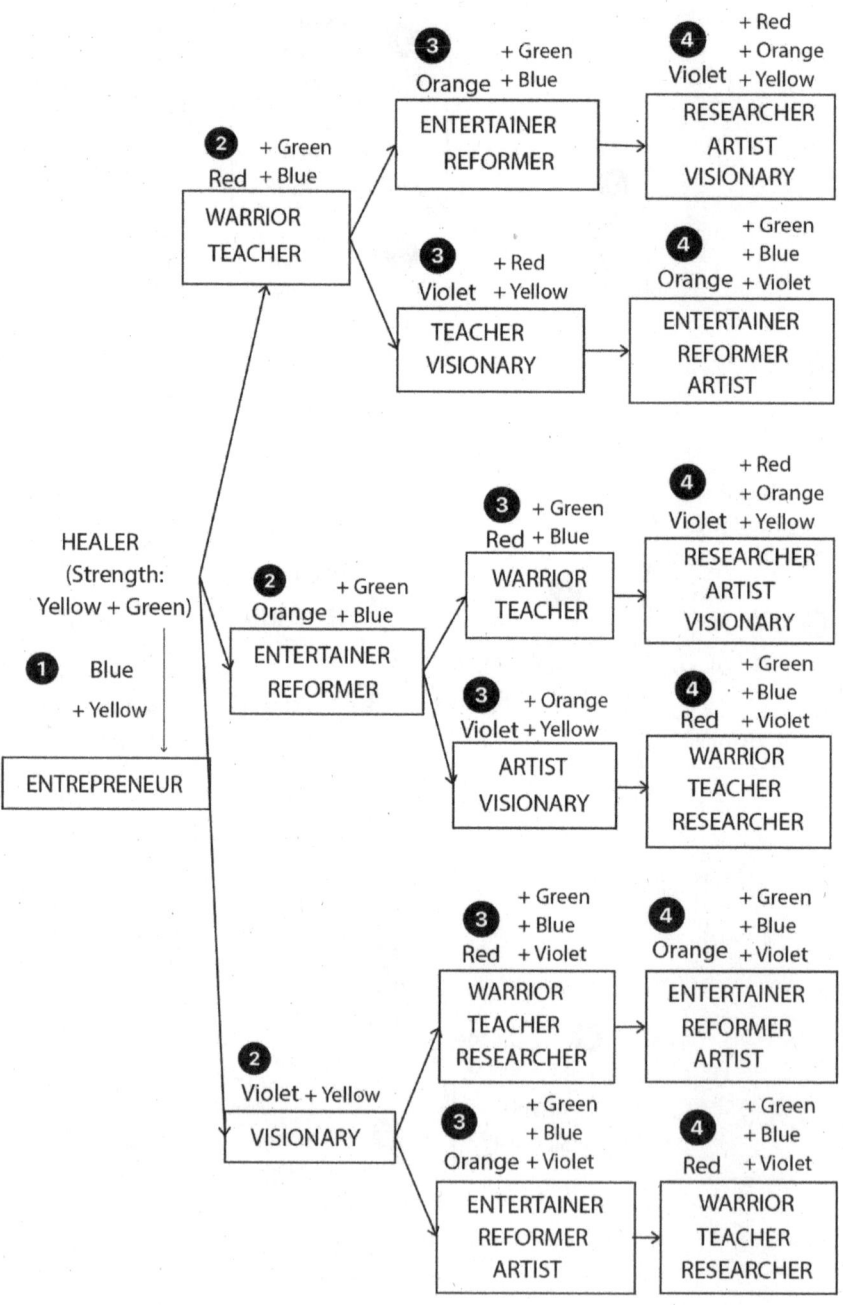

Healer Archetype

Healer Soul Gift Archetype Evolution Path 4

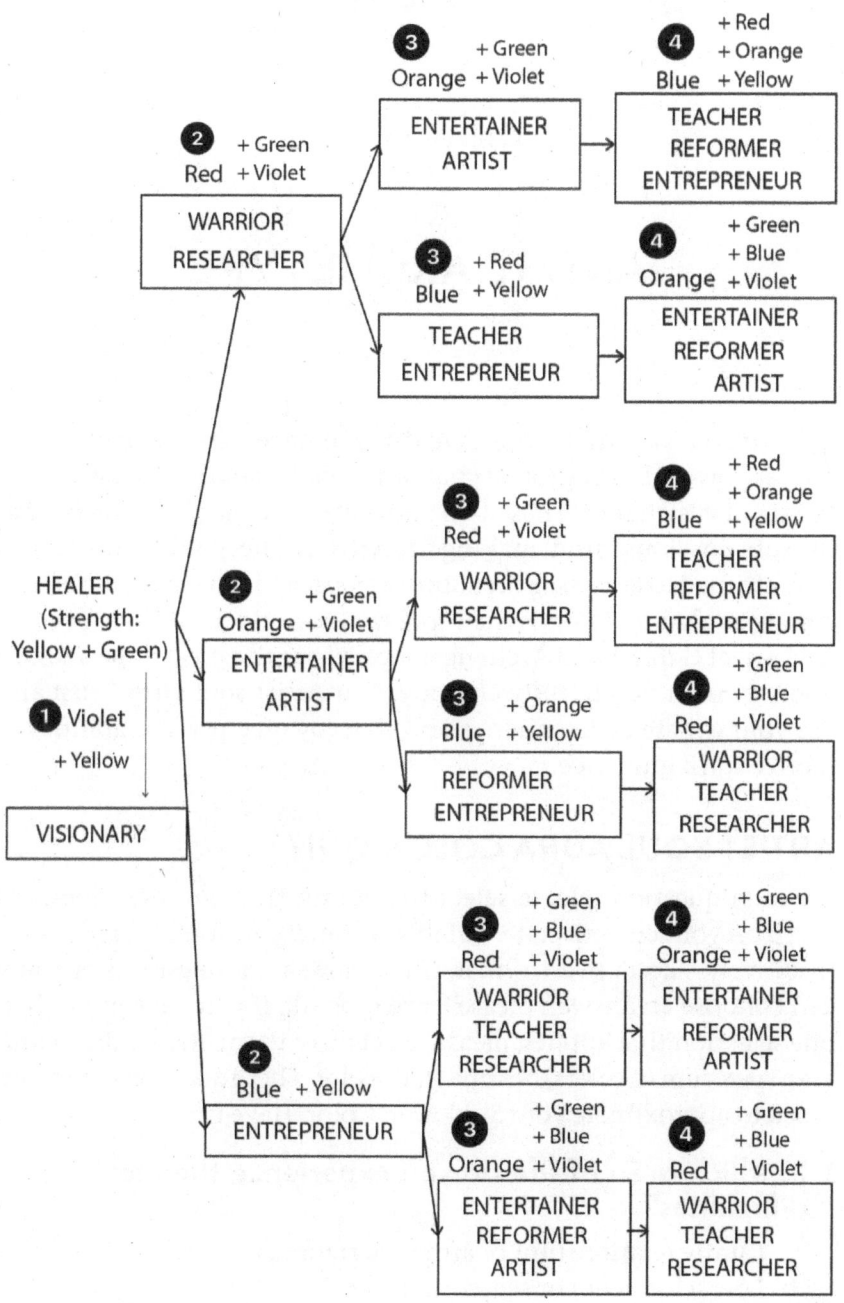

CHAPTER 7

ARTIST ARCHETYPE

If your Soul Gift Archetype is Artist, you have a strong orange aura layer powered by the sacral chakra and violet aura layer powered by the third eye chakra. These two aura layers are deeply connected to the subconscious mind, making the Artist Archetype the most naturally attuned to accessing the subconscious field. The main difference among Soul Aura Colors is their soul wound and soul lessons for each. Archangel Gabriel and Archangel Jophiel are the great angels to call upon to assist you to fully embody your Artist soul gifts. Trust and use your innate clairsentience and clairvoyance psychic abilities to receive spirit guidance.

ARTIST SOUL AURA COLOR QUIZ

For each question, please select the option that best describes you based on your current state. I highly recommend you pick an answer intuitively—don't overthink it. If you have a few questions or really can't choose an answer, please leave it blank. If you have more than one selection that applies, please select all of them. Remember, auras are a spectrum of colors, not one static color. These questions are channeled to approximate your Soul Aura Color. Have fun!

1. In which area of life do you experience the most difficulties?
    a. Family relationships or ancestral traumas
    b. Low self-esteem or self-confidence

c. Being vulnerable, giving and receiving love
   d. Speaking my truth without being self-conscious or worrying about what other people think of me

2. **Where do you feel discomfort or illness most often?**
   a. Legs, feet, bone structure
   b. Digestion, liver, spleen, gallbladder, pancreas
   c. Heart, chest, breast, asthma, blood pressure
   d. Throat, nose, ears, teeth, neck, mouth, jaw

3. **Which circumstances cause the most discomfort?**
   a. Fitting in with my family, feeling out of place
   b. Standing up for myself or something I value
   c. Having intimate relationships
   d. Expressing myself with clarity in public

4. **What are you most afraid of feeling?**
   a. Lack of safety and security
   b. Low motivation and self-image
   c. Jealousy, desire to please others, sadness
   d. Shyness, suppressing communication or talking too much, ADHD

5. **What are you missing that prevents you from living life to the fullest?**
   a. A sense of being grounded and centered
   b. Confidence and motivation
   c. Vulnerability and forgiveness
   d. Truthful communications

6. **Which emotional blocks do you feel most often?**
   a. Anxiety or depression
   b. Anger, frustration, or low energy
   c. Jealousy, or fear of inadequacies
   d. Nervousness, unease, or lingering trauma

THE AURA COLOR WHEEL

7. Which issues do you frequently encounter?
   a. Insecurity, doubt, low self-worth
   b. Low self-esteem, confidence, or energy
   c. Difficulty having hope or faith
   d. Inability to relax, the need to always be doing something

8. Which superpower would change your life?
   a. The power to stay present and bring spiritual knowledge into daily actions
   b. The power of courage and inner strength to take action and weather storms
   c. The power of connection and harmony with my loved ones and community
   d. The power to communicate with the Divine and spirits

9. If you could change one thing about yourself, what would it be?
   a. I want to have the courage to move forward in life: career, new adventures and opportunities, etc.
   b. I want to be able to take actions purposefully according to my beliefs and ideas.
   c. I want to have an intimate connection with my significant other and a loving relationship with myself.
   d. I want to possess strong leadership skills to move society forward according to my ideals.

10. Does your birthday fall in any of the following groups of timing? If not, just leave this blank.
   a. July 26, 1943, 6:42 P.M. – November 17, 1944, 11:23 P.M.
      March 23, 1945, 10:50 P.M. – July 22, 1945, 12:31 P.M.
      February 8, 1951, 8:26 P.M. – June 18, 1951, 9:13 A.M.
      November 8, 1951, 11:22 P.M. – January 27, 1955, 11:28 A.M.
      September 3, 1993, 1:32 P.M. – September 9, 1995, 10:28 A.M.
      December 11, 2001, 6:04 P.M. – February 21, 2005, 12:33 P.M.
      July 31, 2005, 11:48 P.M. – December 5, 2005, 8:03 P.M.

Artist Archetype

b. September 29, 1940, 11:44 P.M. – December 27, 1940, 12:59 P.M.
June 16, 1941, 2:34 P.M. – July 26, 1943, 6:42 P.M.
April 1, 1968, 2:08 P.M. – October 18, 1968, 6:36 P.M.
January 30, 1969, 3:12 A.M. – May 28, 1976, 7:10 A.M.
October 13, 1976, 6:46 P.M. – March 28, 1977, 2:05 P.M.
July 21, 1991, 11:54 P.M. – September 3, 1993, 1:32 P.M.
April 17, 2018, 4:09 P.M. – September 25, 2018, 8:12 P.M.
February 18, 2019, 4:07 P.M. – June 19, 2026, 5:17 P.M.
September 17, 2026, 9:54 P.M. – April 14, 2027, 10:56 P.M.

c. November 27, 1944, 11:23 P.M. – March 23, 1945, 10:50 P.M.
July 22, 1945, 12:31 P.M. – November 10, 1946, 2:14 A.M.
March 26, 1960, 8:39 P.M. – August 19, 1960, 2:31 A.M.
January 20, 1961, 8:50 P.M. – April 1, 1968, 2:08 A.M.
October 18, 1968, 6:36 P.M. – January 30, 1969, 3:12 P.M.
September 9, 1995, 10:28 P.M. – December 29, 1996, 6:16 P.M.
April 4, 1997, 11:50 A.M. – September 2, 1997, 11:24 P.M.
April 20, 2010, 2:28 A.M. – July 20, 2010, 5:46 P.M.
February 8, 2011, 2:55 P.M. – April 17, 2018, 4:09 A.M.
September 25, 2018, 8:12 P.M. – February 18, 2019, 4:07 A.M.

d. January 27, 1955, 11:28 A.M. – March 26, 1960, 8:39 A.M.
August 19, 1960, 2:31 A.M. – January 20, 1961, 8:50 P.M.
June 21, 1983, 9:54 A.M. – November 29, 1983, 8:19 A.M.
April 10, 1984, 11:19 P.M. – June 21, 1988, 5:40 A.M.
February 21, 2005, 12:33 P.M. – July 31, 2005, 11:48 P.M.

Please mark down how many of each selection you have:

a. _____ c. _____
b. _____ d. _____

- If you chose mostly A answers, your aura color is 12: *Apple.*
- If you chose mostly B answers, your aura color is 31: *Magenta.*
- If you chose mostly C answers, your aura color is 35: *Rose.*
- If you chose mostly D answers, your aura color is 05: *Tangerine.*

If you have two or more equal selections, it can mean one of the following:

1. You have two or more aura colors in your auric field. Please read the descriptions and intuitively pick which one resonates with you the most to work with now.
2. You are in transition from one aura color to another within the same Soul Gift Archetype. This happens when you heal a certain aura layer soul wound and are now working on another aura layer soul wound or soul lesson. Remember, soul wounds are just deeper soul lessons.

APPLE AURA COLOR SOULS

If your Soul Aura Color is Apple, you are creative and innovative. When you tap into the inner reservoir of your soul gifts, your creations will surprise and amaze others. You resist conforming to societal norms and prefer to live in the flow. You are curious and brave in experimenting with different forms, mediums, and ways to express yourself. You have powerful visualization skills due to your strong violet aura layer, and creativity with your strong orange aura layer. Wearing apple-colored clothing or accessories and decorating your home or office space with apple green colors accentuate your soul gifts. Working with crystals like labradorite, red tiger's eye, and super seven strengthens your soul gifts.

Your deep soul wound is the red aura layer powered by the root chakra. Because of your wild imagination, people may believe you're not grounded. As a child, you sometimes found it hard to belong, as if you were outside of the family pack. Clearing ancestral and karmic wounds are part of your soul-healing journey. Tending to your physical health and honoring your uniqueness are important. You need to develop a sense of security in your own skin to heal any anxiety or depression you experience. Learning and incorporating Ayurveda and Feng Shui into your life is beneficial. Wearing clothing or accessories in shades of red helps bring in the color energy while you are healing your soul wound. Bloodstone and rainbow hematite are great crystal companions for your soul-healing journey.

Artist Archetype

Your main soul lessons are the yellow, green, and blue aura layers powered by the solar plexus, heart, and throat chakras. Opening your heart to be vulnerable to give and receive unconditional love and learning to trust that process is one of your biggest soul lessons. Reclaiming your self-esteem through self-empowerment and daily affirmation practices is key to your soul growth. You need to learn how to let go of outside judgment and express your truth authentically.

If your soul chooses to work on your red aura layer soul wound first, once you have healed your soul wound, the red aura layer will become one of your strengths in your Soul Aura Color composition. Because aura layers work in pairs, with one layer from the higher three chakras and one layer from the lower three chakras, at this point your soul can choose to combine your red and violet aura layers so that you can become a Researcher Soul Gift Archetype.

Once you have learned your yellow aura layer soul lesson, you can blend your violet and yellow aura layers and shape-shift into a Visionary. When you learn your green aura layer soul lesson, you can combine it with the orange aura strength to become an Entertainer or the red aura strength to become a Warrior. The same is true of your blue aura layer soul lesson. Once you've learned it, your blue aura layer can be a strength, and you can mix it with your orange aura strength to become a Reformer or your red aura strength to become a Teacher.

MAGENTA AURA COLOR SOULS

If your Soul Aura Color is Magenta, you are exuberant and bold! You're not afraid to show off your true colors, and you live life to the fullest. A joyful spirit, you express your artistic talent in various ways—the beautiful interior of your home, the soundtracks you choose for the party, or your fashion sense. You have good taste in all things. Wearing magenta-colored clothing or accessories and decorating your home or office space with magenta colors accentuate your soul gifts. Working with crystals like cobaltoan calcite, tiffany stone, and phosphosiderite strengthens your soul gifts.

Your deep soul wound is the yellow aura layer powered by the solar plexus chakra. Self-acceptance is your soul growth journey. Although flamboyant in nature, you are also self-conscious and receptive to other people's opinions about you. Depending on the family you grew up with, your self-esteem varies by environment. Gaining that true sense of self-confidence is key to healing your soul wound. Studying spiritual wisdom of the true self or your soul's purpose (Western and Vedic astrology, Chinese Zodiac, Feng Shui Birth Element and Kua Number, Human Design, Enneagram, Gene Keys, Numerology) is helpful for you to clear limiting beliefs and have a healthy relationship with the self. Wearing clothing or accessories in shades of yellow helps bring in the color energy while you are healing your soul wound. Imperial topaz and sulfur are wonderful crystal companions for your soul-healing journey.

Your main soul lessons are the red, green, and blue aura layers powered by the root, heart, and throat chakras. You are likely to have some long-term physical issues to work on that may have started when you were a child. Parent-child relationships can be difficult for you. Expressing yourself authentically and setting healthy boundaries are important soul lessons in this lifetime. Establishing a healthy lifestyle, keeping a gratitude journal, and practicing daily affirmations are wonderful remedies for your soul.

If your soul chooses to work on your yellow aura layer soul wound first, once you have healed your soul wound, the yellow aura layer will become one of your strengths in your Soul Aura Color composition. Because aura layers work in pairs, with one layer from the higher three chakras and one layer from the lower three chakras, at this point your soul can choose to combine the yellow and violet aura layers so that you can become a Visionary Soul Gift Archetype.

Once you have learned your red aura layer soul lesson, you can blend your violet and red aura layers and shape-shift into a Researcher. When you learn your green aura layer soul lesson, you can combine it with your orange aura strength to become an Entertainer or your yellow aura strength to become a Healer. The same is true of your blue aura layer soul lesson. Once you've learned it, your blue aura layer can be a strength, and you can mix it with the orange aura strength to become a Reformer or the yellow aura strength to become an Entrepreneur.

ROSE AURA COLOR SOULS

If your Soul Aura Color is Rose, you have a vivid imagination. You are romantic and drawn to beauty, and you may be a poet, painter, or musician. You long for romantic and passionate love. You enjoy all the good things in life, and you are graceful and elegant and have good taste. Wearing rose-colored clothing or accessories and decorating your home or office space with rose colors accentuate your soul gifts. Working with crystals like pink aura quartz, vanadinite, and auralite 23 strengthens your soul gifts.

Your deep soul wound is the green aura layer powered by the heart chakra. Intimate relationships have been a challenge in your life. Due to childhood trauma or karmic wounds, you shield your heart for protection. Learning to trust and be open to give and receive love is your soul-healing journey in this lifetime. Practicing self-compassion, forgiveness, and healing the inner child are remedies for your soul. Shadow work can help you embrace every aspect of yourself. Wearing clothing or accessories in shades of green helps bring in the color energy while you are healing your soul wound. Rhodochrosite and morganite are great crystal companions for your soul-healing journey.

Your main soul lessons are the red, yellow, and blue aura layers powered by the root, solar plexus, and throat chakras. Because you have a vivid imagination, you may often live in your dreams. Sometimes others may find you aloof. A daily grounding practice and spending time in nature are beneficial for you. Reclaiming your personal power by setting healthy boundaries is another soul lesson for you. Accept yourself fully, love yourself unconditionally, and express yourself authentically, and you will thrive and shine your unique light.

If your soul chooses to work on your green aura layer soul wound first, once you have healed your soul wound, the green aura layer will become one of your strengths in your Soul Aura Color composition. Because aura layers work in pairs, with one layer from the higher three chakras and one layer from the lower three chakras, at this point your soul can choose to combine your green and orange aura layers so that you can become an Entertainer Soul Gift Archetype.

THE AURA COLOR WHEEL

Once you have learned your red aura layer soul lesson, you can blend your red aura layer strength and violet aura layers and shapeshift into a Researcher or your red and green aura layers to transform into a Warrior. When you learn your yellow aura layer soul lesson, you can combine it with your violet aura strength to become a Visionary, or with your green aura strength to become a Healer. The same is true of your blue aura layer soul lesson. Once you've learned it, your blue aura layer can be your strength, and you can mix it with your orange aura strength to become a Reformer.

TANGERINE AURA COLOR SOULS

If your Soul Aura Color is Tangerine, you are a passionate creative on planet Earth. You dance with the flow spontaneously. You enjoy all the good things in life: cuisine, art, music, interior design, fashion, and accessories. You love to create. Because of your joyful energy, you attract people to appreciate your creations. The world is a more beautiful place because of you! You tend to have vivid visuals in your third eye of what you want to create, or sometimes hear melodies in your mind to channel through a musical composition. Your innate sense of divine connection is strong. Wearing tangerine-colored clothing or accessories and decorating your home or office space with tangerine colors accentuate your soul gifts. Working with crystals like tangerine aura quartz, Picasso jasper, and amphibole quartz strengthens your soul gifts.

Your deep soul wound is the blue aura layer powered by the throat chakra. Communicating your truth is sometimes challenging for you. Instead, you use your creativity to channel your thoughts and emotions. You tend to have physical issues related to the throat, sinuses, thyroid gland, neck, shoulders, or nervous system. Practicing daily affirmations, sound baths, and processing any childhood emotional trauma can be mind and spiritual medicine for your soul. Wearing clothing or accessories in shades of blue helps bring in the color energy while you are healing your soul wound. Blue lace agate and blue topaz are great crystal companions for your soul-healing journey.

Your main soul lessons are the red, yellow, and green aura layers powered by the root, solar plexus, and heart chakras. As a child, you sometimes found it difficult navigating your place in the world. You felt unsettled and distanced from family and friends. In extreme circumstances, addictions, phobias, and obsessions developed. Cultivating a healthy lifestyle, learning and integrating Ayurveda and Feng Shui, and having a group of positive, empowered friends can be beneficial. You may need to go through some relationship challenges before learning what love really is. For you to be open to unconditional love, you need to first learn to forgive yourself and release any grief you are holding.

If your soul chooses to work on your blue aura layer soul wound first, once you have healed your soul wound, the blue aura layer will become one of your strengths in your Soul Aura Color composition. Because aura layers work in pairs, with one layer from the higher three chakras and one layer from the lower three chakras, at this point your soul can choose to combine your blue and orange aura layers so that you can become a Reformer Soul Gift Archetype.

Once you have learned your red aura layer soul lesson, you can blend your violet and red aura layers and shape-shift into a Researcher or your blue and red aura layers to transform into a Teacher. When you learn your yellow aura layer soul lesson, you can combine it with the violet aura strength to become a Visionary or the blue aura strength to become an Entrepreneur. The same is true of your green aura layer soul lesson. Once you've learned it, your green aura layer can be a strength, and you can mix it with your orange aura strength to become an Entertainer.

ARTIST EVOLUTION PATHS

The following diagrams show the four possible starting points and different paths for your Soul Gift Archetype evolution journey. You can choose to work on your soul wound first or learn one of the three soul lessons. As your soul grows, more aura layers will become your strength. When your soul works on healing soul wounds or learning soul lessons, and these aspects are completed to a satisfactory degree, free will can be exercised to combine aura layer strengths to embody different Soul Gift Archetypes. Of course, you can also choose to remain the Soul Gift Archetype you were born with but just have more light quotient in your Soul Aura Color composition, thus magnetizing high vibrational opportunities in your life and manifesting faster.

THE AURA COLOR WHEEL

Artist Soul Gift Archetype Evolution Path 1

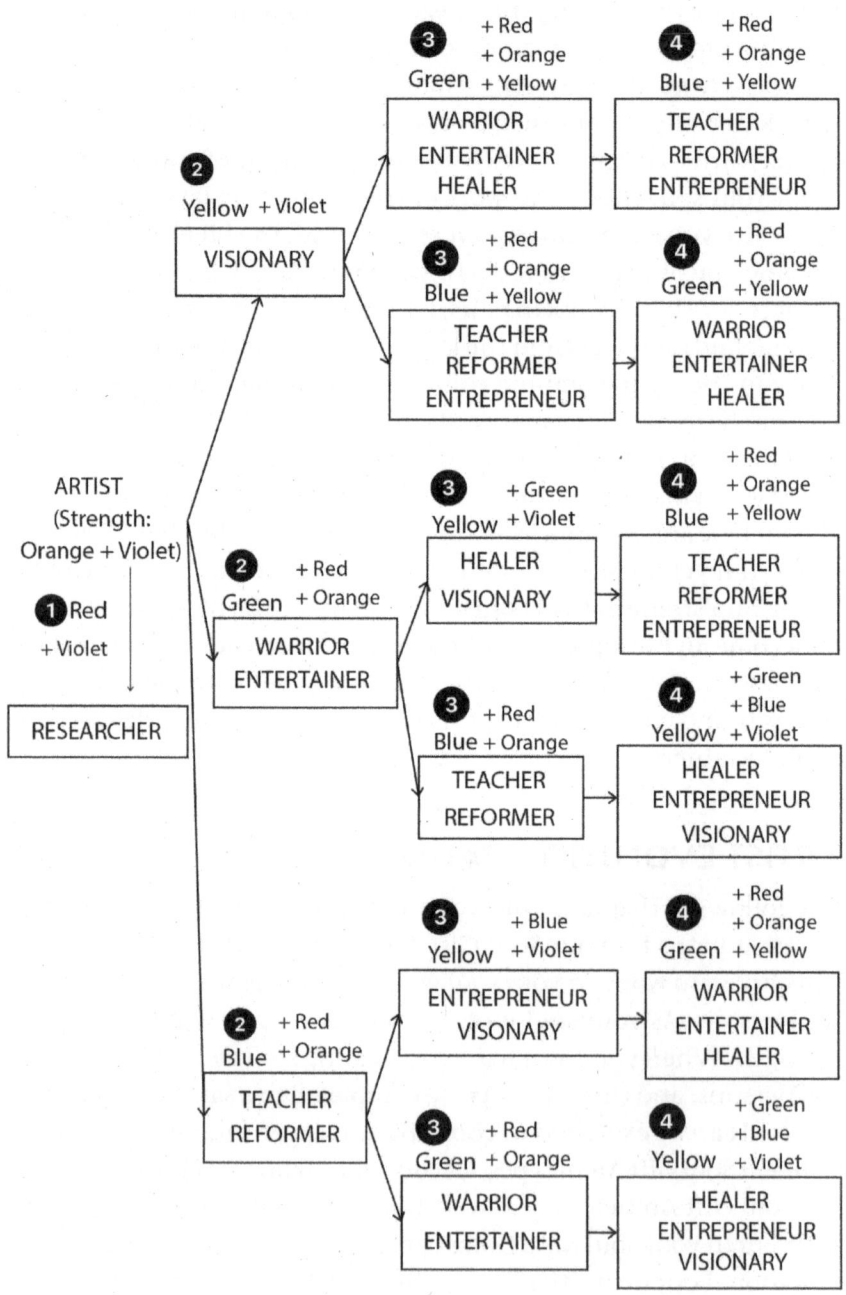

Artist Archetype

Artist Soul Gift Archetype Evolution Path 2

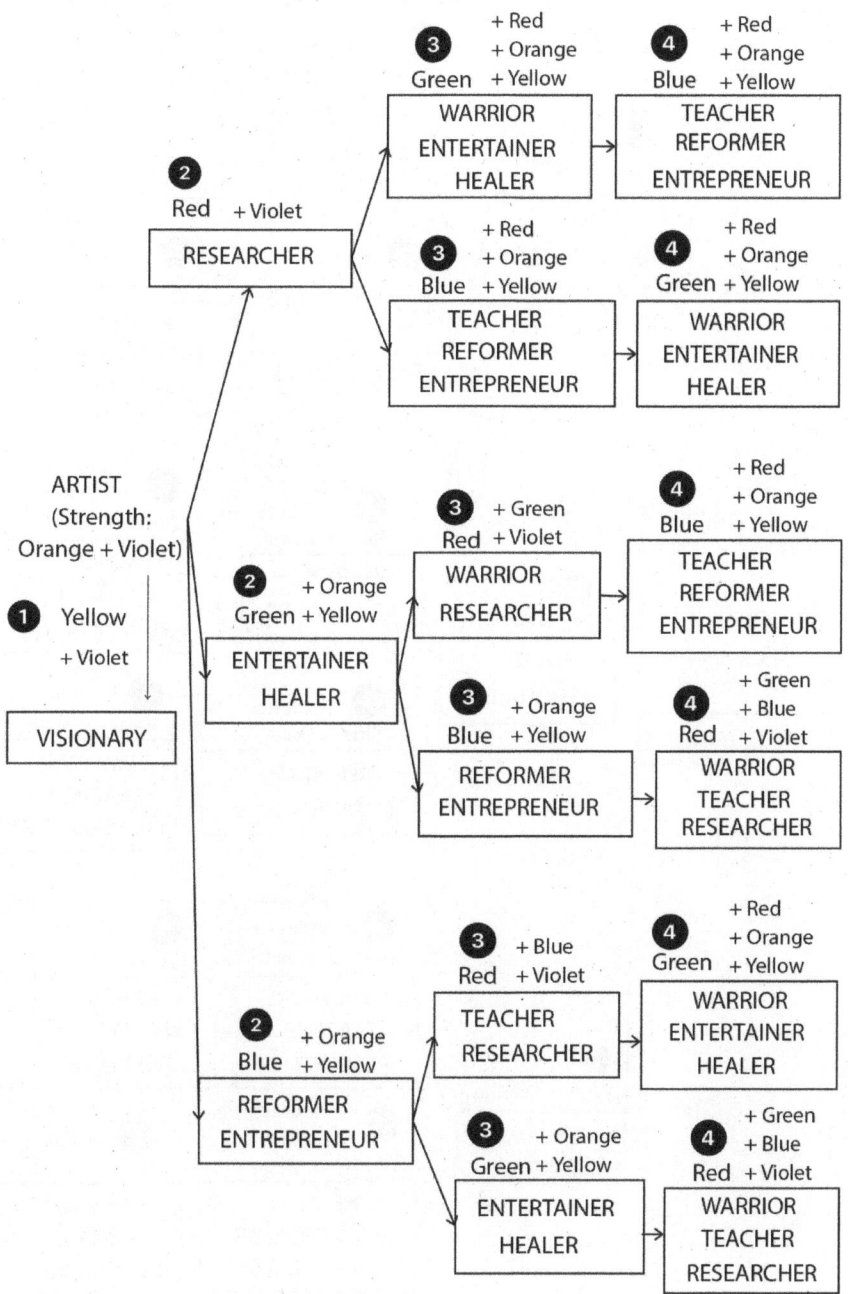

THE AURA COLOR WHEEL

Artist Soul Gift Archetype Evolution Path 3

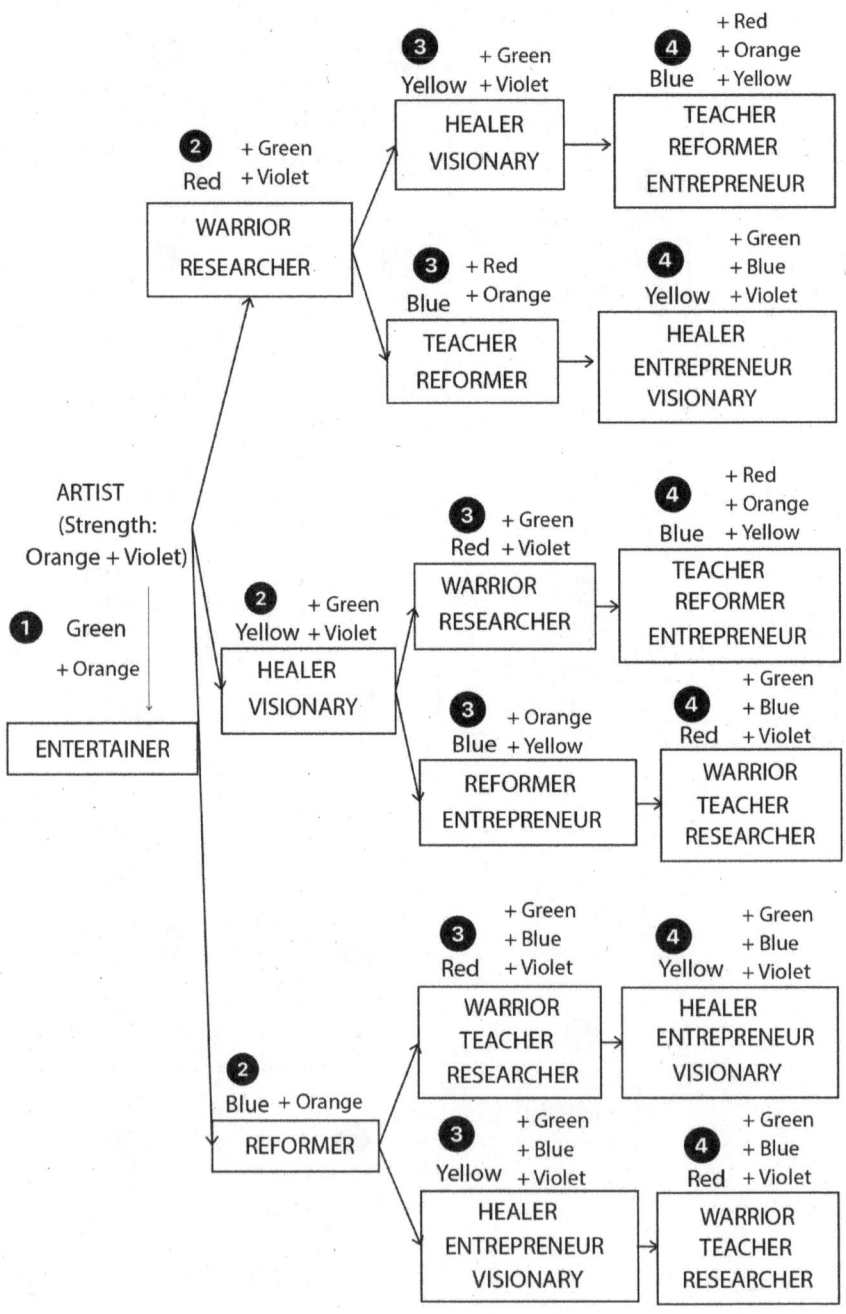

Artist Archetype

Artist Soul Gift Archetype Evolution Path 4

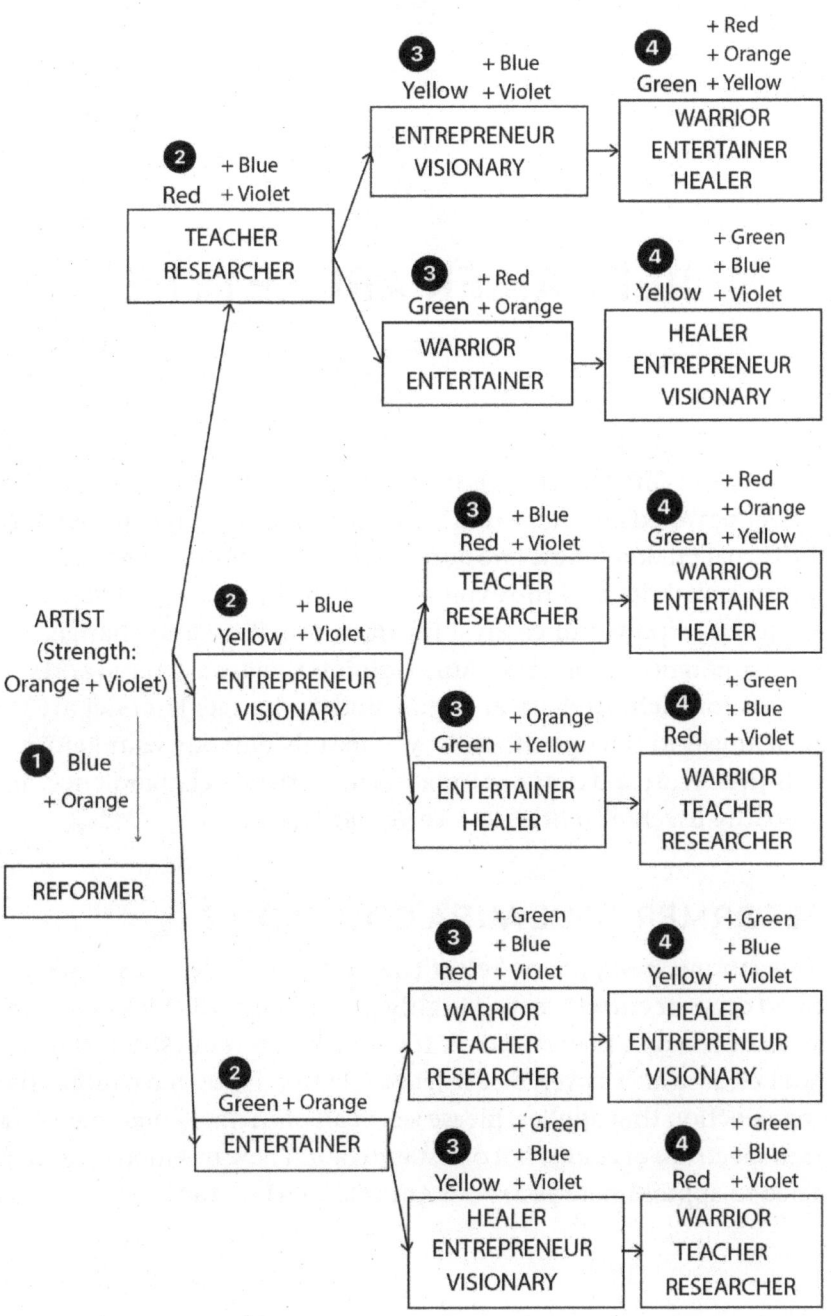

CHAPTER 8

REFORMER ARCHETYPE

If your Soul Gift Archetype is Reformer, you have a strong orange aura layer powered by the sacral chakra and blue aura layer powered by the throat chakra. These two aura layers are deeply connected to passionate creativity and the expression of truth, making the Reformer Archetype a powerful catalyst for transformation and change. The main difference among Soul Aura Colors is their soul wound and soul lessons for each. Archangel Raguel and Archangel Jeremiel are the great angels to call upon to assist you to fully embody your Reformer soul gifts. Trust and use your innate clairsentience, clairaudience, and telepathy psychic abilities to receive spirit guidance.

REFORMER SOUL AURA COLOR QUIZ

For each question, please select the option that best describes you based on your current state. I highly recommend you pick an answer intuitively—don't overthink it. If you have a few questions or really can't choose an answer, please leave it blank. If you have more than one selection that applies, please select all of them. Remember, auras are a spectrum of colors, not one static color. These questions are channeled to approximate your Soul Aura Color. Have fun!

Reformer Archetype

1. **In which area of life do you experience the most difficulties?**
   a. Family relationships or ancestral traumas
   b. Low self-esteem or self-confidence
   c. Being vulnerable, giving and receiving love
   d. Planning and visualizing the future

2. **Where do you feel discomfort or illness most often?**
   a. Legs, feet, bone structure
   b. Digestion, liver, spleen, gallbladder, pancreas
   c. Heart, chest, breast, asthma, blood pressure
   d. Sinuses, headaches, scalp, hair, autoimmune diseases, skin

3. **Which circumstances cause the most discomfort?**
   a. Fitting in with my family, feeling out of place
   b. Standing up for myself or something I value
   c. Having intimate relationships
   d. Sensing other people's energy

4. **What are you most afraid of feeling?**
   a. Lack of safety and security
   b. Low motivation or self-image
   c. Jealousy, desire to please others, sadness
   d. Paranoia or bad feelings about the future

5. **What are you missing that prevents you from living life to the fullest?**
   a. A sense of being grounded and centered
   b. Confidence and motivation
   c. Vulnerability and forgiveness
   d. Intuition and psychic abilities

6. **Which emotional blocks do you feel most often?**
    a. Anxiety or depression
    b. Anger, frustration, or low energy
    c. Jealousy, or fear of inadequacies
    d. Lack of intuition or inspiration

7. **Which issues do you frequently encounter?**
    a. Insecurity, doubt, low self-worth
    b. Low self-esteem, confidence, or low energy
    c. Lack of hope or faith
    d. Mental fog, feeling stuck or in a rut

8. **Which superpower would change your life?**
    a. The power to stay present and bring spiritual knowledge into daily actions
    b. The power of courage and inner strength to take actions and weather storms
    c. The power of connection and harmony with my loved ones and community
    d. The power to gain vision, clarity, inspiration, and innovation

9. **If you could change one thing about yourself, what would it be?**
    a. I want to have the courage to move forward in life: career, new adventures and opportunities, etc.
    b. I want to be able to take actions purposefully according to my beliefs and ideas.
    c. I want to have an intimate connection with my significant other and a loving relationship with myself.
    d. I want to be open to insights and intuitive guidance from the Divine to better understand myself.

Reformer Archetype

10. Does your birthday fall in any of the following groups of timing? If not, just leave this blank.

a. July 26, 1943, 6:42 P.M. – November 17, 1944, 11:23 P.M.
March 23, 1945, 10:50 P.M. – July 22, 1945, 12:31 P.M.
February 8, 1951, 8:26 P.M. – June 18, 1951, 9:13 A.M.
November 8, 1951, 11:22 P.M. – January 27, 1955, 11:28 A.M.
September 3, 1993, 1:32 P.M. – September 9, 1995, 10:28 A.M.
December 11, 2001, 6:04 P.M. – February 21, 2005, 12:33 P.M.
July 31, 2005, 11:48 P.M. – December 5, 2005, 8:03 P.M.

b. September 29, 1940, 11:44 P.M. – December 27, 1940, 12:59 P.M.
June 16, 1941, 2:34 P.M. – July 26, 1943, 6:42 P.M.
April 1, 1968, 2:08 P.M. – October 18, 1968, 6:36 P.M.
January 30, 1969, 3:12 A.M. – May 28, 1976, 7:10 A.M.
October 13, 1976, 6:46 P.M. – March 28, 1977, 2:05 P.M.
July 21, 1991, 11:54 P.M. – September 3, 1993, 1:32 P.M.
April 17, 2018, 4:09 P.M. – September 25, 2018, 8:12 P.M.
February 18, 2019, 4:07 P.M. – June 19, 2026, 5:17 P.M.
September 17, 2026, 9:54 P.M. – April 14, 2027, 10:56 P.M.

c. November 27, 1944, 11:23 P.M. – March 23, 1945, 10:50 P.M.
July 22, 1945, 12:31 P.M. – November 10, 1946, 2:14 A.M.
March 26, 1960, 8:39 P.M. – August 19, 1960, 2:31 A.M.
January 20, 1961, 8:50 P.M. – April 1, 1968, 2:08 A.M.
October 18, 1968, 6:36 P.M. – January 30, 1969, 3:12 P.M.
September 9, 1995, 10:28 P.M. – December 29. 1996, 6:16 P.M.
April 4, 1997, 11:50 A.M. – September 2, 1997, 11:24 P.M.
April 20, 2010, 2:28 A.M. – July 20, 2010, 5:46 P.M.
February 8, 2011, 2:55 P.M. – April 17, 2018, 4:09 A.M.
September 25, 2018, 8:12 P.M. – February 18, 2019, 4:07 A.M.

d. November 10, 1946, 2:14 P.M. – February 8, 1951, 8:26 P.M.
January 18, 1951, 9:13 A.M. – November 8, 1951, 11:22 P.M.
December 29, 1996, 6:16 A.M. – April 4, 1997, 11:50 A.M.
September 2, 1997, 11:24 P.M. – December 11, 2001, 6:04 P.M.

THE AURA COLOR WHEEL

Please mark down how many of each selection you have:

a. _____ c. _____
b. _____ d. _____

- If you chose mostly A answers, your aura color is 21: *Sky*.
- If you chose mostly B answers, your aura color is 25: *Indigo*.
- If you chose mostly C answers, your aura color is 23: *Azure*.
- If you chose mostly D answers, your aura color is 13: *Green*.

If you have two or more equal selections, it can mean one of the following:

1. You have two or more aura colors in your auric field. Please read the descriptions and intuitively pick which one resonates with you the most to work with now.
2. You are in transition from one aura color to another within the same Soul Gift Archetype. This happens when you heal a certain aura layer soul wound and are now working on another aura layer soul wound or soul lesson. Remember, soul wounds are just deeper soul lessons.

SKY AURA COLOR SOULS

If your Soul Aura Color is Sky, you are an idealist on planet Earth. You are here to help raise the vibrations of collective consciousness. You have an internal moral compass and are passionate about your calling. Standing firm with your concept of right and wrong, you live by your high standards. You are a great friend, and friends and family trust you. Wearing sky-colored clothing or accessories and decorating your home or office space with sky colors accentuate your soul gifts. Working with crystals like angelite, orange kyanite, and lithium quartz strengthens your soul gifts.

Your deep soul wound is the red aura layer powered by the root chakra. As a child, you tended to have long-term, lingering physical issues. Tending to your body and cultivating a healthy lifestyle are important. Learning and incorporating Ayurveda and Feng Shui are beneficial for healing your soul wound. Sometimes you feel lonely on the path and experience a sense of insecurity or a feeling of not belonging. Clearing ancestral and past-life wounds is one of your soul missions in this lifetime. Wearing clothing or accessories in shades of red helps bring in the color energy while you are healing your soul wound. Chiastolite and red jasper are great crystal companions for your soul-healing journey.

Your main soul lessons are the yellow, green, and violet aura layers powered by the solar plexus, heart, and third eye chakras. Learning to embrace your personal power and accept yourself in totality, including the shadow side, is one of your soul lessons. Establishing a daily spiritual practice like meditation will help you open your heart to give and receive unconditional love, develop your intuition and psychic abilities, and surrender to the divine plan for your soul during this lifetime.

If your soul chooses to work on your red aura layer soul wound first, once you have healed your soul wound, the red aura layer will become one of your strengths in your Soul Aura Color composition. Because aura layers work in pairs, with one layer from the higher three chakras and one layer from the lower three chakras, at this point your soul can choose to combine your red and blue aura layers so that you can become a Teacher Soul Gift Archetype.

Once you have learned your yellow aura layer soul lesson, you can blend your blue and yellow aura layers and shape-shift into an Entrepreneur. When you learn your green aura layer soul lesson, you can combine it with your orange aura strength to become an Entertainer or your red aura strength to become a Warrior. The same is true of your violet aura layer soul lesson. Once you've learned it, your violet aura layer can be a strength, and you can mix it with your orange aura strength to become an Artist or your red aura strength to become a Researcher.

INDIGO AURA COLOR SOULS

If your Soul Aura Color is Indigo, you are here with the mission to raise the vibrations of planet Earth, to serve as an example, and to lead humanity to a higher path. You are the catalyst of change in society. Leading a group of like-minded people with passion and conviction toward goals brings you fulfillment. Wearing indigo-colored clothing or accessories and decorating your home or office space with indigo colors accentuate your soul gifts. Working with crystals like pietersite, azurite, and copper strengthens your soul gifts.

Your deep soul wound is the yellow aura layer powered by the solar plexus chakra. Self-acceptance, healthy self-esteem, and confidence are recurring themes for your soul's growth and may have been especially challenging areas during childhood. Depending on your relationship with your family members, the education you received, and the culture you grew up in, you may have various issues to resolve to heal your soul wound. On a spiritual level, some collective ancestral and past-life wounds need to be healed in this lifetime. The good news is, once you are healed, the entire lineage of your family will thank you for the work you've done. Studying spiritual wisdom like Western and Vedic astrology, Chinese Zodiac, Feng Shui Birth Element and Kua Number, Human Design, Enneagram, Gene Keys, and Numerology is helpful for you to understand your soul's purpose in this lifetime. Wearing clothing or accessories in shades of yellow helps bring in the color energy while you are healing your soul wound. Serpentine and dendritic agate are great crystal companions for your soul-healing journey.

Your main soul lessons are the red, green, and violet aura layers powered by the root, heart, and third eye chakras. Keeping a daily spiritual practice like meditation is beneficial for you to ground yourself, open your heart, and connect with the Divine. Clearing ancestral, karmic, and past-life wounds is one of your soul missions. Learning how to open your heart to give and receive love and trusting the divine timing and path of everything are other soul lessons for you. Embracing the shadow side of yourself and accepting yourself completely will make you shine from deep within.

If your soul chooses to work on your yellow aura layer soul wound first, once you have healed your soul wound, the yellow aura layer will become one of your strengths in your Soul Aura Color composition. Because aura layers work in pairs, with one layer from the higher three chakras and one layer from the lower three chakras, at this point your soul can choose to combine your yellow and blue aura layers so that you can become an Entrepreneur Soul Gift Archetype.

Once you have learned your red aura layer soul lesson, you can blend your red and blue aura layers and shape-shift into an inspiring Teacher. When you learn your green aura layer soul lesson, you can combine it with your orange aura strength to become an Entertainer, or with your yellow aura strength to become a Healer. The same is true of your violet aura layer soul lesson. Once you've learned it, your violet aura layer can be a strength, and you can mix it with the orange aura strength to become an Artist or the yellow aura strength to become a Visionary.

AZURE AURA COLOR SOULS

If your Soul Aura Color is Azure and you step into your true self, you can be a great public speaker. You speak with passion and conviction, and people are touched by you. You use your speech to move people to achieve a common goal or make societal change. Creating a better community fulfills you. Wearing azure-colored clothing or accessories and decorating your home or office space with azure accentuate your soul gifts. Working with crystals like larimar, ruby in kyanite, and ocean jasper strengthens your soul gifts.

Your deep soul wound is the green aura layer powered by the heart chakra. Being vulnerable and having heart-to-heart relationships are challenging. You might have had a tough childhood, during which you learned to shield yourself for protection. Healing your inner child, clearing self-limiting beliefs, and practicing self-compassion and self-love are crucial for you to heal your soul wound. Learning to forgive and letting go are recurring themes for your soul-healing journey. Wearing clothing or accessories in shades of green helps bring in the color energy while you are healing your soul wound. Smithsonite and mangano calcite are great crystal companions for your soul-healing journey.

Your main soul lessons are the red, yellow, and violet aura layers powered by the root, solar plexus, and third eye chakras. Clearing ancestral, karmic, and past-life wounds, having a strong sense of self-identity, and developing your intuition and psychic abilities to find your soul family and connect with your spirit team are some of the recurring themes of your soul lessons in this lifetime.

If your soul chooses to work on your green aura layer soul wound first, once you have healed your soul wound, the green aura layer will become one of your strengths in your Soul Aura Color composition. Because aura layers work in pairs, with one layer from the higher three chakras and one layer from the lower three chakras, at this point your soul can choose to combine your green and orange aura layers so that you can become an Entertainer Soul Gift Archetype.

Once you have learned your red aura layer soul lesson, you can blend your red and blue aura layers and shape-shift into a Teacher or your red and green aura layers to transform into a Warrior. When you learn your yellow aura layer soul lesson, you can combine it with your blue aura strength to become an Entrepreneur or your green aura strength to become a Healer. The same is true of your violet aura layer soul lesson. Once you've learned it, your violet aura layer can be a strength, and you can mix it with your orange aura strength to become an Artist.

GREEN AURA COLOR SOULS

If your Soul Aura Color is Green, you have deep love and compassion for humanity. You are courageous and will stand up for your beliefs or your chosen community. You are a great friend and family member, willing to share authentic advice with those you care about. People feel understood and safe around you. Wearing green-colored clothing or accessories and decorating your home or office space with green accentuate your soul gifts. Working with crystals like malachite, blue fluorite, and ocean jasper strengthens your soul gifts.

Reformer Archetype

Your deep soul wound is the violet aura layer powered by the third eye chakra. Although you have good intentions, you find it challenging to maintain a clear vision of where you are headed. Because of this sense of lacking higher guidance, your thoughts tend to escalate and lead to anxiety. Past-life regression and healing can be beneficial for you to clear out some deep-rooted wounds. Finding your own soul family or star family will bring out the complete and fulfilling potential of your soul gifts. Wearing clothing or accessories in shades of violet helps bring in the color energy while you are healing your soul wound. Lepidolite and spirit quartz are great crystal companions for your soul-healing journey.

Your main soul lessons are the red, yellow, and green aura layers powered by the root, solar plexus, and heart chakras. Tending to your body, cultivating healthy self-esteem and confidence, and accepting who you are with unconditional love are some of the soul lessons you need to learn. Learning and practicing Ayurveda and Feng Shui, nurturing a healthy sense of the self, clearing limiting beliefs, and embracing the shadow self are great spiritual practices for your soul's self-growth journey.

If your soul chooses to work on your violet aura layer soul wound first, once you have healed your soul wound, the violet aura layer will become one of your strengths in your Soul Aura Color composition. Because aura layers work in pairs, with one layer from the higher three chakras and one layer from the lower three chakras, at this point your soul can choose to combine your violet and orange aura layers so that you can become an Artist Soul Gift Archetype.

Once you have learned your red aura layer soul lesson, you can blend your red and blue aura layers and shape-shift into a Teacher or your red and violet aura layers to transform into a Researcher. When you learn your yellow aura layer soul lesson, you can combine it with the blue aura strength to become an Entrepreneur or your violet aura strength to become a Visionary. The same is true of your green aura layer soul lesson. Once you've learned it, your green aura layer can be a strength, and you can mix it with your orange aura strength to become an Entertainer.

REFORMER EVOLUTION PATHS

The following diagrams show the four possible starting points and different paths for your Soul Gift Archetype evolution journey. You can choose to work on your soul wound first or learn one of the three soul lessons. As your soul grows, more aura layers will become your strength. When your soul works on healing soul wounds or learning soul lessons, and these aspects are completed to a satisfactory degree, free will can be exercised to combine aura layer strengths to embody different Soul Gift Archetypes. Of course, you can also choose to remain the Soul Gift Archetype you were born with but just have more light quotient in your Soul Aura Color composition, thus magnetizing high vibrational opportunities in your life and manifesting faster.

Reformer Archetype

Reformer Soul Gift Archetype Evolution Path 1

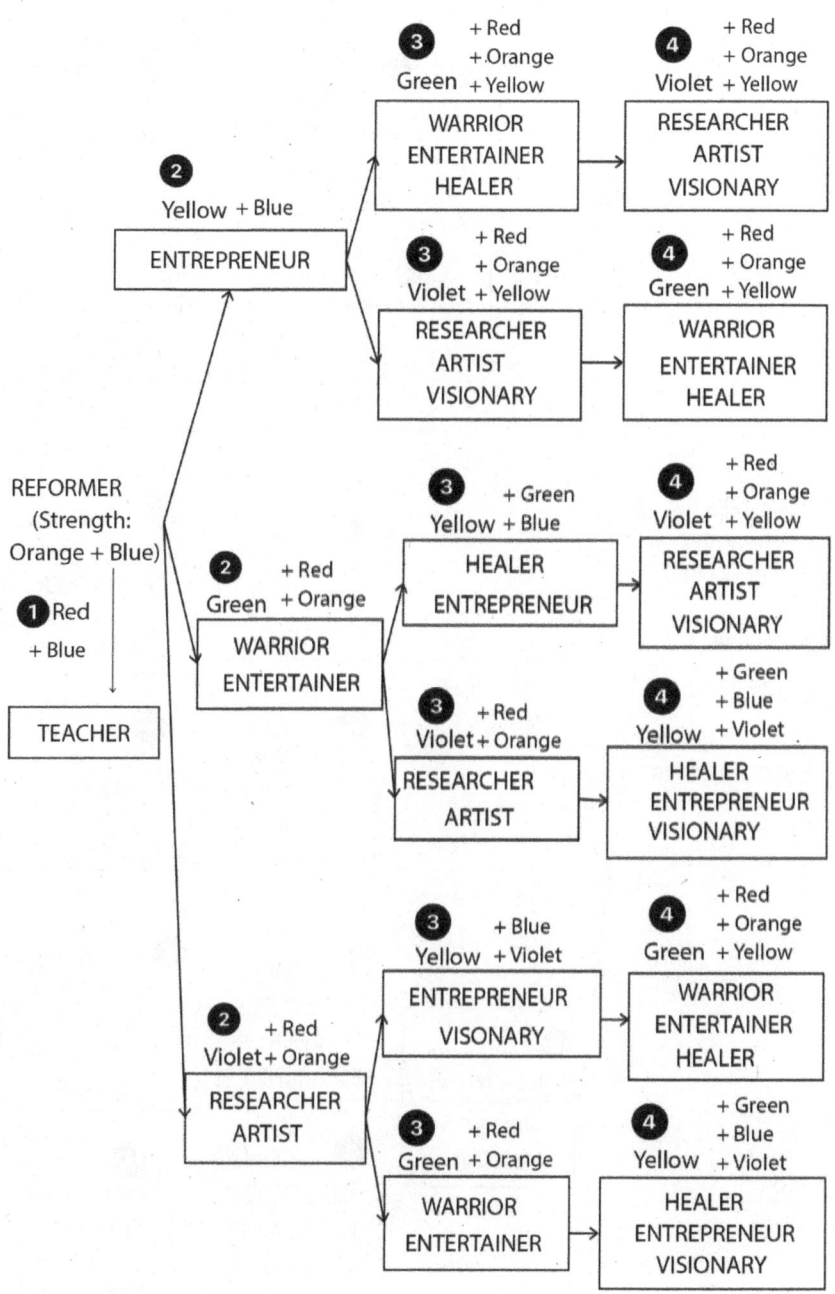

THE AURA COLOR WHEEL

Reformer Soul Gift Archetype Evolution Path 2

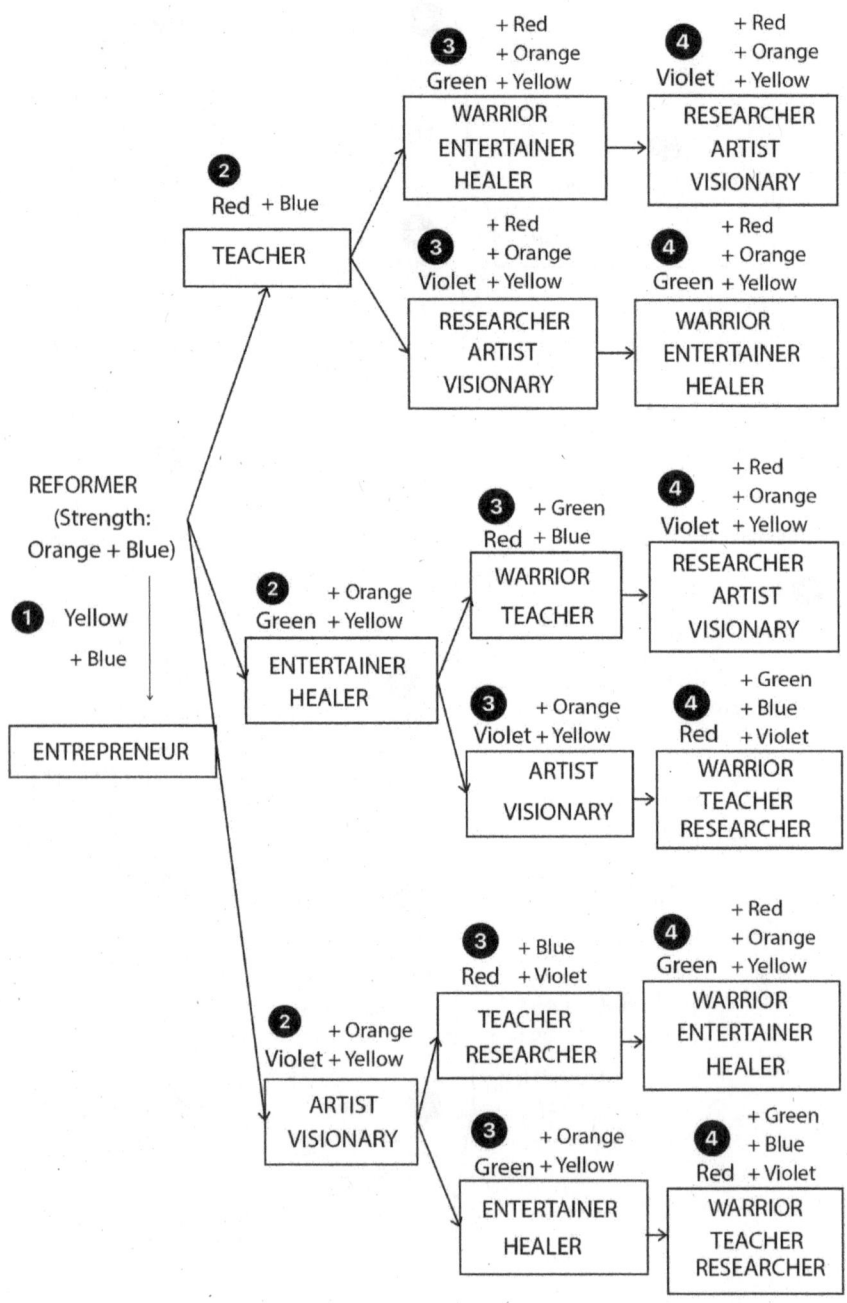

Reformer Soul Gift Archetype Evolution Path 3

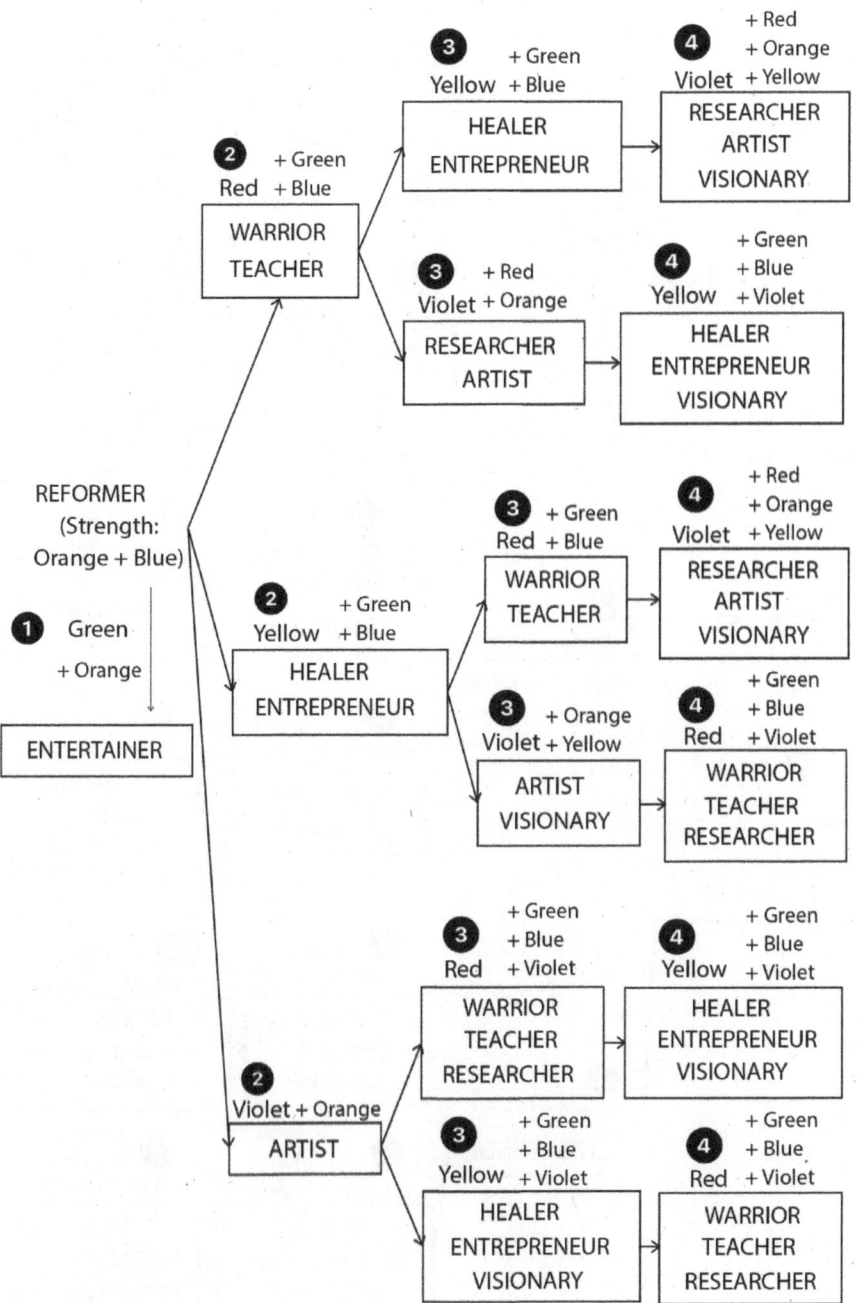

THE AURA COLOR WHEEL

Reformer Soul Gift Archetype Evolution Path 4

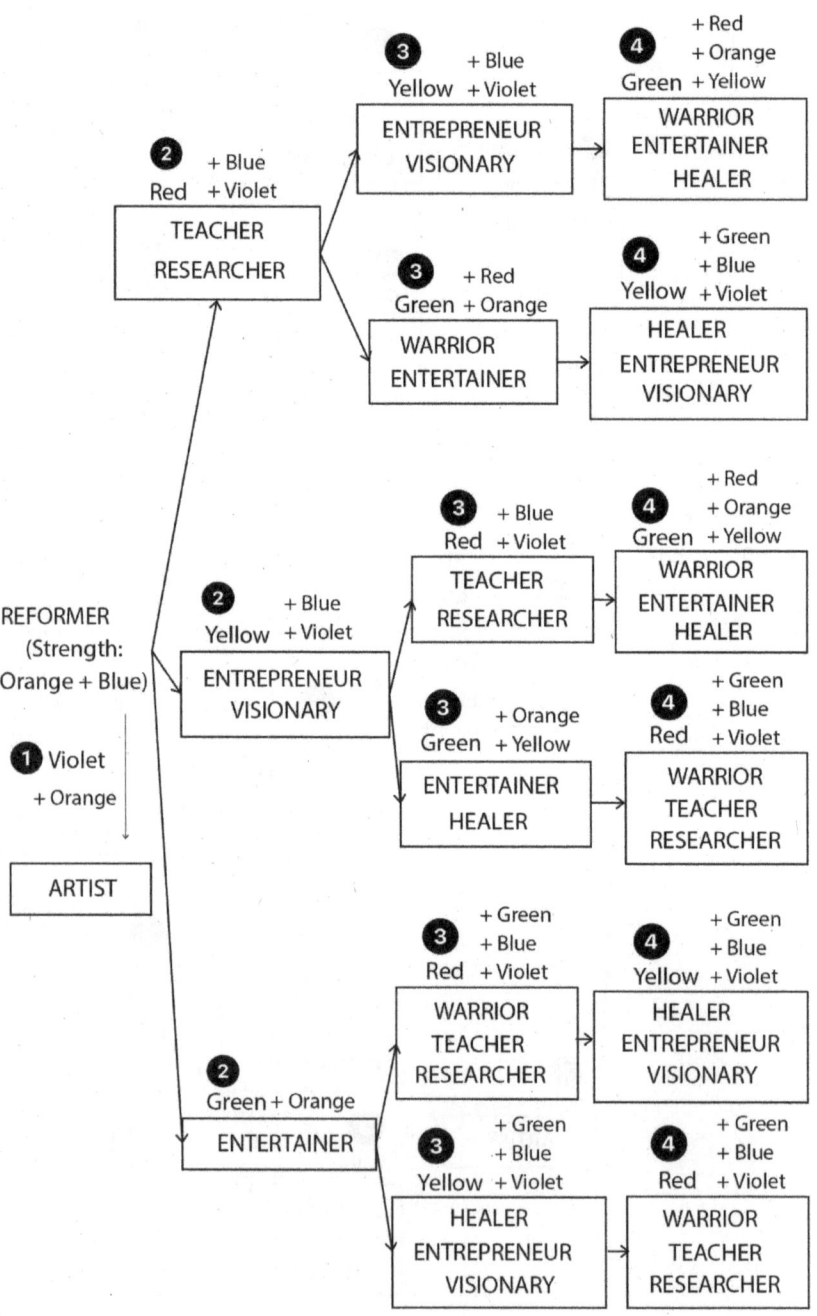

CHAPTER 9

ENTERTAINER ARCHETYPE

If your Soul Gift Archetype is Entertainer, you have a strong orange aura layer powered by the sacral chakra and green aura layer powered by the heart chakra. These two aura layers are strongly connected to love, so it's no surprise that the Entertainer Archetype often attracts and experiences passionate love affairs. The main difference among Soul Aura Colors is their soul wound and soul lessons for each. Archangel Jophiel and Archangel Sandalphon are the great angels to call upon to assist you to fully embody your Entertainer soul gifts. Trust and use your innate clairsentience, clairgustance, and claircognizance psychic abilities to receive spirit guidance.

ENTERTAINER SOUL AURA COLOR QUIZ

For each question, please select the option that best describes you based on your current state. I highly recommend you pick an answer intuitively—don't overthink it. If you have a few questions or really can't choose an answer, please leave it blank. If you have more than one selection that applies, please select all of them. Remember, auras are a spectrum of colors, not one static color. These questions are channeled to approximate your Soul Aura Color. Have fun!

THE AURA COLOR WHEEL

1. **In which area of life do you experience the most difficulties?**
   a. Family relationships or ancestral traumas
   b. Low self-esteem
   c. Speaking my truth without self-consciousness or worry about what other people think of me
   d. Planning and visualizing the future

2. **Where do you feel discomfort or illness most often?**
   a. Legs, feet, bone structure
   b. Digestion, liver, spleen, gallbladder, pancreas
   c. Throat, nose, ears, teeth, neck, mouth, jaw
   d. Sinuses, headaches, scalp, hair, autoimmune diseases, skin

3. **Which circumstances cause the most discomfort?**
   a. Fitting in with my family, feeling out of place
   b. Standing up for myself or something I value
   c. Expressing myself with clarity in public
   d. Sensing other people's energy

4. **What are you most afraid of feeling?**
   a. Lack of safety and security
   b. Low motivation or self-image
   c. Shyness, inability to speak the truth, ADHD
   d. Paranoia or bad feelings about the future

5. **What are you missing that prevents you from living life to the fullest?**
   a. A sense of being grounded and centered
   b. Confidence and motivation
   c. Truthful communication
   d. Intuition and psychic abilities

6. Which emotional blocks do you feel most often?

   a. Anxiety or depression
   b. Anger, frustration, or low energy
   c. Nervousness, unease, or lingering trauma
   d. Lack of intuition or inspiration

7. Which issues do you frequently encounter?

   a. Insecurity, doubt, low self-worth
   b. Low self-esteem or confidence, low energy
   c. Inability to relax, the need to always be doing something
   d. Mental fog, feeling stuck or in a rut

8. Which superpower would change your life?

   a. The power to stay present and bring spiritual knowledge into daily actions
   b. The power of courage and inner strength to take action and weather storms
   c. The power to communicate with the Divine and spirits
   d. The power to gain vision, clarity, inspiration, and innovation

9. If you could change one thing about yourself, what would it be?

   a. I want to have the courage to move forward in life: career, new adventures and opportunities, etc.
   b. I want to be able to take action purposefully according to my beliefs and ideas.
   c. I want to possess strong leadership skills to move society forward according to my ideals.
   d. I want to be open to insights and intuitive guidance from the Divine to better understand myself.

THE AURA COLOR WHEEL

10. **Does your birthday fall in any of the following groups of timing? If not, just leave this blank.**

    a. July 26, 1943, 6:42 P.M. – November 17, 1944, 11:23 P.M.
    March 23, 1945, 10:50 P.M. – July 22, 1945, 12:31 P.M.
    February 8, 1951, 8:26 P.M. – June 18, 1951, 9:13 A.M.
    November 8, 1951, 11:22 P.M. – January 27, 1955, 11:28 A.M.
    September 3, 1993, 1:32 P.M. – September 9, 1995, 10:28 A.M.
    December 11, 2001, 6:04 P.M. – February 21, 2005, 12:33 P.M.
    July 31, 2005, 11:48 P.M. – December 5, 2005, 8:03 P.M.

    b. September 29, 1940, 11:44 P.M. – December 27, 1940, 12:59 P.M.
    June 16, 1941, 2:34 P.M. – July 26, 1943, 6:42 P.M.
    April 1, 1968, 2:08 P.M. – October 18, 1968, 6:36 P.M.
    January 30, 1969, 3:12 A.M. – May 28, 1976, 7:10 A.M.
    October 13, 1976, 6:46 P.M. – March 28, 1977, 2:05 P.M.
    July 21, 1991, 11:54 P.M. – September 3, 1993, 1:32 P.M.
    April 17, 2018, 4:09 P.M. – September 25, 2018, 8:12 P.M.
    February 18, 2019, 4:07 P.M. – June 19, 2026, 5:17 P.M.
    September 17, 2026, 9:54 P.M. – April 14, 2027, 10:56 P.M.

    c. January 27, 1955, 11:28 A.M. – March 26, 1960, 8:39 A.M.
    August 19, 1960, 2:31 A.M. – January 20, 1961, 8:50 P.M.
    June 21, 1983, 9:54 A.M. – November 29, 1983, 8:19 A.M.
    April 10, 1984, 11:19 P.M. – June 21, 1988, 5:40 A.M.
    February 21, 2005, 12:33 P.M. – July 31, 2005, 11:48 P.M.
    December 5, 2005, 8:03 P.M. – April 20, 2010, 2:28 P.M.
    July 20, 2010, 5:46 A.M. – February 8, 2011, 2:55 P.M.
    July 19, 2033, 9:35 A.M. – October 23, 2033, 6:21 P.M.
    May 5, 2034, 5:50 P.M. – July 22, 2038, 1:49 A.M.

    d. November 10, 1946, 2:14 P.M. – February 8, 1951, 8:26 P.M.
    January 18, 1951, 9:13 A.M. – November 8, 1951, 11:22 P.M.
    December 29, 1996, 6:16 A.M. – April 4, 1997, 11:50 A.M.
    September 2, 1997, 11:24 P.M. – December 11, 2001, 6:04 P.M.

    Please mark down how many of each selection you have:
    a. _____   c. _____
    b. _____   d. _____

Entertainer Archetype

- If you chose mostly A answers, your aura color is 10: *Chartreuse.*
- If you chose mostly B answers, your aura color is 32: *Fuchsia.*
- If you chose mostly C answers, your aura color is 06: *Peach.*
- If you chose mostly D answers, your aura color is 08: *Lemon.*

If you have two or more equal selections, it can mean one of the following:

1. You have two or more aura colors in your auric field. Please read the descriptions and intuitively pick which one resonates with you the most to work with now.
2. You are in transition from one aura color to another within the same Soul Gift Archetype. This happens when you heal a certain aura layer soul wound and are now working on another aura layer soul wound or soul lesson. Remember, soul wounds are just deeper soul lessons.

CHARTREUSE AURA COLOR SOULS

If your Soul Aura Color is Chartreuse, you are charming, witty, creative, and lively. Your passion makes you ready to engage fully in life. You make people laugh and lift their spirits, and you can easily become the center of attention. You might be a great singer, stand-up comedian, or other kind of performer. Wearing chartreuse-colored clothing or accessories and decorating your home or office space with chartreuse accentuate your soul gifts. Working with crystals like peridot, green quartz (prasiolite), and orange calcite strengthens your soul gifts.

Your deep soul wound is the red aura layer powered by the root chakra. You have had deep and powerful emotions since you were a child. Some of these emotions—like anger, aggression, anxiety, and paranoia—are the ones you are here to heal. You also need to watch for the tendency toward greed, hoarding, and controlling. Some of you also have had eating disorders in different stages of your life. Cultivating a healthy lifestyle is crucial to healing your soul wound, and learning and practicing Ayurveda and Feng Shui can help. Wearing clothing or accessories in shades of red helps bring in the color energy while you are healing your soul wound. Smoky quartz and zircon are great crystal companions for your soul-healing journey.

Your main soul lessons are the yellow, blue, and violet aura layers powered by the solar plexus, throat, and third eye chakras. Having healthy self-esteem, expressing your truth authentically, and healing past-life wounds are your soul lessons in this lifetime. Self-awareness and mastery studies like Western and Vedic astrology, Chinese Zodiac, Feng Shui Birth Element and Kua Number, Human Design, Enneagram, Gene Keys, and Numerology practices are beneficial. Past-life regression work will bring you healing and self-identity clarity. Daily meditation will not only calm your emotions but also enhance your psychic abilities and strengthen your divine connection.

If your soul chooses to work on your red aura layer soul wound first, once you have healed your soul wound, the red aura layer will become one of your strengths in your Soul Aura Color composition. Because aura layers work in pairs, with one layer from the higher three chakras and one layer from the lower three chakras, at this point your soul can choose to combine your red and green aura layers so that you can become a Warrior Soul Gift Archetype.

Once you have learned your yellow aura layer soul lesson, you can blend your yellow and green aura layers and shape-shift into a Healer. When you learn your blue aura layer soul lesson, you can combine it with the orange aura strength to become a Reformer or your red aura strength to become a Teacher. The same is true of your violet aura layer soul lesson. Once you've learned it, your violet aura layer can be a strength, and you can mix it with your orange aura strength to become an Artist, or with your red aura strength to become a Researcher.

FUCHSIA AURA COLOR SOULS

If your Soul Aura Color is Fuchsia, you are passionate and full of life. You believe in enjoying life to the fullest. The beautiful energy radiating from your heart attracts others. You are a born actor, whether on stage or in movies, television shows, or daily life. You are sociable and ready for any adventure life brings. Wearing fuchsia-colored clothing or accessories and decorating your home or office space with fuchsia accentuate your soul gifts. Working with crystals like pink aura quartz, thulite, and chrysoprase strengthens your soul gifts.

Your deep soul wound is the yellow aura layer powered by the solar plexus chakra. You often feel insecure or self-conscious, and you care about how other people see you. Establishing healthy self-esteem and learning to stand in your own personal power is your soul-healing journey in this lifetime. Studying spiritual wisdom like Western and Vedic astrology, Chinese Zodiac, Feng Shui Birth Element and Kua Number, Human Design, Enneagram, Gene Keys, and Numerology helps you understand your soul's purpose. Wearing clothing or accessories in shades of yellow helps bring in the color energy while you are healing your soul wound. Heliodor and yellow jade are great crystal companions for your soul-healing journey.

Your main soul lessons are the red, blue, and violet aura layers powered by the root, throat, and third eye chakras. You tend to have long-term health issues you are working to heal. Establishing a healthy lifestyle and learning and practicing Ayurveda and Feng Shui are beneficial to you. Clearing self-limiting beliefs, speaking up for yourself in a loving way, and clearing past-life negative patterns are your soul lessons in this lifetime. Daily meditation with a mantra or sound bath that grounds you and enhances your intuition is ideal for your soul and can help you gain clarity and direction for your life.

If your soul chooses to work on your yellow aura layer soul wound first, once you have healed your soul wound, the yellow aura layer will become one of your strengths in your Soul Aura Color composition. Because aura layers work in pairs, with one layer from the higher three chakras and one layer from the lower three chakras, at this point your soul can choose to combine your yellow and green aura layers so that you can become a Healer Soul Gift Archetype.

Once you have learned your red aura layer soul lesson, you can blend your red and green aura layers and shape-shift into a Warrior. When you learn your blue aura layer soul lesson, you can combine it with your orange aura strength to become a Reformer or your yellow aura strength to become an Entrepreneur. The same is true of your violet aura layer soul lesson. Once you've learned it, your violet aura layer can be a strength, and you can mix it with the orange aura strength to become an Artist or the yellow aura strength to become a Visionary.

PEACH AURA COLOR SOULS

If your Soul Aura Color is Peach, you embody a soul that reflects the sweetness of life. You have a wild imagination and are full of creative ideas. Generally gentle and calm, you can completely lose yourself in different forms of art: music, painting, dance, acting, or storytelling. Creating and speaking from your heart is how you attract others in life. Wearing peach-colored clothing or accessories and decorating your home or office space with peach colors accentuate your soul gifts. Working with crystals like peach moonstone and green and pink fluorite strengthens your soul gifts.

Your deep soul wound is the blue aura layer powered by the throat chakra. Expressing yourself authentically is challenging for you, and this was especially true when you were a child. Sometimes you feel strong emotions but have difficulty communicating them clearly. Daily positive affirmations and healthy boundary-setting are good practices for your soul. Mantra meditation and sound baths also aid your communication with the Divine. Wearing clothing or accessories in shades of blue helps bring in the color energy while you are healing your soul wound. Blue aragonite and hemimorphite are great crystal companions for your soul-healing journey.

Your main soul lessons are the red, yellow, and violet aura layers powered by the root, solar plexus, and third eye chakras. Clearing ancestral and karmic wounds, cultivating healthy self-esteem, and developing your intuition and psychic abilities are your soul lessons in this lifetime. Through your soul-healing journey, your sense of confidence will increase. Self-trust is the foundation for you to trust a higher intelligence and surrender to the divine plan for your soul.

If your soul chooses to work on your blue aura layer soul wound first, once you have healed your soul wound, the blue aura layer will become one of your strengths in your Soul Aura Color composition.

Because aura layers work in pairs, with one layer from the higher three chakras and one layer from the lower three chakras, at this point your soul can choose to combine your blue and orange aura layers so that you can become a Reformer Soul Gift Archetype.

Once you have learned your red aura layer soul lesson, you can blend your red and green aura layer strengths and shape-shift into a Warrior or your red and blue aura layer strengths to transform into a Teacher. When you learn your yellow aura layer soul lesson, you can combine it with your green aura strength to become a Healer or your blue aura strength to become an Entrepreneur. The same is true of your violet aura layer soul lesson. Once you've learned it, your violet aura layer can be a strength, and you can mix it with your orange aura strength to become an Artist.

LEMON AURA COLOR SOULS

If your Soul Aura Color is Lemon, your soul emanates the joy of life. You are exuberant and lively, a dancer of life, ready for any new adventure. You are curious and love to explore, and others are captivated by your joyful spirit. If you fully lean in to your soul gifts, you can be the star on any stage you choose. Wearing lemon-colored clothing or accessories and decorating your home or office space with lemon colors accentuate your soul gifts. Working with crystals like lemon quartz, lemon calcite, and epidote strengthens your soul gifts.

Your deep soul wound is the violet aura layer powered by the third eye chakra. You tend to have vivid dreams or nightmares, and this was especially true when you were a child. Although passionate about life, you sometimes lack direction. Having a daily spiritual practice like meditation will help improve your intuition and connection with higher guidance. Wearing clothing or accessories in shades of violet helps bring in the color energy while you are healing your soul wound. Purple or white opal and chevron amethyst are great crystal companions for your soul-healing journey.

Your main soul lessons are the red, yellow, and blue aura layers powered by the root, solar plexus, and throat chakras. Learning to trust yourself and firmly expressing yourself with healthy boundaries are your soul lessons. Due to karmic and ancestral traumas, you tend to self-doubt and sometimes feel insecure and lonely. Daily affirmations and self-empowerment practices are beneficial for your soul-growth journey.

If your soul chooses to work on your violet aura layer soul wound first, once you have healed your soul wound, the violet aura layer will become one of your strengths in your Soul Aura Color composition. Because aura layers work in pairs, with one layer from the higher three chakras and one layer from the lower three chakras, at this point your soul can choose to combine your violet and orange aura layers so that you can become an Artist Soul Gift Archetype.

Once you have learned your red aura layer soul lesson, you can blend your red and green aura layers and shape-shift into a Warrior or your red and violet aura layers to transform into a Researcher. When you learn your yellow aura layer soul lesson, you can combine it with the green aura strength to become a Healer or the violet aura strength to become a Visionary. The same is true of your blue aura layer soul lesson. Once you've learned it, your blue aura layer can be a strength, and you can mix it with your orange aura strength to become a Reformer.

ENTERTAINER EVOLUTION PATHS

The following diagrams show the four possible starting points and different paths for your Soul Gift Archetype evolution journey. You can choose to work on your soul wound first or learn one of the three soul lessons. As your soul grows, more aura layers will become your strength. When your soul works on healing soul wounds or learning soul lessons, and these aspects are completed to a satisfactory degree, free will can be exercised to combine aura layer strengths to embody different Soul Gift Archetypes. Of course, you can also choose to remain the Soul Gift Archetype you were born with but just have more light quotient in your Soul Aura Color composition, thus magnetizing high vibrational opportunities in your life and manifesting faster.

Entertainer Soul Gift Archetype Evolution Path 1

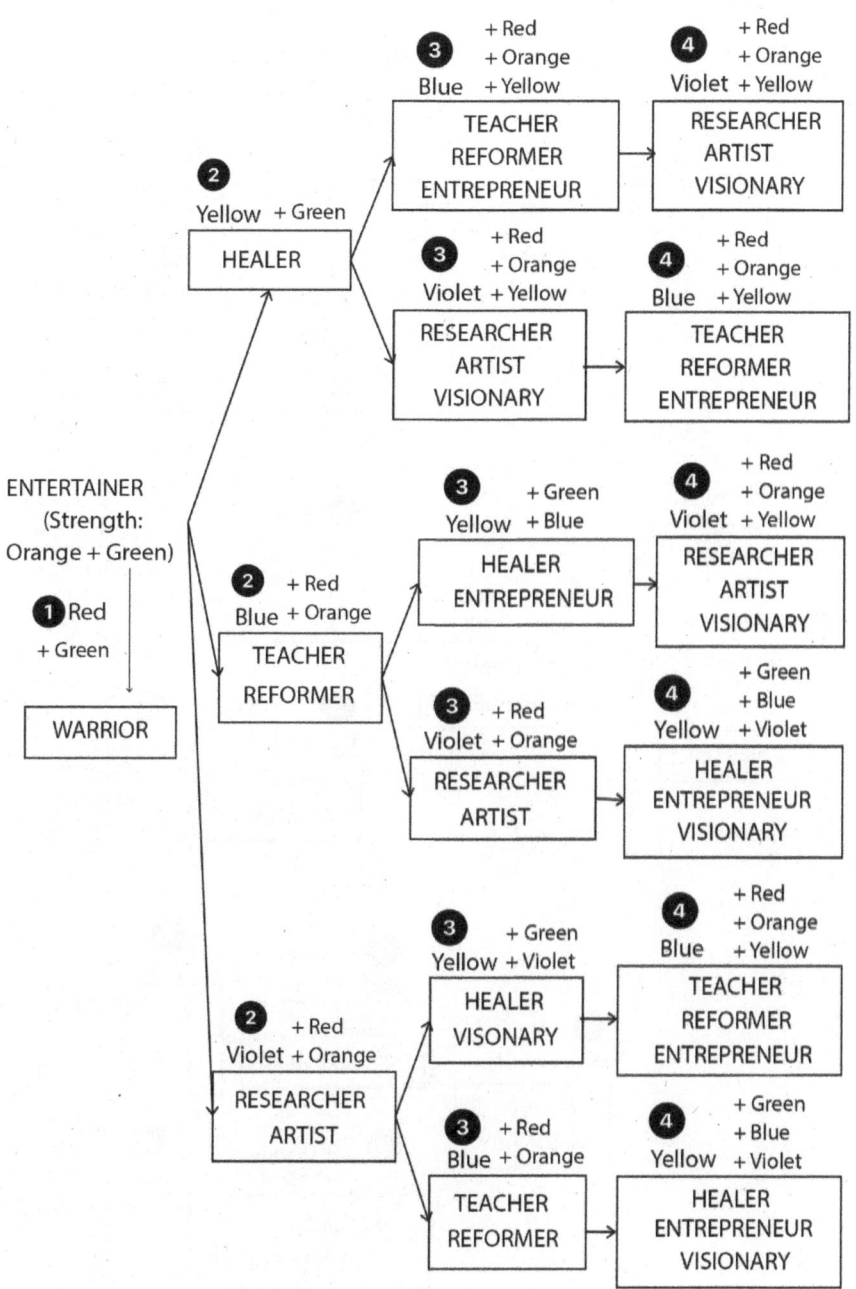

THE AURA COLOR WHEEL

Entertainer Soul Gift Archetype Evolution Path 2

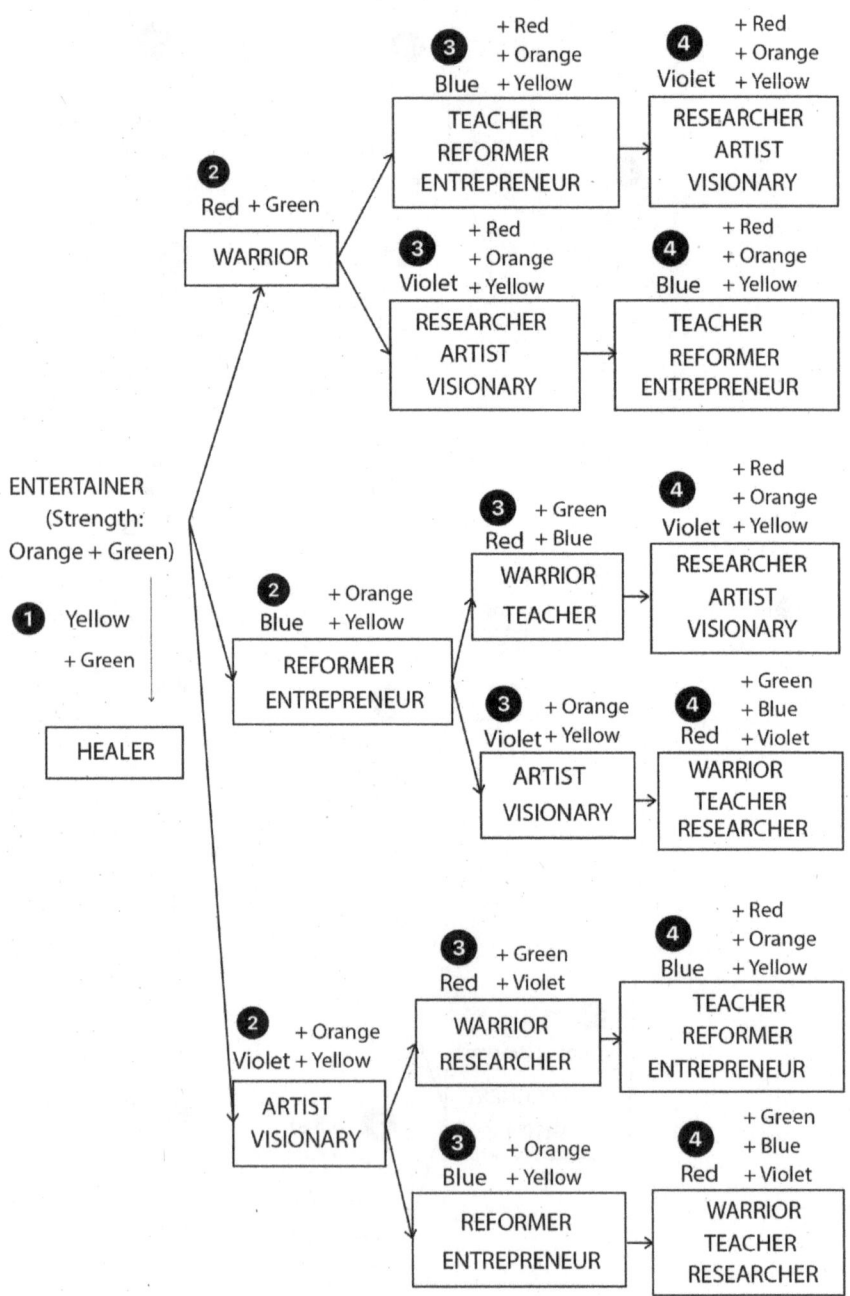

Entertainer Archetype

Entertainer Soul Gift Archetype Evolution Path 3

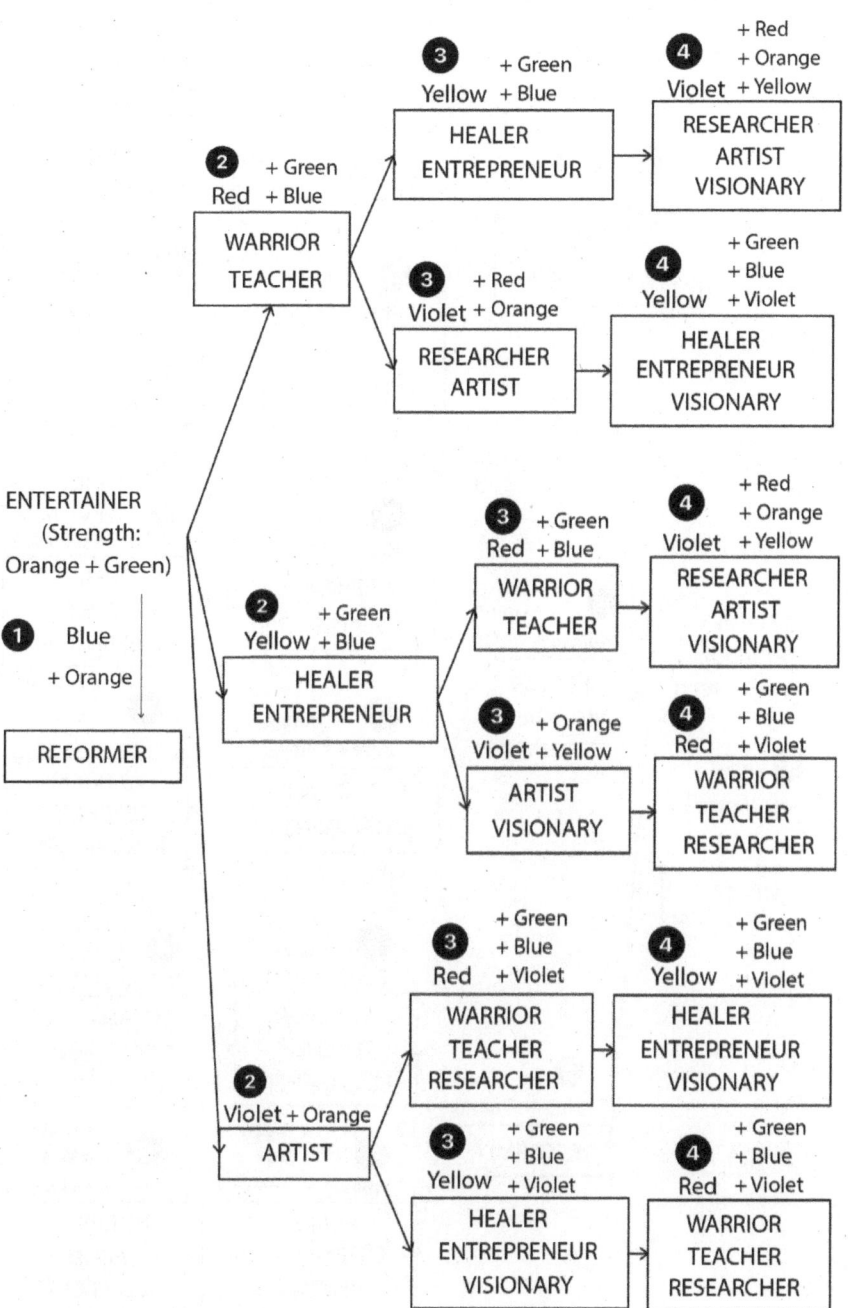

THE AURA COLOR WHEEL

Entertainer Soul Gift Archetype Evolution Path 4

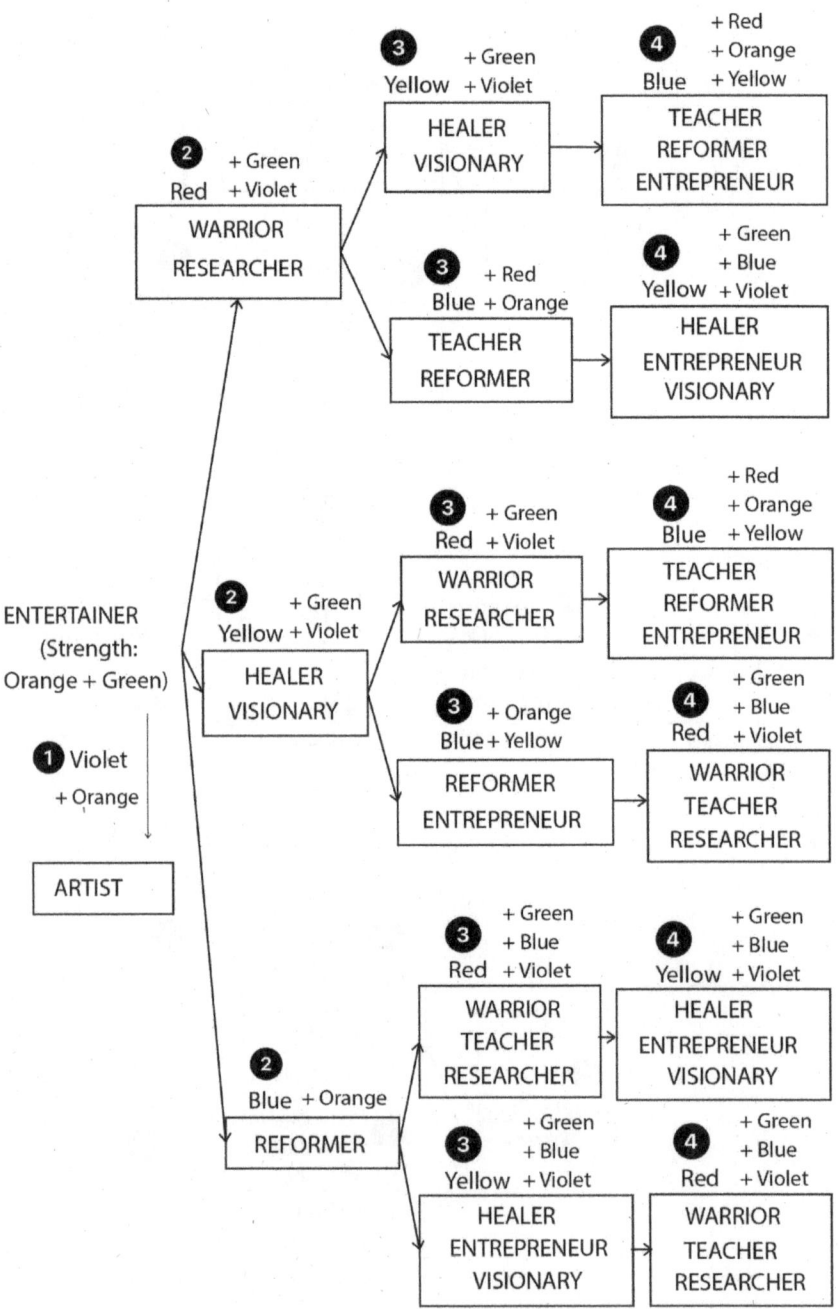

CHAPTER 10

RESEARCHER ARCHETYPE

If your Soul Gift Archetype is Researcher, you have a strong red aura layer powered by the root chakra and violet aura layer powered by the third eye chakra. These two aura layers are deeply interconnected, bridging vision and reality through grounded actions, which makes the Researcher Archetype exceptionally skilled at uncovering insights and conducting meaningful research. The main difference among Soul Aura Colors is their soul wound and soul lessons for each. Archangel Raziel and Archangel Metatron are the great angels to call upon to assist you to fully embody your Researcher soul gifts. Trust and use your innate clairsalience, clairvoyance, and psychometry psychic abilities to receive spirit guidance.

RESEARCHER SOUL AURA COLOR QUIZ

For each question, please select the option that best describes you based on your current state. I highly recommend you pick an answer intuitively—don't overthink it. If you have a few questions or really can't choose an answer, please leave it blank. If you have more than one selection that applies, please select all of them. Remember, auras are a spectrum of colors, not one static color. These questions are channeled to approximate your Soul Aura Color. Have fun!

THE AURA COLOR WHEEL

1. **In which area of life do you experience the most difficulties?**
   a. Regulating emotions
   b. Low self-esteem or self-confidence
   c. Being vulnerable, giving and receiving love
   d. Speaking my truth without self-consciousness or worry about how other people see me

2. **Where do you feel discomfort or illness most often?**
   a. Hormones, reproductive system, lower back
   b. Digestion, liver, spleen, gallbladder, pancreas
   c. Heart, chest, breast, asthma, blood pressure
   d. Throat, nose, ears, teeth, neck, mouth, jaw

3. **Which circumstances cause the most discomfort?**
   a. Sharing emotions, being too emotional, empathizing with others
   b. Standing up for myself or something I value
   c. Having intimate relationships
   d. Expressing myself with clarity in public

4. **What are you most afraid of feeling?**
   a. Guilt and shame
   b. Low motivation and self-image
   c. Jealousy, desire to please others, sadness
   d. Shyness, suppressing communication or speaking too much, ADHD

5. **What are you missing that prevents you from living life to the fullest?**
   a. Creativity and spontaneity
   b. Confidence and motivation
   c. Vulnerability and forgiveness
   d. Truthful communication

6. Which emotional blocks do you feel most often?
   a. Sadness, isolation, or emotional eating
   b. Anger, frustration, or low energy
   c. Jealousy, or fear of inadequacies
   d. Nervousness, unease, or lingering trauma

7. Which issues do you frequently encounter?
   a. Inability to say no to others, feeling guilty
   b. Low self-esteem, confidence, low energy
   c. Lack of hope or faith
   d. Inability to relax, a need to always be doing something

8. Which superpower would change your life?
   a. The power to find calm and peace in everyday life
   b. The power of courage and inner strength to take action and weather storms
   c. The power of connection and harmony with my loved ones and community
   d. The power to communicate with the Divine and spirits

9. If you could change one thing about yourself, what would it be?
   a. I want to feel inspired, creative, decisive, and flowing with life.
   b. I want to be able to take actions purposefully according to my beliefs and ideas.
   c. I want to have an intimate connection with my significant other and a loving relationship with myself.
   d. I want to possess strong leadership skills to move society forward according to my ideals.

THE AURA COLOR WHEEL

10. **Does your birthday fall in any of the following groups of timing? If not, just leave this blank.**

   a. May 28, 1938, 8:39 A.M. – September 29, 1940, 11:44 P.M.
   December 27, 1940, 12:59 A.M. – June 16, 1941, 2:34 P.M.
   May 28, 1977, 2:05 P.M. – June 21, 1983, 8:19 A.M.
   November 29, 1983, 8:19 A.M. – April 10, 1984, 11:19 P.M.
   June 21, 1988, 5:40 A.M. – July 21, 1991, 11:54 A.M.
   June 19, 2026, 5:17 P.M. – September 17, 2026, 9:54 P.M.
   April 14, 2027, 10:56 P.M. – July 19, 2033, 9:35 A.M.

   b. September 29, 1940, 11:44 P.M. – December 27, 1940, 12:59 P.M.
   June 16, 1941, 2:34 P.M. – July 26, 1943, 6:42 P.M.
   April 1, 1968, 2:08 P.M. – October 18, 1968, 6:36 P.M.
   January 30, 1969, 3:12 A.M. – May 28, 1976, 7:10 A.M.
   October 13, 1976, 6:46 P.M. – March 28, 1977, 2:05 P.M.
   July 21, 1991, 11:54 P.M. – September 3, 1993, 1:32 P.M.
   April 17, 2018, 4:09 P.M. – September 25, 2018, 8:12 P.M.
   February 18, 2019, 4:07 P.M. – June 19, 2026, 5:17 P.M.
   September 17, 2026, 9:54 P.M. – April 14, 2027, 10:56 P.M.

   c. November 27, 1944, 11:23 P.M. – March 23, 1945, 10:50 P.M.
   July 22, 1945, 12:31 P.M. – November 10, 1946, 2:14 A.M.
   March 26, 1960, 8:39 P.M. – August 19, 1960, 2:31 A.M.
   January 20, 1961, 8:50 P.M. – April 1, 1968, 2:08 A.M.
   October 18, 1968, 6:36 P.M. – January 30, 1969, 3:12 P.M.
   September 9, 1995, 10:28 P.M. – December 29. 1996, 6:16 P.M.
   April 4, 1997, 11:50 A.M. – September 2, 1997, 11:24 P.M.
   April 20, 2010, 2:28 A.M. – July 20, 2010, 5:46 P.M.
   February 8, 2011, 2:55 P.M. – April 17, 2018, 4:09 A.M.
   September 25, 2018, 8:12 P.M. – February 18, 2019, 4:07 A.M.

   d. January 27, 1955, 11:28 A.M. – March 26, 1960, 8:39 A.M.
   August 19, 1960, 2:31 A.M. – January 20, 1961, 8:50 P.M.
   June 21, 1983, 9:54 A.M. – November 29, 1983, 8:19 A.M.
   April 10, 1984, 11:19 P.M. – June 21, 1988, 5:40 A.M.
   February 21, 2005, 12:33 P.M. – July 31, 2005, 11:48 P.M.
   December 5, 2005, 8:03 P.M. – April 20, 2010, 2:28 P.M.
   July 20, 2010, 5:46 A.M. – February 8, 2011, 2:55 P.M.
   July 19, 2033, 9:35 A.M. – October 23, 2033, 6:21 P.M.
   May 5, 2034, 5:50 P.M. – July 22, 2038, 1:49 A.M.

Researcher Archetype

Please mark down how many of each selection you have:
a. _____ c. _____
b. _____ d. _____

- If you chose mostly A answers, your aura color is 29: *Orchid*.
- If you chose mostly B answers, your aura color is 24: *Ocean*.
- If you chose mostly C answers, your aura color is 34: *Ruby*.
- If you chose mostly D answers, your aura color is 36: *Carnation*.

If you have two or more equal selections, it can mean one of the following:

1. You have two or more aura colors in your auric field. Please read the descriptions and intuitively pick which one resonates with you the most to work with now.

2. You are in transition from one aura color to another within the same Soul Gift Archetype. This happens when you heal a certain aura layer soul wound and are now working on another aura layer soul wound or soul lesson. Remember, soul wounds are just deeper soul lessons.

ORCHID AURA COLOR SOULS

If your Soul Aura Color is Orchid, you have a clear vision, and you can take daily grounded actions to achieve that vision. You love doing research when inspiration hits. You're not satisfied with superficial facts about a subject that interests you and like to dig deeply into topics and investigate everything you need to know. You're a good student because you love to study, and continued education is important to you. Wearing orchid-colored clothing or accessories and decorating your home or office space with orchid colors accentuate your soul gifts. Working with crystals like red chalcedony, cherry creek jasper, and purpurite strengthens your soul gifts.

THE AURA COLOR WHEEL

Your deep soul wound is the orange aura layer powered by the sacral chakra. You tend to have strong emotions and difficulty regulating them, and this was especially true when you were a child. Learning to face emotional storms instead of either blowing up or suppressing them is a healthy way to mature your soul. You also tend to have hormonal issues and challenging menstrual cycles if you are a female. Learning to live with the seasons (Wheel of the Year), the moon cycles, and days of the week is beneficial. Wearing clothing or accessories in shades of orange helps bring in the color energy while you are healing your soul wound. Botswana agate and halite are great crystal companions for your soul-healing journey.

Your main soul lessons are the yellow, green, and blue aura layers powered by the solar plexus, heart, and throat chakras. Self-compassion and self-love are crucial to your soul growth. When your love of self grows, your self-confidence and self-acceptance will too. Then you will be able to express your truth authentically and courageously. Healing your inner child, clearing self-limiting beliefs, and embracing the shadow self are some of your soul lessons in this lifetime.

If your soul chooses to work on your orange aura layer soul wound first, once you have healed your soul wound, the orange aura layer will become one of your strengths in your Soul Aura Color composition. Because aura layers work in pairs, with one layer from the higher three chakras and one layer from the lower three chakras, at this point your soul can choose to combine your orange and violet aura layers so that you can become an Artist Soul Gift Archetype.

Once you have learned your yellow aura layer soul lesson, you can blend your yellow and violet aura layers and shape-shift into a Visionary. When you learn your green aura layer soul lesson, you can combine it with the red aura strength to become a Warrior or with the orange aura strength to become an Entertainer. The same is true of your blue aura layer soul lesson. Once you've learned it, your blue aura layer can be a strength, and you can mix it with your red aura strength to become a Teacher or your orange aura strength to become a Reformer.

OCEAN AURA COLOR SOULS

If your Soul Aura Color is Ocean, you are calm and logical. You're a great analyst and thorough and patient at your work. You tend to have a long-term research agenda with the mission to advance your area of expertise. If you lean fully into your soul gifts, you can achieve your goals through daily grounded actions. Moving your field of expertise forward brings you fulfillment. Wearing ocean-colored clothing or accessories and decorating your home or office space with ocean colors accentuate your soul gifts. Working with crystals like shattuckite, lazulite, and chrysanthemum stone strengthens your soul gifts.

Your deep soul wound is the yellow aura layer powered by the solar plexus chakra. Lacking a sense of self-identity was a struggle during your childhood. You've been working on cultivating healthy self-esteem and self-confidence. Manifesting what you want doesn't come easily, because it's a soul wound you are here to heal. Learning some spiritual self-discovery tools like Western and Vedic astrology, Chinese Zodiac, Human Design, Enneagram, Numerology, and Gene Keys is beneficial for you. Wearing clothing or accessories in shades of yellow helps bring in the color energy while you are healing your soul wound. Golden healer quartz and yellow jasper are great crystal companions for your soul-healing journey.

Your main soul lessons are the orange, green, and blue aura layers powered by the sacral, heart, and throat chakras. Regulating your emotions, cultivating self-compassion and self-love, and expressing your truth authentically are your soul lessons in this lifetime. Clearing emotional trauma, healing your inner child, and rewiring your self-limiting beliefs into positive affirmations are beneficial for your soul's growth.

If your soul chooses to work on your yellow aura layer soul wound first, once you have healed your soul wound, the yellow aura layer will become one of your strengths in your Soul Aura Color composition. Because aura layers work in pairs, with one layer from the higher three chakras and one layer from the lower three chakras, at this point your soul can choose to combine your yellow and violet aura layers so that you can become a Visionary Soul Gift Archetype.

Once you have learned your orange aura layer soul lesson, you can blend your orange and violet aura layers and shape-shift into an Artist. When you learn your green aura layer soul lesson, you can combine it with your red aura strength to become a Warrior or your yellow aura strength to become a Healer. The same is true of your blue aura layer soul lesson. Once you've learned it, your blue aura layer can be a strength, and you can mix it with your red aura strength to become a Teacher or your yellow aura strength to become an Entrepreneur.

RUBY AURA COLOR SOULS

If your Soul Aura Color is Ruby, you have a clear vision of what you want. You are determined and hardworking. Learning and researching areas of interest bring fulfillment, and you're often found in your garage or home studio figuring out something new. Knowledge and discovery inspire you. Wearing ruby-colored clothing or accessories and decorating your home or office space with ruby colors accentuate your soul gifts. Working with crystals like ruby, eudialyte, and stichtite strengthens your soul gifts.

Your deep soul wound is the green aura layer powered by the heart chakra. Being vulnerable and having heart-to-heart relationships doesn't come easily for you. When you were a child, you had tough relationships with your family or childhood trauma that blocks you from trusting other people. Healing your inner child and learning how to give and receive love unconditionally are your soul's deepest yearnings. Practicing self-compassion, working through your shadows to embrace every part of yourself, and clearing self-limiting beliefs are useful tools to heal your soul wound. Wearing clothing or accessories in shades of green helps bring in the color energy while you are healing your soul wound. Chrysocolla, pink opal, and unakite are great crystal companions for your soul-healing journey.

Your main soul lessons are the orange, yellow, and blue aura layers powered by the sacral, solar plexus, and throat chakras. Regulating your emotions, cultivating healthy self-esteem and self-confidence, and communicating your truth authentically are your soul lessons in this lifetime. Healing your emotional trauma will bring forth your

Researcher Archetype

self-confidence without the weight of shame or guilt. Daily affirmations, mantra meditations, and sound baths are beneficial spiritual tools for your soul growth.

If your soul chooses to work on your green aura layer soul wound first, once you have healed your soul wound, the green aura layer will become one of your strengths in your Soul Aura Color composition. Because aura layers work in pairs, with one layer from the higher three chakras and one layer from the lower three chakras, at this point your soul can choose to combine your green and red aura layers so that you can become a Warrior Soul Gift Archetype.

Once you have learned your orange aura layer soul lesson, you can blend your orange and violet aura layers and shape-shift into an Artist or your orange and green aura layers to transform into an Entertainer. When you learn your yellow aura layer soul lesson, you can combine it with your violet aura strength to become a Visionary or your green aura strength to become a Healer. The same is true of your blue aura layer soul lesson. Once you've learned it, your blue aura layer can be a strength, and you can mix it with your red aura strength to become a Teacher.

CARNATION AURA COLOR SOULS

If your Soul Aura Color is Carnation, you are a practical researcher. You typically work behind the scenes and possess a deep body of knowledge within the area of your expertise. You have high standards and work hard to maintain them. You are intuitive, persevering, and resilient. Working on a project that involves new discoveries excites you. Wearing carnation-colored clothing or accessories and decorating your home or office space with carnation colors accentuate your soul gifts. Working with crystals like sardonyx, conglomerate, howlite, and sugilite strengthens your soul gifts.

Your deep soul wound is the blue aura layer powered by the throat chakra. Speaking up for yourself is not your strong suit. Because of your high standards, you can be critical of yourself and the people around you. Some of you have recurring physical illnesses related to the throat chakra, such as strep throat, serious allergies, or sinus issues.

Practicing daily affirmations, immersing yourself in sound baths, and clearing any ancestral and life-limiting beliefs from the past are great mind and spiritual medicine for your soul. Wearing clothing or accessories in shades of blue helps bring in the color energy while you are healing your soul wound. Blue kyanite and zeusite are great crystal companions for your soul-healing journey.

Your main soul lessons are the orange, yellow, and green aura layers powered by the sacral, solar plexus, and heart chakras. Healing your emotional and childhood traumas will allow you to experience unconditional love. When you can love yourself completely and compassionately—even your shadow self—your self-esteem and confidence will shine through. Clearing self-limiting beliefs is beneficial for the growth of your soul.

If your soul chooses to work on your blue aura layer soul wound first, once you have healed your soul wound, the blue aura layer will become one of your strengths in your Soul Aura Color composition. Because aura layers work in pairs, with one layer from the higher three chakras and one layer from the lower three chakras, at this point your soul can choose to combine your blue and red aura layers so that you can become a Teacher Soul Gift Archetype.

Once you have learned your orange aura layer soul lesson, you can blend your orange and violet aura layers and shape-shift into an Artist or your orange and blue aura layers to transform into a Reformer. When you learn your yellow aura layer soul lesson, you can combine it with the violet aura strength to become a Visionary or your blue aura strength to become an Entrepreneur. The same is true of your green aura layer soul lesson. Once you've learned it, your green aura layer can be a strength, and you can mix it with your red aura strength to become a Warrior.

RESEARCHER EVOLUTION PATHS

The following diagrams show the four possible starting points and different paths for your Soul Gift Archetype evolution journey. You can choose to work on your soul wound first or learn one of the three soul lessons. As your soul grows, more aura layers will become your strength. When your soul works on healing soul wounds or learning soul lessons, and these aspects are completed to a satisfactory degree, free will can be exercised to combine aura layer strengths to embody different Soul Gift Archetypes. Of course, you can also choose to remain the Soul Gift Archetype you were born with but just have more light quotient in your Soul Aura Color composition, thus magnetizing high vibrational opportunities in your life and manifesting faster.

THE AURA COLOR WHEEL

Researcher Soul Gift Archetype Evolution Path 1

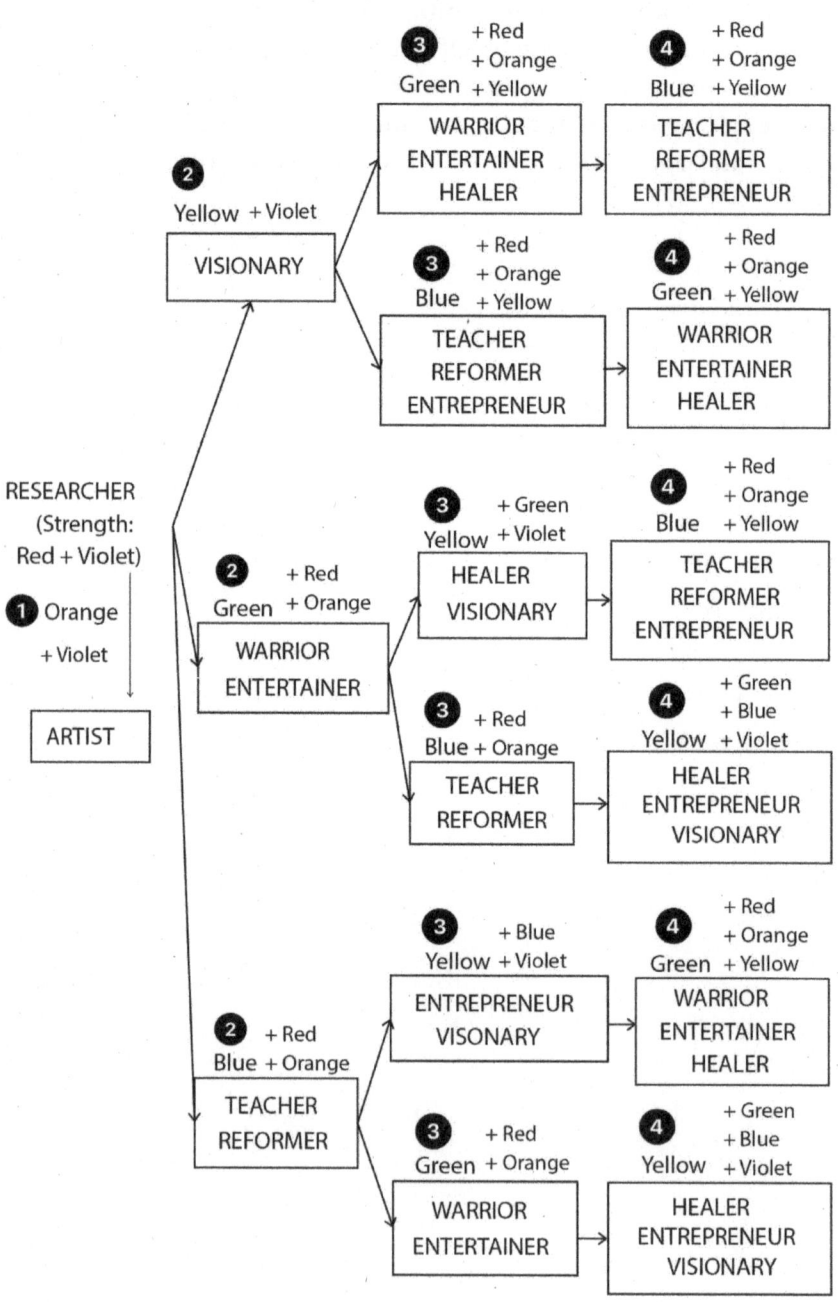

Researcher Archetype

Researcher Soul Gift Archetype Evolution Path 2

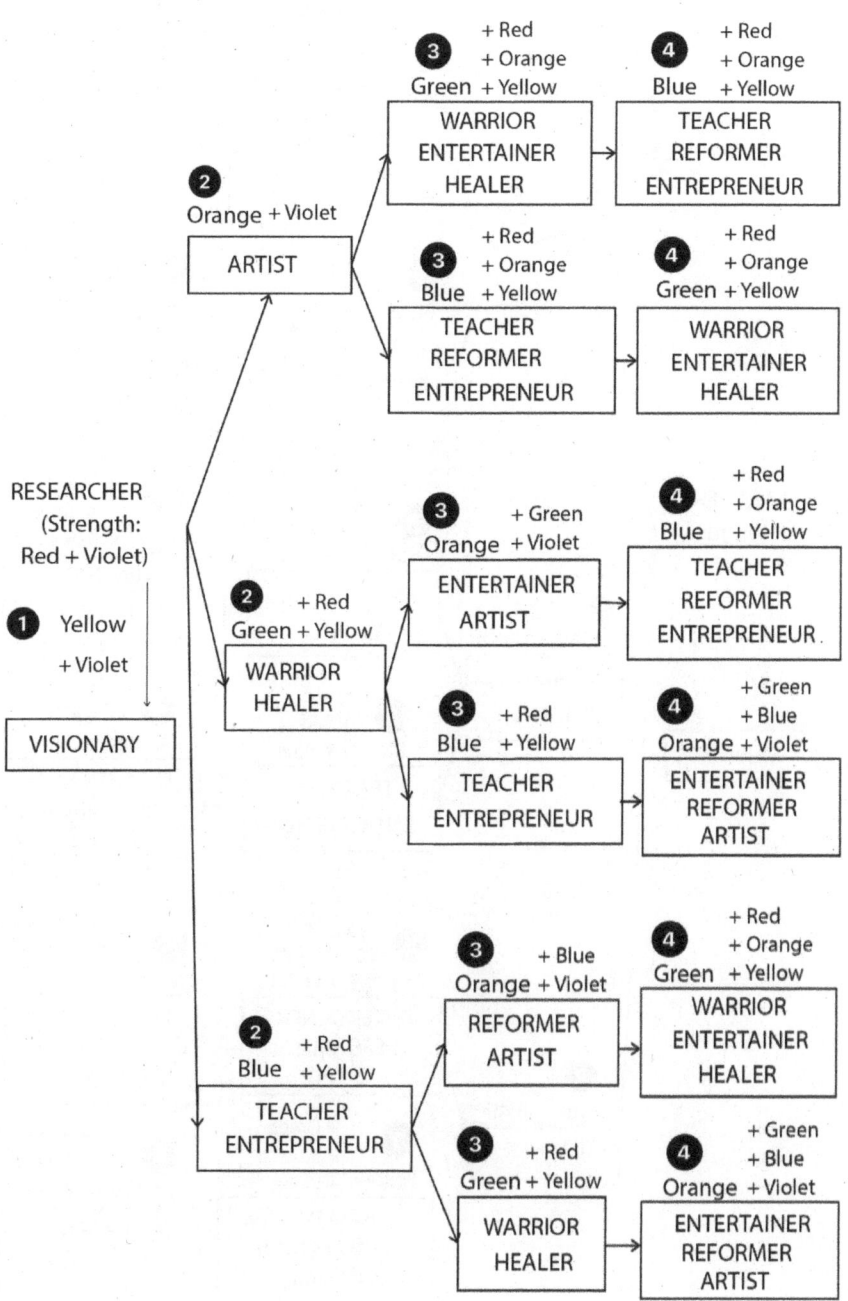

THE AURA COLOR WHEEL

Researcher Soul Gift Archetype Evolution Path 3

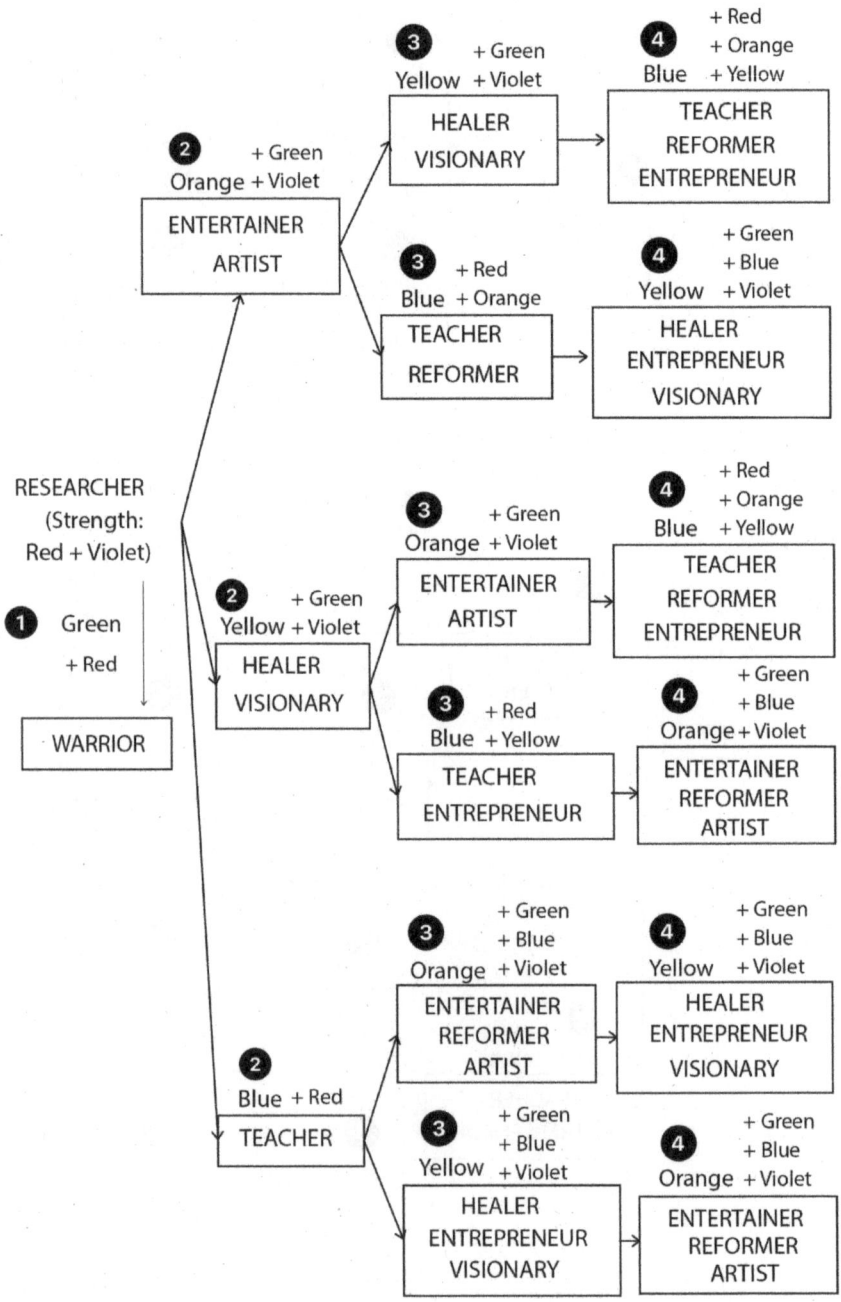

Researcher Archetype

Researcher Soul Gift Archetype Evolution Path 4

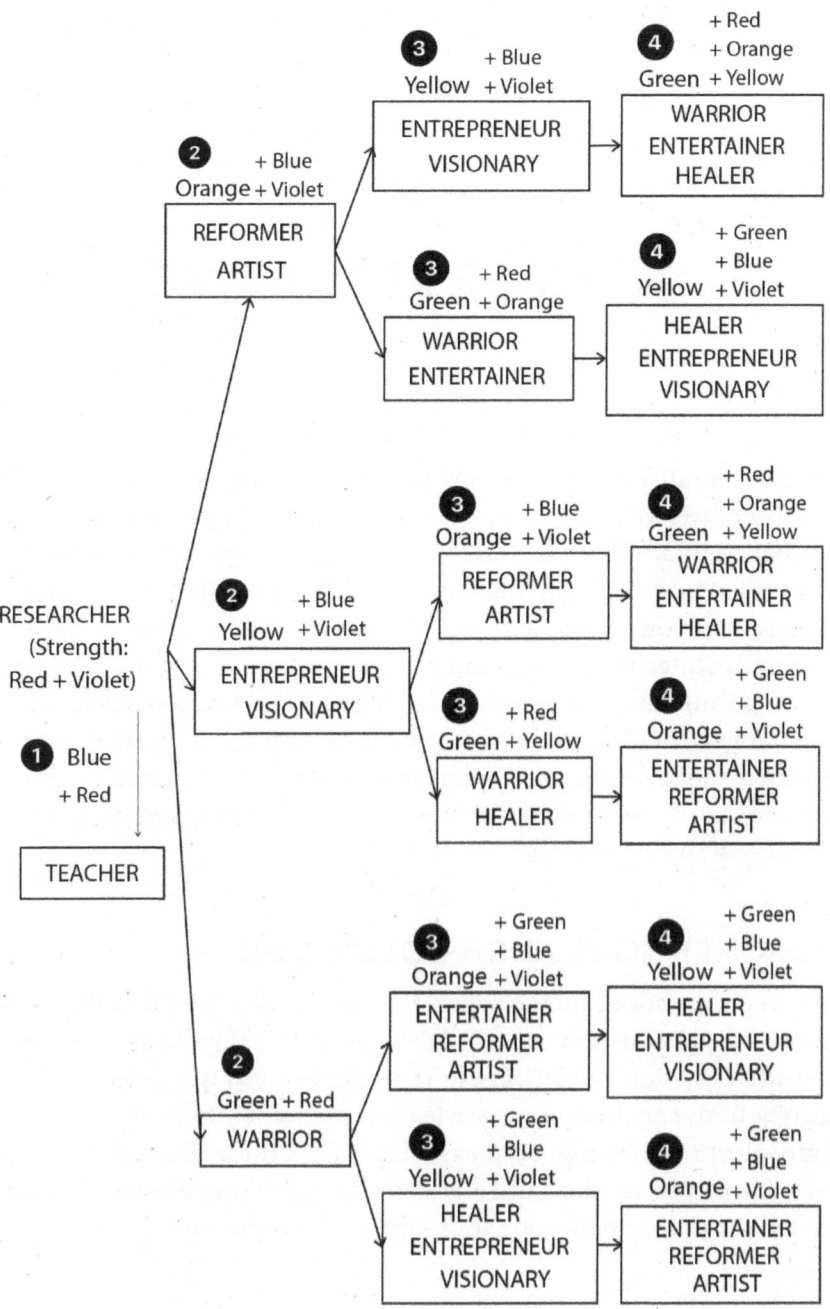

CHAPTER 11

TEACHER ARCHETYPE

If your Soul Gift Archetype is Teacher, you have a strong red aura layer powered by the root chakra and blue aura layer powered by the throat chakra. These two aura layers are deeply connected to feeling grounded in your identity and confidently expressing your thoughts, needs, and boundaries without fear, making the Teacher Archetype perfectly suited for guiding and inspiring others. The main difference among Soul Aura Colors is their soul wound and soul lessons for each. Archangel Uriel and Archangel Haniel are the great angels to call upon to assist you to fully embody your Teacher soul gifts. Trust and use your innate clairsalience, clairaudience, and channeling psychic abilities to receive spirit guidance.

TEACHER SOUL AURA COLOR QUIZ

For each question, please select the option that best describes you based on your current state. I highly recommend you pick an answer intuitively—don't overthink it. If you have a few questions or really can't choose an answer, please leave it blank. If you have more than one selection that applies, please select all of them. Remember, auras are a spectrum of colors, not one static color. These questions are channeled to approximate your Soul Aura Color. Have fun!

Teacher Archetype

1. **In which area of life do you experience the most difficulties?**
   a. Regulating emotions
   b. Low self-esteem or self-confidence
   c. Being vulnerable, giving and receiving love
   d. Planning and visualizing the future

2. **Where do you feel discomfort or illness most often?**
   a. Hormones, reproductive system, lower back
   b. Digestion, liver, spleen, gallbladder, pancreas
   c. Heart, chest, breast, asthma, blood pressure
   d. Sinuses, headaches, scalp, hair, autoimmune diseases, skin

3. **Which circumstances cause the most discomfort?**
   a. Sharing emotions, being too emotional, empathizing with others
   b. Standing up for myself or something I value
   c. Having intimate relationships
   d. Sensing other people's energy

4. **What are you most afraid of feeling?**
   a. Guilt and shame
   b. Low motivation and self-image
   c. Jealousy, desire to please others, sadness
   d. Paranoia or bad feelings about the future

5. **What are you missing that prevents you from living life to the fullest?**
   a. Creativity and spontaneity
   b. Confidence and motivation
   c. Vulnerability and forgiveness
   d. Intuition and psychic abilities

THE AURA COLOR WHEEL

6. Which emotional blocks do you feel most often?
  a. Sadness, isolation, or emotional eating
  b. Anger, frustration, or low energy
  c. Jealousy, or fear of inadequacies
  d. Lack of intuition or inspiration

7. Which issues do you frequently encounter?
  a. Inability to say no, guilt
  b. Low self-esteem or confidence, low energy
  c. Lack of hope or faith
  d. Mental fog, feeling stuck or in a rut

8. Which superpower would change your life?
  a. The power to find calm and peace in everyday life
  b. The power of courage and inner strength to take action and weather storms
  c. The power of connection and harmony with my loved ones and community
  d. The power to gain vision, clarity, inspiration, and innovation

9. If you could change one thing about yourself, what would it be?
  a. I want to feel inspired, creative, decisive, and flowing with life.
  b. I want to be able to take action purposefully according to my beliefs and ideas.
  c. I want to have an intimate connection with my significant other and a loving relationship with myself.
  d. I want to be open to insights and intuitive guidance from the Divine to better understand myself.

Teacher Archetype

10. **Does your birthday fall in any of the following groups of timing? If not, just leave this blank.**
    a. May 28, 1938, 8:39 A.M. – September 29, 1940, 11:44 P.M.
       December 27, 1940, 12:59 A.M. – June 16, 1941, 2:34 P.M.
       May 28, 1977, 2:05 P.M. – June 21, 1983, 8:19 A.M.
       November 29, 1983, 8:19 A.M. – April 10, 1984, 11:19 P.M.
       June 21, 1988, 5:40 A.M. – July 21, 1991, 11:54 A.M.
       June 19, 2026, 5:17 P.M. – September 17, 2026, 9:54 P.M.
       April 14, 2027, 10:56 P.M. – July 19, 2033, 9:35 A.M.
    b. September 29, 1940, 11:44 P.M. – December 27, 1940, 12:59 P.M.
       June 16, 1941, 2:34 P.M. – July 26, 1943, 6:42 P.M.
       April 1, 1968, 2:08 P.M. – October 18, 1968, 6:36 P.M.
       January 30, 1969, 3:12 A.M. – May 28, 1976, 7:10 A.M.
       October 13, 1976, 6:46 P.M. – March 28, 1977, 2:05 P.M.
       July 21, 1991, 11:54 P.M. – September 3, 1993, 1:32 P.M.
       April 17, 2018, 4:09 P.M. – September 25, 2018, 8:12 P.M.
       February 18, 2019, 4:07 P.M. – June 19, 2026, 5:17 P.M.
       September 17, 2026, 9:54 P.M. – April 14, 2027, 10:56 P.M.
    c. November 27, 1944, 11:23 P.M. – March 23, 1945, 10:50 P.M.
       July 22, 1945, 12:31 P.M. – November 10, 1946, 2:14 A.M.
       March 26, 1960, 8:39 P.M. – August 19, 1960, 2:31 A.M.
       January 20, 1961, 8:50 P.M. – April 1, 1968, 2:08 A.M.
       October 18, 1968, 6:36 P.M. – January 30, 1969, 3:12 P.M.
       September 9, 1995, 10:28 P.M. – December 29, 1996, 6:16 P.M.
       April 4, 1997, 11:50 A.M. – September 2, 1997, 11:24 P.M.
       April 20, 2010, 2:28 A.M. – July 20, 2010, 5:46 P.M.
       February 8, 2011, 2:55 P.M. – April 17, 2018, 4:09 A.M.
       September 25, 2018, 8:12 P.M. – February 18, 2019, 4:07 A.M.
    d. November 10, 1946, 2:14 P.M. – February 8, 1951, 8:26 P.M.
       January 18, 1951, 9:13 A.M. – November 8, 1951, 11:22 P.M.
       December 29, 1996, 6:16 A.M. – April 4, 1997, 11:50 A.M.
       September 2, 1997, 11:24 P.M. – December 11, 2001, 6:04 P.M.

THE AURA COLOR WHEEL

Please mark down how many of each selection you have:
a. _____   c. _____
b. _____   d. _____

- If you chose mostly A answers, your aura color is 22: *Blue*.
- If you chose mostly B answers, your aura color is 27: *Lilac*.
- If you chose mostly C answers, your aura color is 30: *Lavender*.
- If you chose mostly D answers, your aura color is 33: *Pink*.

If you have two or more equal selections, it can mean one of the following:

1. You have two or more aura colors in your auric field. Please read the descriptions and intuitively pick which one resonates with you the most to work with now.
2. You are in transition from one aura color to another within the same Soul Gift Archetype. This happens when you heal a certain aura layer soul wound and are now working on another aura layer soul wound or soul lesson. Remember, soul wounds are just deeper soul lessons.

BLUE AURA COLOR SOULS

If your Soul Aura Color is Blue, you are a natural teacher. You like to share your knowledge, experience, and stories through communicating. You love spending time with like-minded souls, discussing subjects of interest. You are well-read or experienced and eager to share what you've learned with your family and friends. Wearing blue-colored clothing or accessories and decorating your home or office space with blue colors accentuate your soul gifts. Working with crystals like lapis lazuli, snowflake obsidian, and fancy jasper strengthens your soul gifts.

Your deep soul wound is the orange aura layer powered by the sacral chakra. You tend to suppress negative emotions and remain calm most of the time. However, all human beings need to process and release

Teacher Archetype

emotions to keep a healthy balance. Clearing any emotional trauma and learning to live with nature's cycles (Wheel of the Year, moon cycles, and days of the week) can help you heal. Wearing clothing or accessories in shades of orange helps bring in the color energy while you are healing your soul wound. Stilbite and flower agate are great crystal companions for your soul-healing journey.

Your main soul lessons are the yellow, green, and violet aura layers powered by the solar plexus, heart, and third eye chakras. Self-compassion and self-love are your biggest soul lessons in this lifetime. Once you heal your inner child, clear all the self-limiting beliefs, and open your heart to trust, you will receive inner wisdom from your soul. Studying spiritual wisdom, such as Western and Vedic astrology, Chinese Zodiac, Feng Shui Birth Element and Kua Number, Human Design, Enneagram, Gene Keys, and Numerology, helps you understand your soul. Your intuition will grow and higher guidance will flow. You will become self-empowered and manifest your desires in life.

If your soul chooses to work on your orange aura layer soul wound first, once you have healed your soul wound, the orange aura layer will become one of your strengths in your Soul Aura Color composition. Because aura layers work in pairs, with one layer from the higher three chakras and one layer from the lower three chakras, at this point your soul can choose to combine your orange and blue aura layers so that you can become a Reformer Soul Gift Archetype.

Once you have learned your yellow aura layer soul lesson, you can blend your yellow and blue aura layers and shape-shift into an Entrepreneur. When you learn your green aura layer soul lesson, you can combine it with your red aura strength to become a Warrior or your orange aura strength to become an Entertainer. The same is true of your violet aura layer soul lesson. Once you've learned it, your violet aura layer can be a strength and you can mix it with your red aura strength to become a Researcher or your orange aura layer strength to become an Artist.

LILAC AURA COLOR SOULS

If your Soul Aura Color is Lilac, you are a great teacher. You are curious and interested in studying a variety of subjects. You are happy spending time in bookstores, museums, or historical sites if the subject matter is intriguing. You like to synthesize what you learn to share with other people, and you can serve as a channel of higher wisdom. Wearing lilac-colored clothing or accessories and decorating your home or office space with lilac colors accentuate your soul gifts. Working with crystals like blue chalcedony, gem silica, and tree agate strengthens your soul gifts.

Your deep soul wound is the yellow aura layer powered by the solar plexus chakra. Healing this soul wound will result in finding your self-identity and growing self-empowerment. You are here to cultivate healthy self-esteem and confidence by clearing childhood or past-life traumas. Learning self-discovery spiritual tools like Western and Vedic astrology, Chinese Zodiac, Numerology, Human Design, Enneagram, and Gene Keys will help you understand your true self. Wearing clothing or accessories in shades of yellow helps bring in the color energy while you are healing your soul wound. Yellow apatite and amber are great crystal companions for your soul-healing journey.

Your main soul lessons are the orange, green, and violet aura layers powered by the sacral, heart, and third eye chakras. Regulating your emotions, opening your heart for unconditional love, and cultivating a connection with higher wisdom are your soul lessons in this lifetime. Processing stuck emotions, clearing limiting beliefs, and embracing the shadow self will bring inner peace and strengthen your connection with the Divine. Keeping a gratitude journal is beneficial to your soul growth journey.

If your soul chooses to work on your yellow aura layer soul wound first, once you have healed your soul wound, the yellow aura layer will become one of your strengths in your Soul Aura Color composition. Because aura layers work in pairs, with one layer from the higher three chakras and one layer from the lower three chakras, at this point your soul can choose to combine your yellow and blue aura layers so that you can become an Entrepreneur Soul Gift Archetype.

Teacher Archetype

Once you have learned your orange aura layer soul lesson, you can blend your orange and blue aura layers and shape-shift into a Reformer. When you learn your green aura layer soul lesson, you can combine it with your red aura strength to become a Warrior or your yellow aura strength to become a Healer. The same is true of your violet aura layer soul lesson. Once you've learned it, your violet aura layer can be a strength, and you can mix it with your red aura strength to become a Researcher or your yellow aura strength to become a Visionary.

LAVENDER AURA COLOR SOULS

If your Soul Aura Color is Lavender, you are an encouraging teacher. Most likely, you have offered hope to another during dark times. If you truly embrace your soul gifts, you will have the ability to change the trajectory of other lives. Wearing lavender-colored clothing or accessories and decorating your home or office space with lavender colors accentuate your soul gifts. Working with crystals like blue calcite, trolleite, and lavender jade strengthens your soul gifts.

Your deep soul wound is the green aura layer powered by the heart chakra. Becoming vulnerable in heart-to-heart relationships is challenging for you. You probably have a complicated relationship with your parents or family members or experienced challenging relationship issues when you were young. Because of this, you shield yourself from being hurt. Healing your inner child, practicing self-compassion and self-love, clearing limiting beliefs, and embracing your shadow self are part of your soul-healing journey. Wearing clothing or accessories in shades of green helps bring in the color energy while you are healing your soul wound. Green moonstone and lavender rose quartz are beneficial crystal companions for your soul-healing journey.

Your main soul lessons are the orange, yellow, and violet aura layers powered by the sacral, solar plexus, and third eye chakras. You tend to suppress your negative emotions to avoid pain. Addressing stuck emotions from the past is such a soul-healing remedy for you. Forming a healthy self-identity with clarity and confidence, cultivating a connection with a higher wisdom, and clearing past-life traumas are some of the soul lessons for this lifetime.

If your soul chooses to work on your green aura layer soul wound first, once you have healed your soul wound, the green aura layer will become one of your strengths in your Soul Aura Color composition. Because aura layers work in pairs, with one layer from the higher three chakras and one layer from the lower three chakras, at this point your soul can choose to combine your green and red aura layers so that you can become a Warrior Soul Gift Archetype.

Once you have learned your orange aura layer soul lesson, you can blend your orange and blue aura layer strengths to shape-shift into a Reformer or your orange and green aura layer strengths to transform into an Entertainer. When you learn your yellow aura layer soul lesson, you can combine it with your blue aura strength to become an Entrepreneur or your green aura strength to become a Healer. The same is true of your violet aura layer soul lesson. Once you've learned it, your violet aura layer can be a strength, and you can mix it with your red aura strength to become a Researcher.

PINK AURA COLOR SOULS

If your Soul Aura Color is Pink, you are a dedicated teacher. You make an excellent caregiver, especially of children. You are patient and communicative. Generally grounded, you radiate a loving light, attracting gentle souls. Wearing pink-colored clothing or accessories and decorating your home or office space with pink colors accentuate your soul gifts. Working with crystals like rubellite, noreena jasper, and blue quartz strengthens your soul gifts.

Your deep soul wound is the violet aura layer powered by the third eye chakra. You sometimes feel a lack of direction and guidance. Life seems to pass with monotonous, day-to-day activities. Forming a daily spiritual practice like meditation will help you find a sense of direction and connect with your soul family. Healing your past-life wounds and developing your psychic abilities are part of your soul journey in this lifetime. Wearing clothing or accessories in shades of violet helps bring in the color energy while you are healing your soul wound. Purple chalcedony and danburite are great crystal companions for your soul-healing journey.

Your main soul lessons are the orange, yellow, and green aura layers powered by the sacral, solar plexus, and heart chakras. Processing and healing your childhood and emotional trauma will help soften your heart. Developing self-compassion and self-love are your soul lessons. When you learn to embrace yourself—even the shadow side—a healthy self-esteem will form. With the self-confidence and self-trust that will grow through your soul journey, you'll be unstoppable.

If your soul chooses to work on your violet aura layer soul wound first, once you have healed your soul wound, the violet aura layer will become one of your strengths in your Soul Aura Color composition. Because aura layers work in pairs, with one layer from the higher three chakras and one layer from the lower three chakras, at this point your soul can choose to combine your violet and red aura layers so that you can become a Researcher Soul Gift Archetype.

Once you have learned your orange aura layer soul lesson, you can blend your orange and blue aura layers and shape-shift into a Reformer or your orange and violet aura layers to transform into an Artist. When you learn your yellow aura layer soul lesson, you can combine it with your blue aura strength to become an Entrepreneur or your violet aura strength to become a Visionary. The same is true of your green aura layer soul lesson. Once you've learned it, your green aura layer can be a strength, and you can mix it with your red aura strength to become a Warrior.

TEACHER EVOLUTION PATHS

The following diagrams show the four possible starting points and different paths for your Soul Gift Archetype evolution journey. You can choose to work on your soul wound first or learn one of the three soul lessons. As your soul grows, more aura layers will become your strength. When your soul works on healing soul wounds or learning soul lessons, and these aspects are completed to a satisfactory degree, free will can be exercised to combine aura layer strengths to embody different Soul Gift Archetypes. Of course, you can also choose to remain the Soul Gift Archetype you were born with but just have more light quotient in your Soul Aura Color composition, thus magnetizing high vibrational opportunities in your life and manifesting faster.

THE AURA COLOR WHEEL

Teacher Soul Gift Archetype Evolution Path 1

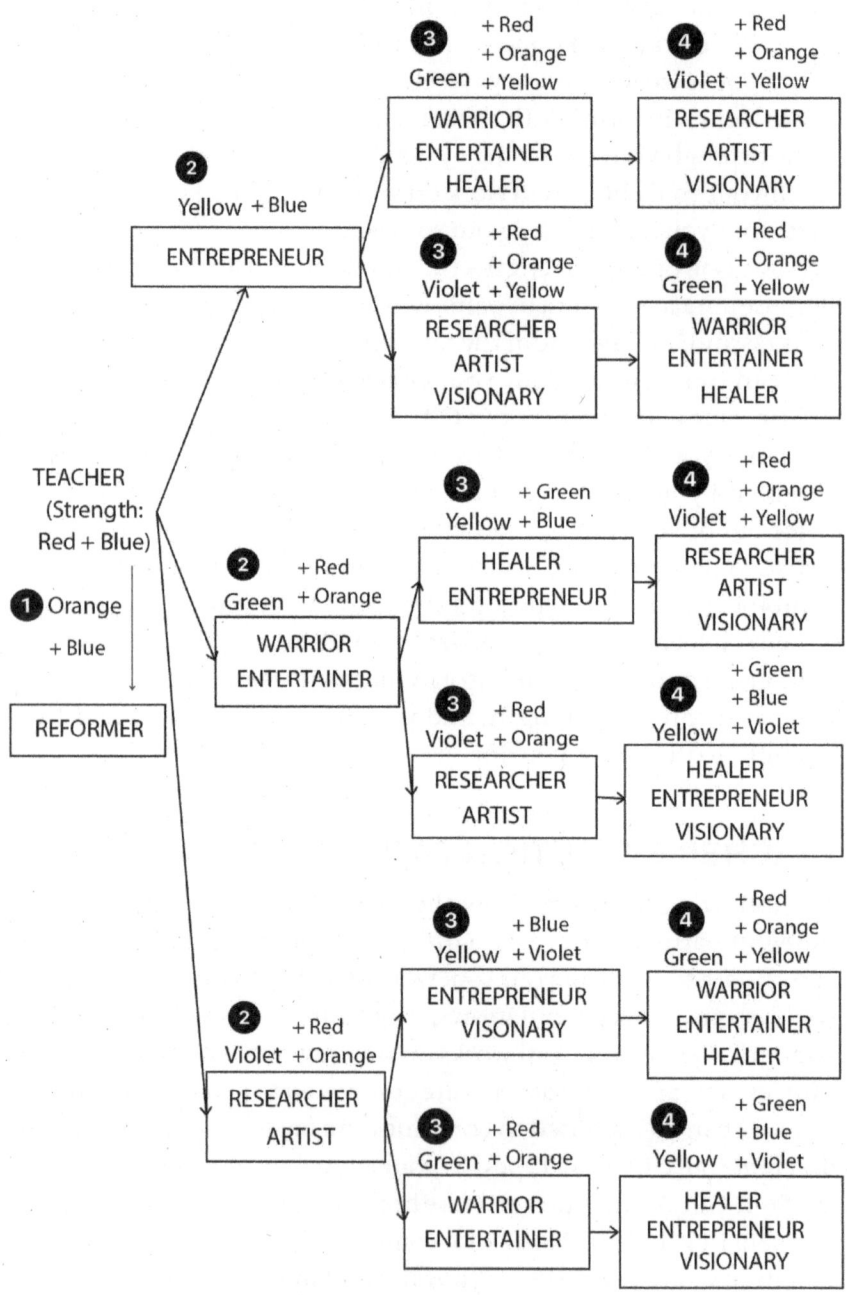

Teacher Soul Gift Archetype Evolution Path 2

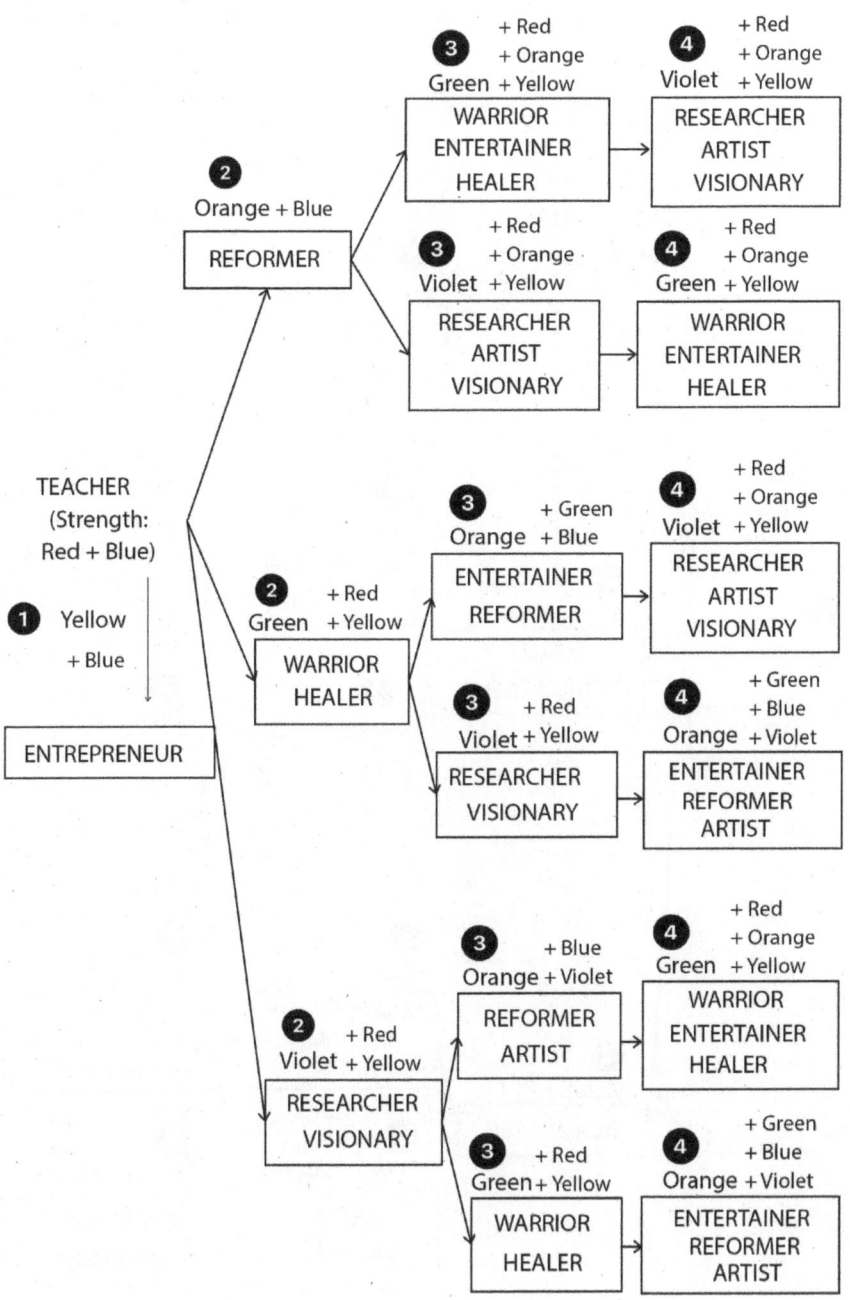

THE AURA COLOR WHEEL

Teacher Soul Gift Archetype Evolution Path 3

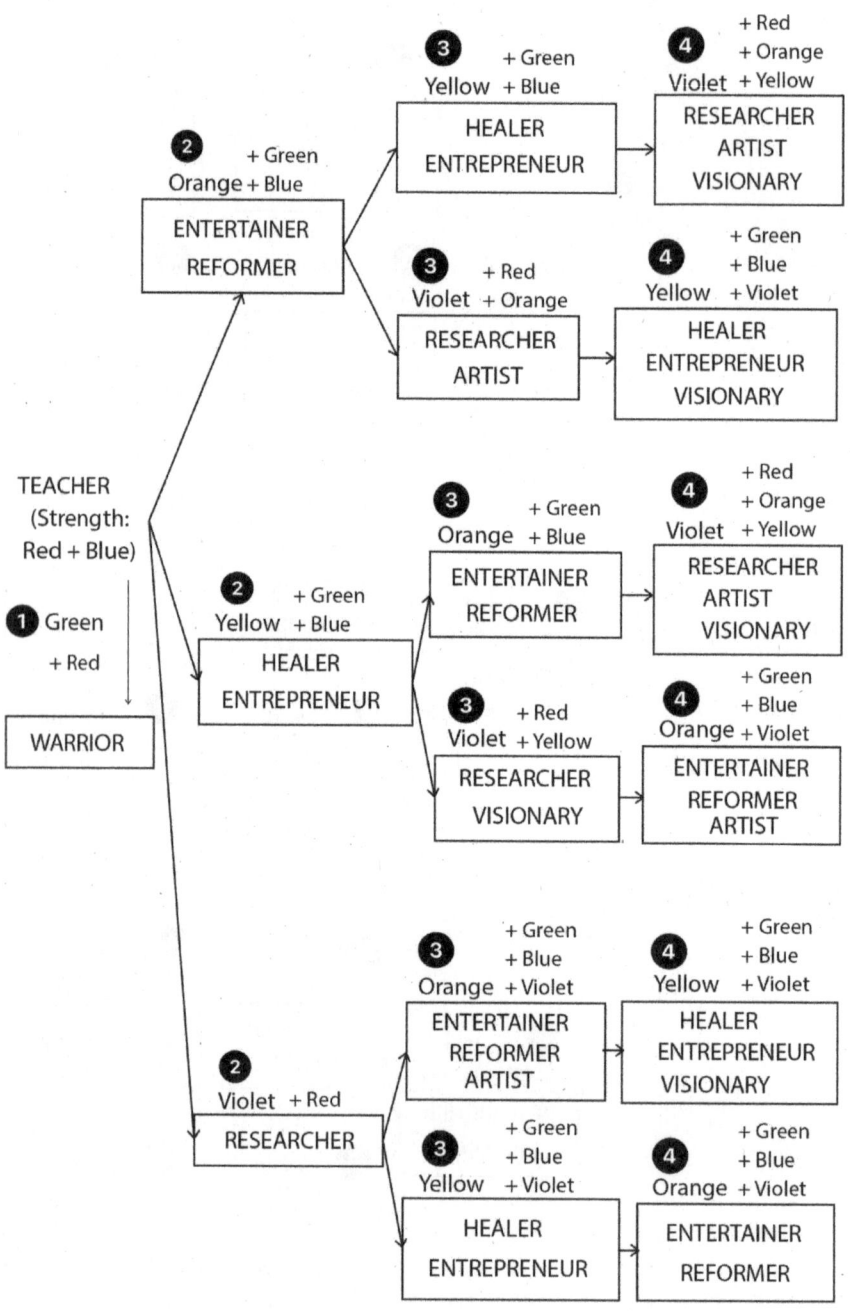

Teacher Archetype

Teacher Soul Gift Archetype Evolution Path 4

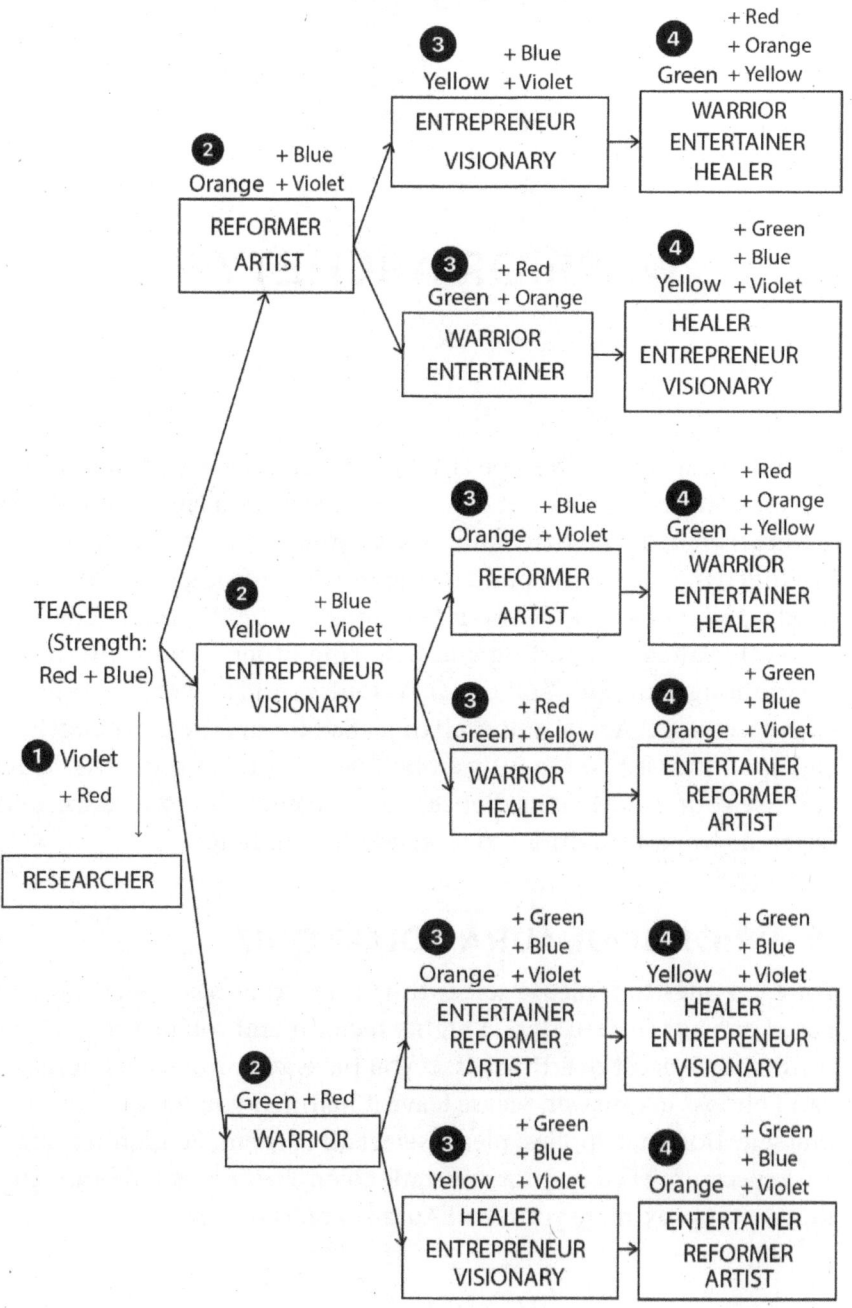

CHAPTER 12

WARRIOR ARCHETYPE

If your Soul Gift Archetype is Warrior, you have a strong red aura layer powered by the root chakra and green aura layer powered by the heart chakra. These two aura layers are deeply connected to feeling grounded in your identity and confidently expressing your thoughts, needs, and boundaries without fear, making the Warrior Archetype perfectly suited for guiding and inspiring others. The main difference among Soul Aura Colors is their soul wound and soul lessons for each. Archangel Azrael and Archangel Zadkiel are the great angels to call upon to assist you to fully embody your Warrior soul gifts. Trust and use your innate clairsalience, clairtangency, clairsentience, and psychic sympathy abilities to receive spirit guidance.

WARRIOR SOUL AURA COLOR QUIZ

For each question, please select the option that best describes you based on your current state. I highly recommend you pick an answer intuitively—don't overthink it. If you have a few questions or really can't choose an answer, please leave it blank. If you have more than one selection that applies, please select all of them. Remember, auras are a spectrum of colors, not one static color. These questions are channeled to approximate your Soul Aura Color. Have fun!

Warrior Archetype

1. **In which area of life do you experience the most difficulties?**
   a. Regulating emotions
   b. Low self-esteem or self-confidence
   c. Speaking my truth without self-consciousness or worry about how other people see me
   d. Planning and visualizing the future

2. **Where do you feel discomfort or illness most often?**
   a. Hormones, reproductive system, lower back
   b. Digestion, liver, spleen, gallbladder, pancreas
   c. Throat, nose, ears, teeth, neck, mouth, jaw
   d. Sinuses, headaches, scalp, hair, autoimmune diseases, skin

3. **Which circumstances cause the most discomfort?**
   a. Sharing emotions, being too emotional, empathizing with others
   b. Standing up for myself or something I value
   c. Expressing myself with clarity in public
   d. Sensing other people's energy

4. **What are you most afraid of feeling?**
   a. Guilt and shame
   b. Low motivation or self-image
   c. Shyness, suppressing communication or speaking too much, ADHD
   d. Paranoia or bad feelings about the future

5. **What are you missing that prevents you from living life to the fullest?**
   a. Creativity and spontaneity
   b. Confidence and motivation
   c. Truthful communication
   d. Intuition and psychic abilities

THE AURA COLOR WHEEL

6. **Which emotional blocks do you feel most often?**
   a. Sadness, isolation, or emotional eating
   b. Anger, frustration, or low energy
   c. Nervousness, unease, or lingering trauma
   d. Lack of intuition or inspiration

7. **Which issues do you frequently encounter?**
   a. Inability to say no, guilt
   b. Low self-esteem or confidence, low energy
   c. Inability to relax, the need to always be doing something
   d. Mental fog, feeling stuck or in a rut

8. **Which superpower would change your life?**
   a. The power to find calm and peace in everyday life
   b. The power of courage and inner strength to take action and weather storms
   c. The power to communicate with the Divine and spirits
   d. The power to gain vision, clarity, inspiration, and innovation

9. **If you could change one thing about yourself, what would it be?**
   a. I want to feel inspired, creative, decisive, and flowing with life.
   b. I want to be able to take action purposefully according to my beliefs and ideas.
   c. I want to possess strong leadership skills to move society forward according to my ideals.
   d. I want to be open to insights and intuitive guidance from the Divine to better understand myself.

Warrior Archetype

10. Does your birthday fall in any of the following groups of timing? If not, just leave this blank.

a. May 28, 1938, 8:39 A.M. – September 29, 1940, 11:44 P.M.
December 27, 1940, 12:59 A.M. – June 16, 1941, 2:34 P.M.
May 28, 1977, 2:05 P.M. – June 21, 1983, 8:19 A.M.
November 29, 1983, 8:19 A.M. – April 10, 1984, 11:19 P.M.
June 21, 1988, 5:40 A.M. – July 21, 1991, 11:54 A.M.
June 19, 2026, 5:17 P.M. – September 17, 2026, 9:54 P.M.
April 14, 2027, 10:56 P.M. – July 19, 2033, 9:35 A.M.

b. September 29, 1940, 11:44 P.M. – December 27, 1940, 12:59 P.M.
June 16, 1941, 2:34 P.M. – July 26, 1943, 6:42 P.M.
April 1, 1968, 2:08 P.M. – October 18, 1968, 6:36 P.M.
January 30, 1969, 3:12 A.M. – May 28, 1976, 7:10 A.M.
October 13, 1976, 6:46 P.M. – March 28, 1977, 2:05 P.M.
July 21, 1991, 11:54 P.M. – September 3, 1993, 1:32 P.M.
April 17, 2018, 4:09 P.M. – September 25, 2018, 8:12 P.M.
February 18, 2019, 4:07 P.M. – June 19, 2026, 5:17 P.M.
September 17, 2026, 9:54 P.M. – April 14, 2027, 10:56 P.M.

c. January 27, 1955, 11:28 A.M. – March 26, 1960, 8:39 A.M.
August 19, 1960, 2:31 A.M. – January 20, 1961, 8:50 P.M.
June 21, 1983, 9:54 A.M. – November 29, 1983, 8:19 A.M.
April 10, 1984, 11:19 P.M. – June 21, 1988, 5:40 A.M.
February 21, 2005, 12:33 P.M. – July 31, 2005, 11:48 P.M.
December 5, 2005, 8:03 P.M. – April 20, 2010, 2:28 P.M.
July 20, 2010, 5:46 A.M. – February 8, 2011, 2:55 P.M.
July 19, 2033, 9:35 A.M. – October 23, 2033, 6:21 P.M.
May 5, 2034, 5:50 P.M. – July 22, 2038, 1:49 A.M.

d. November 10, 1946, 2:14 P.M. – February 8, 1951, 8:26 P.M.
January 18, 1951, 9:13 A.M. – November 8, 1951, 11:22 P.M.
December 29, 1996, 6:16 A.M. – April 4, 1997, 11:50 A.M.
September 2, 1997, 11:24 P.M. – December 11, 2001, 6:04 P.M.

THE AURA COLOR WHEEL

Please mark down how many of each selection you have:
- a. _____
- b. _____
- c. _____
- d. _____

- If you chose mostly A answers, your aura color is 02: *Crimson*.
- If you chose mostly B answers, your aura color is 01: *Red*.
- If you chose mostly C answers, your aura color is 04: *Orange*.
- If you chose mostly D answers, your aura color is 03: *Coral*.

If you have two or more equal selections, it can mean one of the following:

1. You have two or more aura colors in your auric field. Please read the descriptions and intuitively pick which one resonates with you the most to work with now.
2. You are in transition from one aura color to another within the same Soul Gift Archetype. This happens when you heal a certain aura layer soul wound and are now working on another aura layer soul wound or soul lesson. Remember, soul wounds are just deeper soul lessons.

CRIMSON AURA COLOR SOULS

If your Soul Aura Color is Crimson, you are a powerful protector. You have high energy and good physical strength. Your strong sense of righteousness makes you willing to stand up for your family and friends, and people feel safe and secure around you. Wearing crimson-colored clothing or accessories and decorating your home or office space with crimson colors accentuate your soul gifts. Working with crystals like petrified wood, green onyx, and rhodonite strengthens your soul gifts.

Your deep soul wound is the orange aura layer powered by the sacral chakra. You may struggle with anger and aggression because you are a passionate and compassionate person. You take your work seriously. Learning how to regulate strong emotions is your main soul-healing journey. Learning to live with the seasons (the Wheel of the Year, moon cycles, and days of the week) will help bring balance into your life. Wearing clothing or accessories in shades of orange helps bring in the color energy while you are healing your soul wound. Sphalerite and black moonstone (larvikite) are great crystal companions for your soul-healing journey.

Your main soul lessons are the yellow, blue, and violet aura layers powered by the solar plexus, throat, and third eye chakras. Forming a healthy self-identity and self-esteem, expressing your truth authentically, developing your intuition and psychic abilities, and cultivating a connection with the Divine are your soul lessons in this lifetime. Having a daily spiritual practice like mantra meditations or sound baths helps deepen your connection with your soul and higher wisdom.

If your soul chooses to work on your orange aura layer soul wound first, once you have healed your soul wound, the orange aura layer will become one of your strengths in your Soul Aura Color composition. Because aura layers work in pairs, with one layer from the higher three chakras and one layer from the lower three chakras, at this point your soul can choose to combine your orange and green aura layers so that you can become an Entertainer Soul Gift Archetype.

Once you have learned your yellow aura layer soul lesson, you can blend your yellow and green aura layers and shape-shift into a Healer. When you learn your blue aura layer soul lesson, you can combine it with your red aura strength to become a Teacher or your orange aura strength to become a Reformer. The same is true of your violet aura layer soul lesson. Once you've learned it, your violet aura layer can be a strength, and you can mix it with your red aura strength to become a Researcher or your orange aura strength to become an Artist.

RED AURA COLOR SOULS

If your Soul Aura Color is Red, you are a fighter. You are high energy and full of life. Because of your physical strength, you may be an athlete. You enjoy working up a good sweat and anticipate adventures ahead. Wearing red-colored clothing or accessories and decorating your home or office space with red colors accentuate your soul gifts.

Working with crystals like fire quartz, mahogany obsidian, and ruby in zoisite strengthens your soul gifts.

Your deep soul wound is the yellow aura layer powered by the solar plexus chakra. Because of your physique, you may battle arrogance or controlling acts, which you could mistake for self-confidence. Getting to know your true self—instead of your ego—is part of your soul-healing journey. Healthy self-esteem is based on deep knowledge of the true self, not the ego. Exploring spiritual self-discovery tools like Western and Vedic astrology, Chinese Zodiac, Numerology, Human Design, Enneagram, and Gene Keys is beneficial for you to cultivate a balanced sense of self-identity. Wearing clothing or accessories in shades of yellow helps bring in the color energy while you are healing your soul wound. Sunstone and pyrite are great crystal companions for your soul-healing journey.

Your main soul lessons are the orange, blue, and violet aura layers powered by the sacral, throat, and third eye chakras. Regulating your emotions, expressing your true self authentically, and cultivating a connection with the Divine are your soul lessons. Living with the cycles of nature (Wheel of the Year, moon cycles, and days of the week) nourishes your body and balances your emotions. Daily mantra meditations and sound baths soothe your soul in your active life.

If your soul chooses to work on your yellow aura layer soul wound first, once you have healed your soul wound, the yellow aura layer will become one of your strengths in your Soul Aura Color composition. Because aura layers work in pairs, with one layer from the higher three chakras and one layer from the lower three chakras, at this point your soul can choose to combine your yellow and green aura layers so that you can become a Healer Soul Gift Archetype.

Once you have learned your orange aura layer soul lesson, you can blend your orange and green aura layers and shape-shift into an Entertainer. When you learn your blue aura layer soul lesson, you can combine it with your red aura strength to become a Teacher or your yellow aura strength to become an Entrepreneur. The same is true of your violet aura layer soul lesson. Once you've learned it, your violet aura layer can be a strength, and you can mix it with your red aura strength to become a Researcher or your yellow aura strength to become a Visionary.

ORANGE AURA COLOR SOULS

If your Soul Aura Color is Orange, you are passionate and compassionate. A loyal friend, you enjoy helping others with your physical strengths. You are sociable and full of energy—a happy soul to be around. Wearing orange clothing or accessories and decorating your home or office space with orange colors accentuate your soul gifts. Working with crystals like polychrome jasper, green kyanite, and garnet strengthens your soul gifts.

Your deep soul wound is the blue aura layer powered by the throat chakra. You tend to be either suppressed or prone to outbursts or ADHD, and this was especially true during childhood. Expressing your truth without aggression or suppression doesn't come easily. Positive affirmations, mantras, chanting, and sound healing are beneficial for your soul-healing journey. Wearing clothing or accessories in shades of blue helps bring in the color energy while you are healing your soul wound. K2 jasper and scheelite are great crystal companions for your soul-healing journey.

Your main soul lessons are the orange, yellow, and violet aura layers powered by the sacral, solar plexus, and third eye chakras. Healing your emotional traumas, cultivating healthy self-esteem, and developing your intuition and connection with the Divine are your soul lessons in this lifetime. Living with nature's cycles (Wheel of the Year, moon cycles, and days of the week) balances your emotions and helps you learn patience. Daily self-care and calming activities will restore your energy.

If your soul chooses to work on your blue aura layer soul wound first, once you have healed your soul wound, the blue aura layer will become one of your strengths in your Soul Aura Color composition. Because aura layers work in pairs, with one layer from the higher three chakras and one layer from the lower three chakras, at this point your soul can choose to combine your blue and red aura layers so that you can become a Teacher Soul Gift Archetype.

Once you have learned your orange aura layer soul lesson, you can blend your orange and green aura layers and shape-shift into an Entertainer or your orange and blue aura layers to transform into a

Reformer. When you learn your yellow aura layer soul lesson, you can combine it with your green aura strength to become a Healer or your blue aura strength to become an Entrepreneur. The same is true of your violet aura layer soul lesson. Once you've learned it, your violet aura layer can be a strength, and you can mix it with your red aura strength to become a Researcher.

CORAL AURA COLOR SOULS

If your Soul Aura Color is Coral, you are a natural athlete. You are the dancers of life, ready to engage in any adventure ahead. You have high energy, and normally you're the planner or organizer of a group. Your energy is contagious, and people like to be around you. Wearing coral-colored clothing or accessories and decorating your home or office space with coral colors accentuate your Soul gifts. Working with crystals like coral, pink tourmaline, tourmalinated quartz, and black obsidian strengthens your soul gifts.

Your deep soul wound is the violet aura layer powered by the third eye chakra. You tend to have vivid dreams or nightmares, and this was especially true when you were a child. Although passionate about life, you sometimes feel a lack of direction. Having a daily spiritual practice like meditation will help improve your intuition and a connection with higher guidance. Wearing clothing or accessories in shades of violet helps bring in the color energy while you are healing your soul wound. Iolite and Tibetan quartz are great crystal companions for your soul-healing journey.

Your main soul lessons are the orange, yellow, and blue aura layers powered by the sacral, solar plexus, and throat chakras. Regulating your emotions, finding your true self-identity, forming a healthy self-esteem, and expressing your truth authentically are your soul lessons. Processing stuck emotions from the past will help remove your self-limiting beliefs. Positive affirmations, mantras, chanting practices, and sound healing are great spiritual medicine for your soul.

If your soul chooses to work on your violet aura layer soul wound first, once you have healed your soul wound, the violet aura layer will become one of your strengths in your Soul Aura Color composition.

Warrior Archetype

Because aura layers work in pairs, with one layer from the higher three chakras and one layer from the lower three chakras, at this point your soul can choose to combine your violet and red aura layers so that you can become a Researcher Soul Gift Archetype.

Once you have learned your orange aura layer soul lesson, you can blend your orange and green aura layers and shape-shift into an Entertainer or your orange and violet aura layers to transform into an Artist. When you learn your yellow aura layer soul lesson, you can combine it with your green aura strength to become a Healer or your violet aura strength to become a Visionary. The same is true of your blue aura layer soul lesson. Once you've learned it, your blue aura layer can be your strength, and you can mix it with your red aura strength to become a Teacher.

WARRIOR EVOLUTION PATHS

The following diagrams show the four possible starting points and different paths for your Soul Gift Archetype evolution journey. You can choose to work on your soul wound first or learn one of the three soul lessons. As your soul grows, more aura layers will become your strength. When your soul works on healing soul wounds or learning soul lessons and these aspects are completed to a satisfactory degree, free will can be exercised to combine aura layer strengths to embody different Soul Gift Archetypes. Of course, you can also choose to remain the Soul Gift Archetype you were born with but just have more light quotient in your Soul Aura Color composition, thus magnetizing high vibrational opportunities in your life and manifesting faster.

THE AURA COLOR WHEEL

Warrior Soul Gift Archetype Evolution Path 1

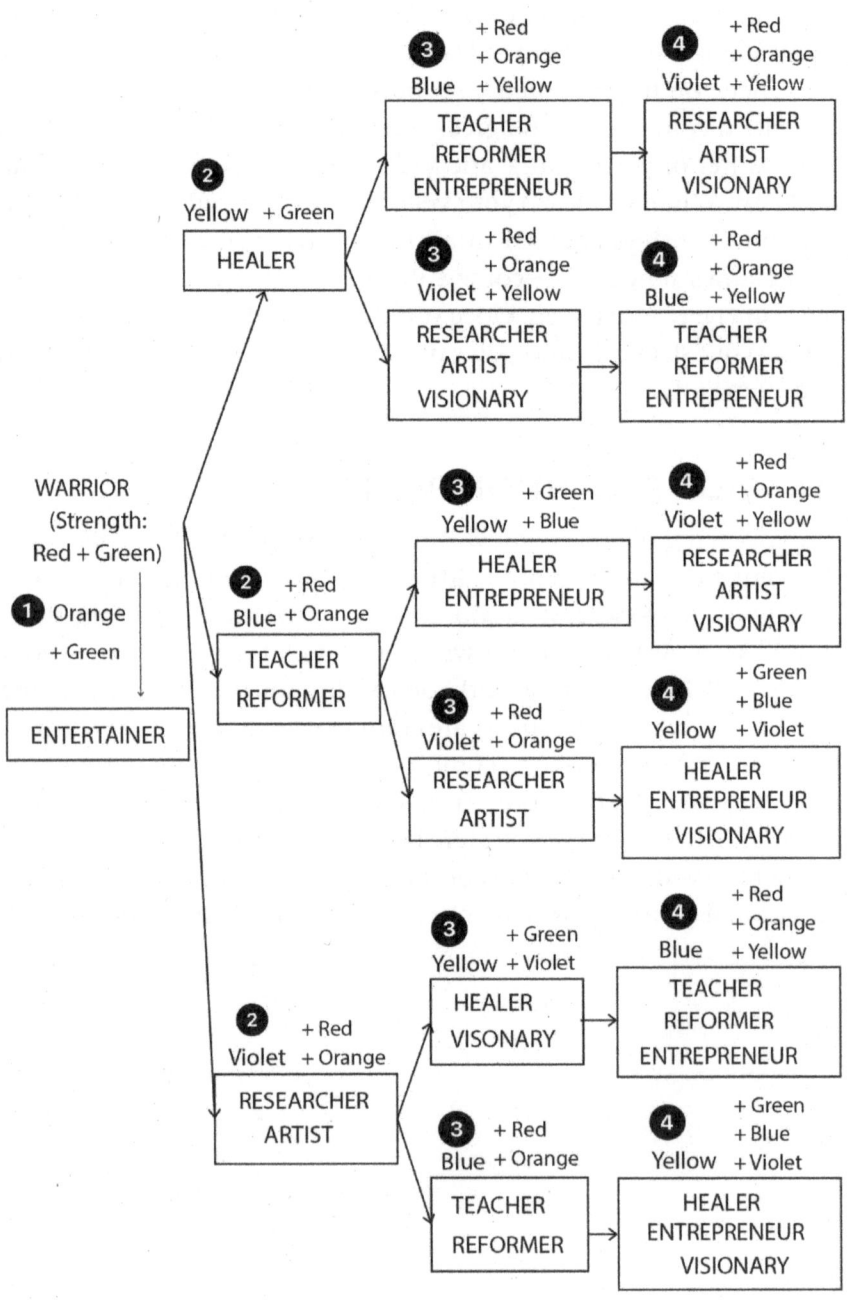

Warrior Archetype

Warrior Soul Gift Archetype Evolution Path 2

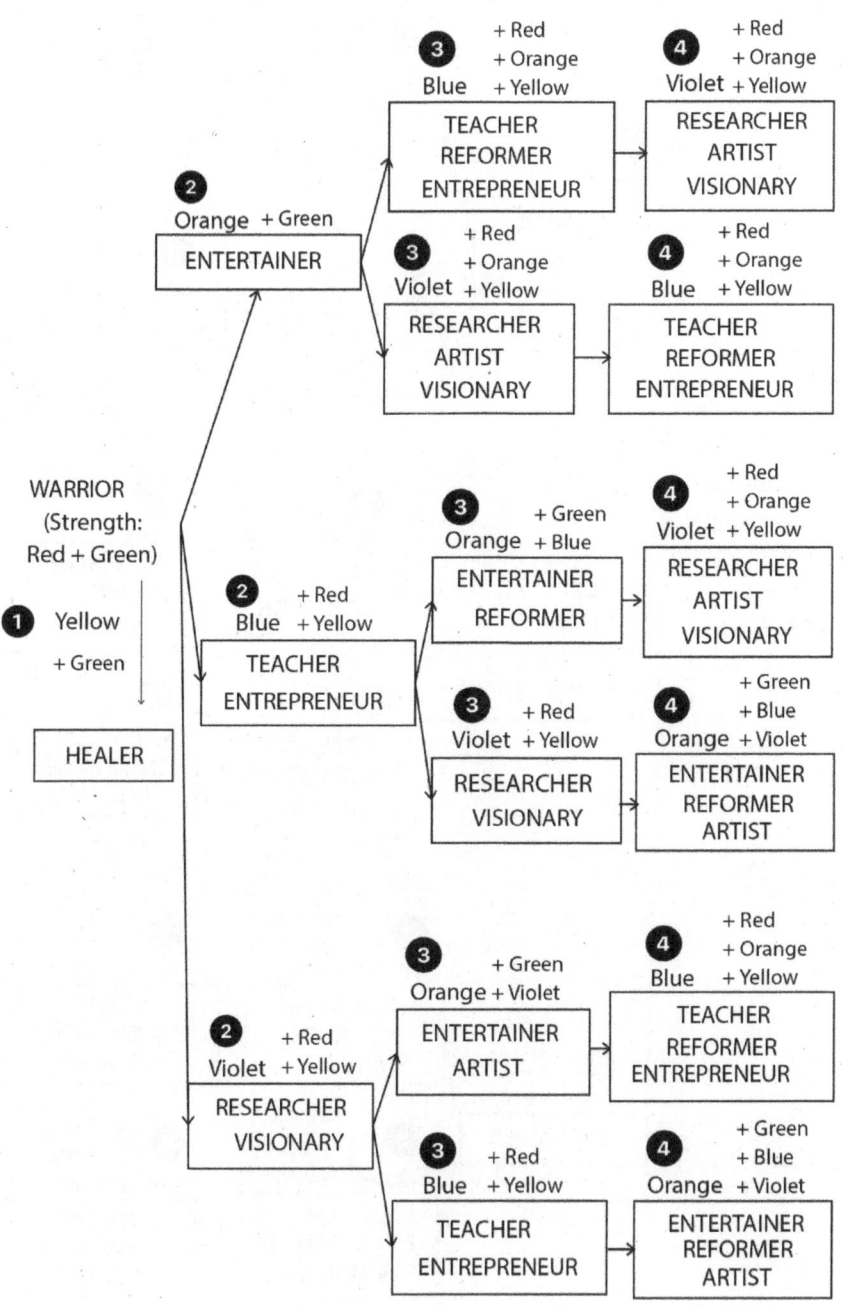

THE AURA COLOR WHEEL

Warrior Soul Gift Archetype Evolution Path 3

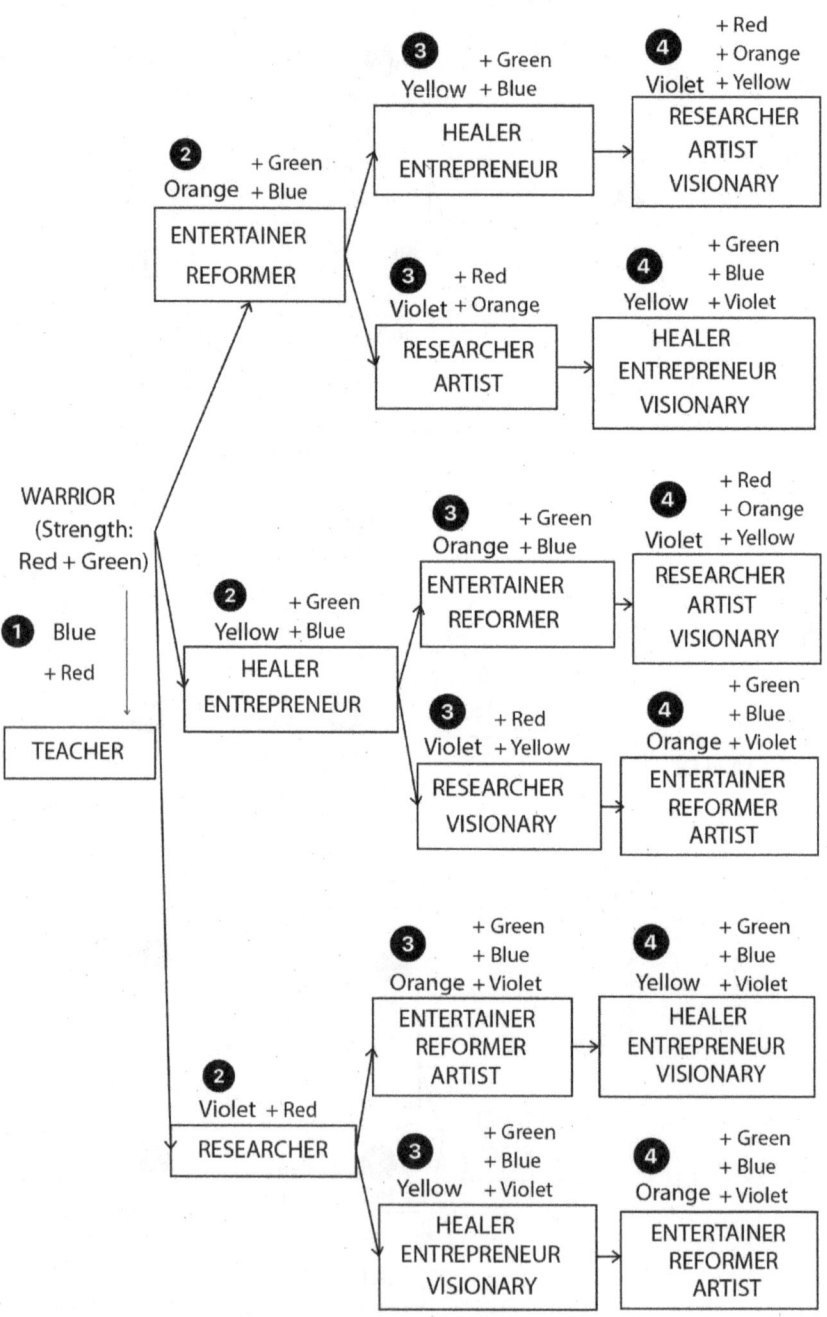

Warrior Soul Gift Archetype Evolution Path 4

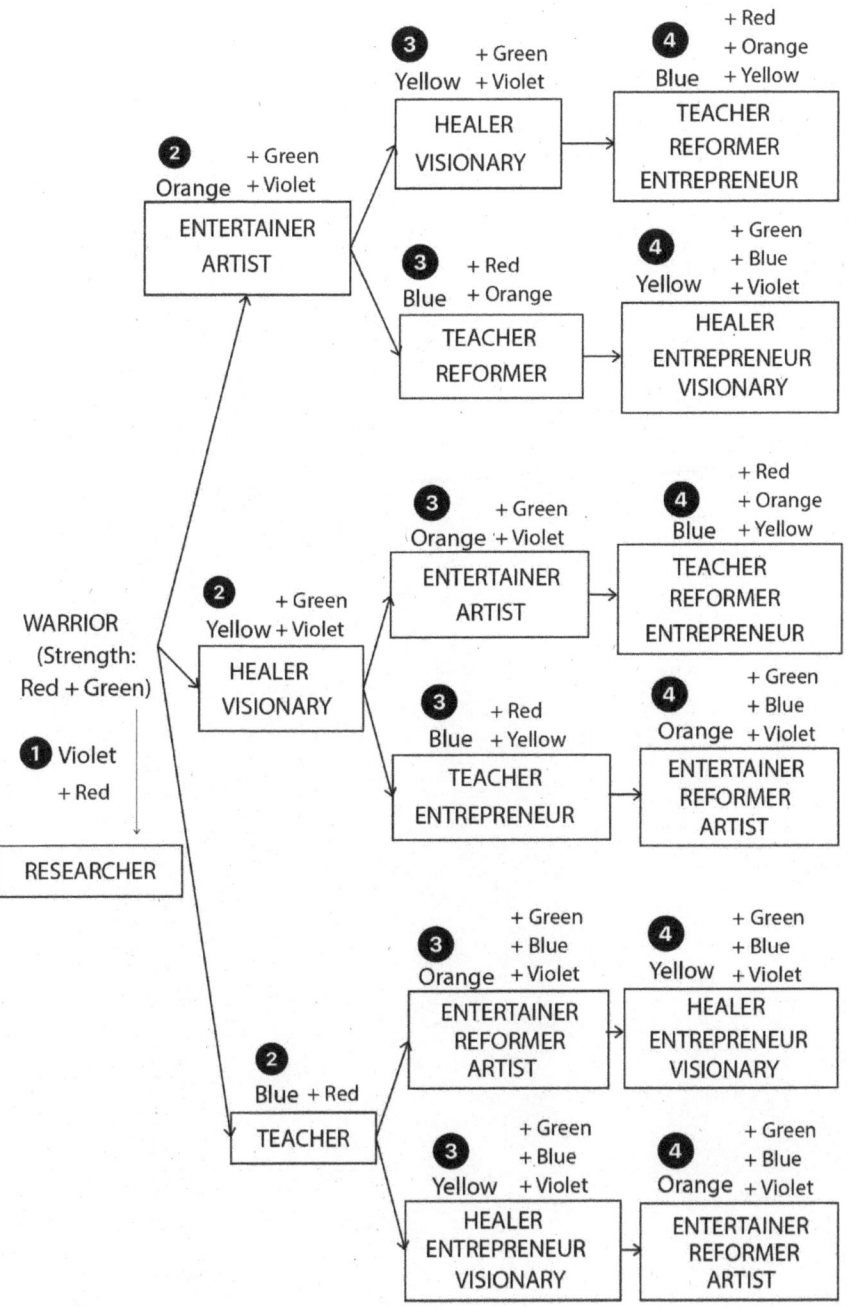

PART III

SPIRITUAL TOOLS FOR YOUR AURA HEALTH

CHAPTER 13

MEDITATION AND JOURNALING

When you work on all of your aura layers on a consistent basis, the four higher chakras—Earth Star Chakra, Gaia Gateway Chakra, Soul Star Chakra, and Stella Gateway Chakra—will activate. You will feel connected to the quantum field through your personal auric field and become a channel of light with Mother Earth and Father Sky's electromagnetic fields. This is also known as the Torus Field—a doughnut-shaped energy loop primarily generated by the heart, creating a continuous flow that connects us with the Earth and the Universe. When your Torus Field is healthy and flows without resistance, you attract all good things in life with ease: health, creativity, joy, abundance, love, beauty, and peace. Eventually, you become a rainbow light body.

With consistent intention and spiritual work, we will all eventually get here. It doesn't mean that our chakra or aura energy will never become imbalanced, but we will quickly know how to return to this radiant rainbow aura state because of all the self-knowledge and spiritual work. We can tap into the wisdom of Earth, connect with the spirit realm in the Universe, and use our own soul guidance for our life decisions. Life flows with ease, joy, and fulfilment.

There are five important energy fields within and around us, and when we harmonize these energy fields in a balanced state, we flow with our rainbow aura state to attract and manifest what we desire easily and effortlessly: our extended body (our immediate environment), physical body, energy body, Mother Earth's energy, and Father Sky's energy. As above, so below, the fundamental principle of the Universe. Our brain is electric, our heart is magnetic, the sun is electric, the earth is magnetic, and we are the conductor between heaven and earth. There are many ways to absorb Mother Earth and Father Sky's energies through nature, eating wholesome organic food, sunbathing, stargazing, and so on.

In this part of the book, I will introduce you to my favorite ways to harmonize these energy fields to maintain your Merkaba light body in the heart chakra and keep all higher chakras activated and connected. In this chapter we will focus on meditation. I will also include some journal prompts to help you reflect on your spiritual journey.

THE POWER OF MEDITATION

Edgar Cayce described prayer as talking to God and meditation as listening to God,[1] highlighting meditation's crucial role in spiritual growth. Tara Brach, Ph.D., clinical psychologist and meditation teacher, says, "Meditation is evolution's strategy to bring out our full potential."[2] I've gained vital insights and soul and spirit guidance, including the Aura Color Wheel system, during meditation—a foundational spiritual practice across all cultures and religions. I stress to students and readers alike the transformative power of meditation; it's the one practice I hope you remember from my teachings.

Personally, meditation has been a remedy for my anxiety and depression, allowing me to discontinue prescription medications within three months. It has quieted my mind, enhanced my clarity, and motivated me to grow into a better version of myself. Through meditation, I began to perceive energies, aura colors, and spirits with my third eye, which revolutionized my life, encouraging me to embrace a greater vision and fulfill my soul's purpose.

Many students express difficulty in sitting still and meditating, a challenge exacerbated by the relentless pace of modern life, particularly in urban settings. However, like any new skill, it becomes more natural over time, evolving into a habit akin to brushing your teeth daily; it's simply about finding the right approach that suits you. If one meditation technique doesn't resonate, explore others until you discover one that feels right. As you gain experience, you may even create a personalized blend of methods that best nurtures your soul.

How to Establish a Meditation Practice

Meditation's primary aim is to calm the mind, not to eliminate thoughts or emotions. Instead, the practice involves observing these thoughts and emotions without attachment, allowing them to arise and pass naturally. This process aligns your brain waves with the Alpha or Theta states, associated with deep relaxation and inward focus. Techniques like listening to solfeggio frequency music in guided meditations can facilitate this state. The Alpha and Theta brain states are notably powerful. The Silva Mind Control Method developed by Jose Silva, and Theta Healing by Vianna Stibal, leverage these states to enhance mental function and facilitate profound healing by reprogramming limiting beliefs through meditative practices similar to hypnosis.

As for duration, there's no one-size-fits-all answer for how long to meditate. It varies depending on individual ability to reach Alpha or Theta states, which could be as quick as five minutes for experienced practitioners. Beginners might start with 20 minutes daily, extending the duration if feeling stressed. Interestingly, the more you meditate, the more you tend to enjoy the prolonged states of peace and oneness, often leading to longer sessions or even retreats.

It generally takes about 21 days to form a meditation habit, although benefits can be felt immediately. Setting specific intentions for each meditation session can greatly enhance its effectiveness. For instance, aiming to connect with your spirit team can facilitate spiritual connections more quickly than meditating without a clear intention.

Finally, creating a dedicated meditation space, whether in your home or a natural setting, can significantly enhance your practice. This space should be a "safe" area where you can easily relax and immerse in meditation, adorned with elements like an altar, pictures of spirit guides, crystals, and flowers to foster a serene environment conducive to meditation.

As a meditation practitioner and teacher with over a decade of experience, I have explored a broad spectrum of techniques, from traditional to contemporary. In teaching beginners, I categorize these techniques based on the layers of consciousness or Koshas (Sanskrit for "sheaths"), as outlined in the Indian wisdom texts, the Upanishads (specifically the Taittiriya from *The Upanishads* translated by Eknath Easwaran). Depending on your level, you can choose techniques that resonate with you and are appropriate for the specific aura layers you might be healing or strengthening. For instance, early in my practice, I gravitated toward mantra meditations, following Deepak Chopra and Oprah Winfrey's 21-Day Meditation Challenges, which I later realized was part of healing my blue aura layer.

I recommend using guided meditations to begin your practice. Once you form a habit of meditating, you can choose to use only background music and set a timer, or better yet, immerse yourself in nature with nature's song surrounding you when meditating.

Meditations for the Five Koshas

Meditation techniques are generally designed to target different levels of consciousness. To explain, according to the Upanishads, humans possess three bodies: the Physical Body, made up of the five primary elements (earth, water, fire, air, and space); the Astral Body, an energy body that acts as a bridge between physical and spiritual realms and contains the chakras; and the Spiritual or Causal Body, which stores karma and connects us to the Divine. Within these three bodies are the five Koshas of consciousness. The Annamaya Kosha, or food sheath, is the first and outermost layer within the physical body. The subsequent three sheaths reside in the Astral Body: the Pranamaya Kosha (vital sheath) sustains life processes like breathing and digestion; the Manomaya Kosha (mental sheath) encompasses our thoughts, emotions, and memories; and the Vijnanamaya Kosha (wisdom sheath) is linked to our intellect and intuition. Finally, the Anandamaya Kosha, or blissful sheath, is the deepest layer, fostering sensations of joy, love, and a sense of oneness, and is located in the Spiritual Body.

The following image is an overview of these three bodies and five Koshas, along with specific meditation techniques suitable for each layer—a comprehensive framework for your practice.

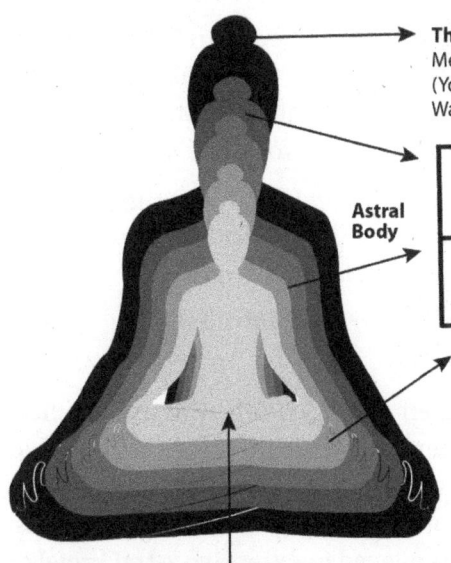

The Physical Body—Annamaya Kosha
Meditation: Body Scan, Moving Meditation (Yoga, Ayurveda, Qigong, Tai Chi, Mindful Walking, Dancing, Painting, Gardening)

Pranamaya Kosha (Energy Body)
Meditation: Breath Work, Chakra Meditation, Kundalini Meditation

Astral Body

Manamaya Kosha (Mental Body)
Meditation: Mindfulness, Mantra, Affirmation, Transcendental Meditation (TM)*

Vijnanamaya Kosha (Wisdom Body)
Meditation: Metta (Loving Kindness), Sound Bath/Solfeggio Frequency, Visualization, Vipassana (Insight Meditation)**

The Spiritual/Causal Body—Anandamaya Kosha (Bliss Body)
Meditation: Akashic Records (Past-Life Regression), Soul Journey, Angel, Oneness Meditation

* Transcendental Meditation is a simple, silent form of meditation that involves the use of a personally assigned mantra to effortlessly transcend, or settle beyond, thought and experience a state of pure consciousness.

** Vipassana Meditation is an ancient form of meditation that focuses on self-observation to understand the impermanent and interconnected nature of all things, aiming to cultivate deep insight and equanimity. It is taught in a 10-day residence setting.

The auric field and chakra system are integral to the Pranamaya Kosha, but each aura layer is closely linked to specific koshas, influencing suitable meditation techniques:

- The red aura layer, energized by the root chakra, aligns with the Annamaya Kosha. Techniques like body scans and moving meditations like yoga, qigong, tai chi, mindful walking, dancing, painting, and gardening are particularly effective for engaging with this physical layer.

- The orange aura layer, driven by the sacral chakra, resonates with the Pranamaya Kosha, making breath work and kundalini meditations beneficial.

- The yellow aura layer, powered by the solar plexus chakra, corresponds to the Manomaya Kosha; here, mindfulness, mantras, and transcendental meditation are optimal for mental clarity.

- The green and blue aura layers, associated with the heart and throat chakras, respectively, align with the Vijnanamaya Kosha. Metta (loving-kindness) meditations, sound baths, and visualization techniques are ideal for these aura layers.
- The violet and white aura layers, energized by the third eye and crown chakras, respectively, connect with the Anandamaya Kosha, making soul journeys, past-life regressions, and angel meditations effective for spiritual connections.

Newcomers to meditation often struggle with stillness, a reflection of their predominant engagement with the physical body and Annamaya Kosha. I recommend starting with a body scan or moving meditations to ease this transition and help ground the awareness. These practices also benefit those engaged in extensive astral travel or channeling, helping them reconnect with their physical body.

Inner Light Meditation

This book doesn't delve into each meditation technique in depth but aims to deepen your understanding of meditation's essential role in spiritual practices and healing. Here is a guided meditation I've developed over the years, effective in cleansing and balancing all five layers of consciousness. Typically lasting 15 to 20 minutes, it can be completed, with practice, in as little as 5 minutes through visualization. It is my daily go-to routine. The Inner Light Meditation is designed to protect, expand, and supercharge your auric field to attract and manifest only the highest good for you. This guided meditation is available for download at www.helencreatesbeauty.com/pages/auracolorwheelbook.

Find a comfortable sitting position with your spine upright. (Ideally, you would practice this meditation either sitting with a straight spine or standing up in nature, but you can do it lying down if your body needs to.)

Close your eyes and take three deep cleansing breaths to tune in to the here and now. Inhale through your nose and exhale through your mouth.

Inhale love, exhale fear.
Inhale peace, exhale worry.
Inhale joy, exhale negativity.

Now bring your awareness to your body and the space around your body.

Bring your awareness to your crown, hair, forehead, face, eyes, nose, ears, mouth, tongue, teeth, and lips. Release any clench of the jaw. Become aware of the space and air around your head and face. Thank every part of your head; thank your brain for serving you every day.

Bring your awareness to your shoulders and neck, release any tension there, let go, and thank them.

Bring your awareness to your upper arms, forearms, wrists, hands, and fingers, and thank them.

Bring your awareness to your upper back, lower back, chest, and heart. Notice your breath coming in and out of your body and your belly coming up and down as you breathe in and out. Notice the space around your upper body and give gratitude to every body part in your torso. Fill them up with luminous, loving light.

Bring your awareness to your lower belly and your digestive and intestinal systems, and thank them for working hard and bringing nutrients to your body.

Notice your buttocks, thighs, legs, ankles, feet, and toes, and thank them for helping you every day (even if you are in a wheelchair). Notice the space around your lower body. Fill it up with luminous, loving light.

Now visualize tree roots growing out from the bottom of your feet or the bottom of your buttocks into Mother Earth. The tree roots are going through the different layers of Mother Earth, the underground waters, the crystals, until they reach the golden center core of Mother Earth. The golden light from Mother Gaia is coming back up through your tree roots into the bottom of your feet, into your lower body, and to your upper body, merging with your soul's light in the center of your heart. It is as if a light switch turns on every organ, bloodstream, and cell inside of your body. Now visualize a golden white light shimmering like a cascading waterfall coming down from the top of your crown to the center of your heart, merging with Mother Gaia and your own soul's light, illuminating your full body from your crown to the bottom of your feet. You are perfectly situated between Mother Earth and Father Sky.

Now visualize your chakra system like wheels of energy spinning clockwise from the bottom of your spine to the crown of your head. Your root chakra is like a red lotus flower opening up, revealing a crystal in the middle; your sacral chakra is like an orange lotus flower opening up, revealing a crystal in the middle; your solar plexus chakra is like a yellow lotus flower opening up, revealing a crystal in the middle; your heart chakra is like a green lotus flower opening up, revealing a crystal in the middle; your throat chakra is like a blue lotus flower opening up, revealing a crystal in the middle; your third eye chakra is like a violet lotus flower opening up, revealing a crystal in the middle; and your crown chakra is like a white lotus flower opening up, revealing a crystal in the middle.

Now call in all the angels and spirit guides who are currently working with you and are of the highest vibrations of resonances to come be with you now. Archangels of the vertical plane: Archangel Metatron of the golden ray of light is above your crown, and Archangel Sandalphon of the copper ray of light is at the bottom of your feet. Archangels of the eight directions: Archangel Michael is in your south with a flaming blue sword, Archangel Uriel is in your north with an orange torch, Archangel Raphael with a green caduceus is in your east, Archangel Gabriel with a white ray of light is in your west, Archangel Ariel with a ruby ray of light is in your southeast, Archangel Chamuel with a pink ray of light is in your southwest, Archangel Haniel of a silvery blue ray of light is in your northeast, and Archangel Jophiel with a yellow ray of light is in your northwest.

All the angels and spirit guides create a bubble of golden white light enveloping your auric field, clearing, charging, and illuminating all layers of your existence across time and space.

If you have a specific question that you seek guidance for, you can speak it now either out loud or silently. Bathe in the light and receive. Thank your angels and spirit guides for assisting you to bring your own soul's light forward. Feeling grateful, energetic, and clear, open your eyes and begin your day with this bubble of light with you.

MY DAILY ROUTINE FOR A RADIANT AURA

Meditation is essentially a spiritual practice that brings your awareness to the present moment so that your intuition is enhanced to sense subtle energies and connect with spirit guidance. An extension of having your daily five minutes to hours-long spiritual practices can be a set of mindfully curated sacred actions you choose to bring into your life.

As an inspiration for you to intentionally choose your own, I want to share my daily routine for maintaining a healthy and radiant aura while staying spiritually connected to the Earth and cosmic energies. These practices can range from as little as five minutes to as long as an hour, with the key being your intention and attention—energy flows where intention and attention go. My hope is that sharing this will encourage you to develop your own daily spiritual routine. It doesn't need to be elaborate; even five minutes a day can make a difference.

Every morning, I start by drinking a glass of crystal elixir that I prepared the night before. I spend 15 minutes doing gentle yoga stretches in my backyard, connecting with nature. This is followed by a 15-minute morning meditation, a variation of the Inner Light Meditation, during which I say a prayer to my spirit team. I also pray for my family, friends, clients, students, and souls who need prayers. I draw a card from my Flowing with My Rainbow Chakra Affirmation Deck and set my intention for the day. I say the affirmation aloud in front of a mirror with a smile. Next, I comb my aura with a selenite bar and choose my clothing color and crystal accessories based on my intention or the aura layer I am working on. I make a cup of tea, turn on the essential oil diffuser, and start my workday; sometimes I put on solfeggio frequencies as background music.

In the evening, before bed, I meditate for 15 minutes, followed by a 15-minute gratitude journaling session or automatic writing, which I refer to as "dates with my spirit guides."

For days when I'm very busy, my five-minute version involves taking a few deep breaths upon waking and saying a prayer to my spirit team for guidance and support on the day's tasks. In the evening, I lie in bed and name five things I am grateful for, thanking my spirit team for their guidance, even amidst challenges.

JOURNALING

Understanding your Soul Aura Color, including its evolution and potential changes, can deepen your self-awareness and enhance your spiritual journey. Journaling can be a helpful tool on this journey, and it can be beneficial for recording any insights that surface during meditation. The guided journal prompts that follow are designed to help you reflect on your personal growth, identify blockages, and align more closely with your soul's purpose. Revisit these questions periodically, especially after significant emotional, mental, or spiritual developments, when you notice a certain aura layer soul wound is healed or a soul lesson is learned. You can download the following journal prompts at www.helencreatesbeauty.com/pages/auracolorwheelbook.

Self-Reflection Guided Journal Prompts

Reflect on the following seven prompts and record your answers in a journal or notebook. If you're having any trouble, meditation can help. After you complete all the prompts, you may also want to meditate to receive guidance on any current issues and/or on who you want to become in the future.

1. *Childhood Joy:* Recall a joyful memory from your childhood. Describe it in detail.
2. *Early Aspirations:* What did you dream of becoming as a child?
3. *Barriers:* Reflect on events that prevented these dreams from materializing. Can you associate these barriers with specific aura layers?
4. *Overcoming Obstacles:* How have you addressed these blockages? Identify the aura layers involved and any shifts in your Soul Aura Color during these times.
5. *Life-Changing Events:* Have any significant events—positive or negative/traumatic—altered your life's path? Identify any major soul wounds healed or lessons learned as well as the corresponding aura layers.

6. *Current Focus:* What aura layer issues are you presently working on?
7. *Future Self:* Visualize who and how you want to be in one, five, and ten years. What changes do you see?

Esther's Self-Reflection

Esther, a second-generation Asian immigrant in the U.S., dreamed of being an artist as a child. However, as the only minority in a suburban neighborhood and kindergarten, she found herself isolated and lacking a sense of safety and security. She couldn't speak English and felt the kids at school watched her like a circus clown. In addition, her first-generation Asian immigrant parents with a survivor mentality did not consider an artist to be a reliable job option to make money, so in college she changed her major from fashion illustration to marketing. As a child, Esther was an Artist Soul Gift Archetype with an Apple Soul Aura Color, and her soul wound was in the red aura layer powered by the root chakra.

In adulthood, Esther pursued a corporate career in the fashion industry in NYC, striving to prove her worth by working harder than anyone else. Despite professional setbacks, Esther remained resilient, leading to significant personal growth. She was working on her yellow aura layer (one of her soul lessons) powered by the solar plexus chakra. She combined her strong violet aura layer powered by the third eye chakra from the Artist Soul Gift Archetype and the yellow aura layer to become a Visionary Soul Gift Archetype with a Forest Soul Aura Color.

There were two major events during her career path that made her feel disheartened by the ethics and business conduct of the fashion industry. One time she was hired by a company who offered her a high-salary job and fired her within a year after the company had gained all her contacts. Another time she lost her investment in a partnership venture. During these stressful times, her mother was diagnosed with breast cancer for the second time. These challenges catalyzed a transformation in Esther's heart chakra (green aura layer), aligning her business practices with her ethical standards. This shifted her into the Healer Soul Gift Archetype with a Jade Soul Aura Color.

Currently, Esther is establishing a successful jewelry business that reflects her values, and she enjoys mentoring newcomers in the fashion industry. She learned her blue aura layer soul lesson powered by the throat chakra, and combining it with her yellow aura layer strength, she shapeshifted into an Entrepreneur Soul Gift Archetype with a Lime Soul Aura Color.

Looking forward, Esther aims to prioritize personal joy and spiritual growth over financial goals, working on healing ancestral trauma associated with her root chakra. She aspires to integrate her strengths across different aura layers, potentially combining her red and blue aura layers and evolving into a Teacher Soul Gift Archetype. Depending on which aura layer is weaker at the time, her Soul Aura Color can be one of these four: Blue, Lilac, Lavender, or Pink. Or, if at this point she can maintain all her aura layer health, she can shape-shift into any Soul Gift Archetype she chooses to become, and her Soul Aura Color will shift toward White.

Your Soul Evolution Aura Health Checkup Journal

This guided journal can help you keep track of your soul evolution journey. Each time you shift into a new Soul Gift Archetype and Soul Aura Color, you can journal about where you are now to help you work through your soul wound and lessons.

1. My current Soul Gift Archetype(s) is/are _____.
2. My current Soul Aura Color(s) is/are _____.
3. The aura layer(s) I am currently working on is/are _____.
4. The way I identify the aura layer I am currently working on is because:
   Physically, I _____.
   Emotionally, I _____.
   Mentally, I _____.
   Spiritually, I _____.

Meditation and Journaling

5. Holistic healing and spiritual practices I have tried to heal or strengthen this aura layer are (repeat this for all aura layers you are working on)
   _____
   _____
   _____.

6. Holistic healing and spiritual practices I have tried and would like to keep in my aura healing toolbox are (repeat this for all aura layers you are working on)
   _____
   _____
   _____
   _____
   _____.

7. What is my soul or spirit team calling me to work on next?
   _____
   _____
   _____

8. What Soul Gift Archetype and Soul Aura Color am I shifting into? _____

The goal of this guided journal is to use the Aura Color Wheel system to help you identify your soul gifts and learn how you can use them to be of service. It helps you be aware of life situations that require you to take conscious action to heal or learn your soul lessons. You can also recognize what you've achieved and which aura layers need more work. By embracing change and aligning with your soul's purpose, you open yourself to greater synchronicities, opportunities, and spiritual healing.

CHAPTER 14

AYURVEDA

Ayurveda is an ancient system of medicine that originated in India over 3,000 years ago. The term *ayurveda* is derived from the Sanskrit words *ayur* (life) and *veda* (knowledge), and it translates to "the knowledge of life." From many holistic practitioners' experiences, Ayurveda seeks to balance the body, mind, and spirit through natural methods, promoting health and preventing illness. It is my go-to for balancing one's physical body, especially when your soul wound tends to manifest in physical discomfort or dis-ease. In this chapter, I include some basic Ayurveda knowledge for you to self-diagnose and rebalance your aura energy through dietary recommendations.

THE THREE PRIMARY DOSHAS

According to Ayurveda, there are three primary doshas, or bioenergies, that govern the body: Vata (air and ether), Pitta (fire and water), and Kapha (water and earth). Each person has a unique balance of these doshas, and an imbalance can lead to health issues. We are all born with a natural composition of Vata, Pitta, and Kapha, just like our Soul Aura Color composition has some strong elements like our soul gift aura layer and some weaker elements like our soul wound aura layer. The following illustration and chart summarize the characteristics for each dosha.

Ayurveda

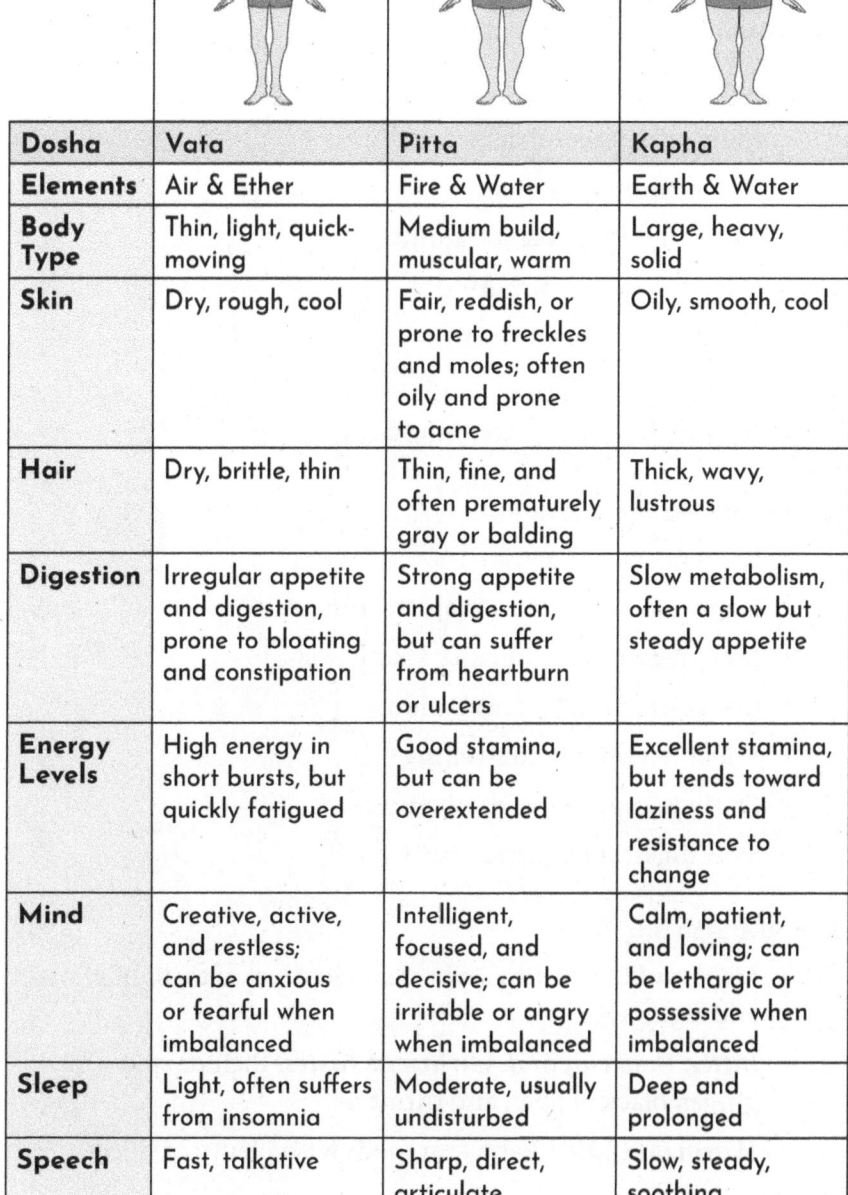

Dosha	Vata	Pitta	Kapha
Elements	Air & Ether	Fire & Water	Earth & Water
Body Type	Thin, light, quick-moving	Medium build, muscular, warm	Large, heavy, solid
Skin	Dry, rough, cool	Fair, reddish, or prone to freckles and moles; often oily and prone to acne	Oily, smooth, cool
Hair	Dry, brittle, thin	Thin, fine, and often prematurely gray or balding	Thick, wavy, lustrous
Digestion	Irregular appetite and digestion, prone to bloating and constipation	Strong appetite and digestion, but can suffer from heartburn or ulcers	Slow metabolism, often a slow but steady appetite
Energy Levels	High energy in short bursts, but quickly fatigued	Good stamina, but can be overextended	Excellent stamina, but tends toward laziness and resistance to change
Mind	Creative, active, and restless; can be anxious or fearful when imbalanced	Intelligent, focused, and decisive; can be irritable or angry when imbalanced	Calm, patient, and loving; can be lethargic or possessive when imbalanced
Sleep	Light, often suffers from insomnia	Moderate, usually undisturbed	Deep and prolonged
Speech	Fast, talkative	Sharp, direct, articulate	Slow, steady, soothing

Kapha Dosha Symptoms and Dietary Recommendations

Kapha in energetic essence is similar to the root and sacral chakras. If your soul wound is in the red or orange aura layers, you tend to have a Kapha imbalance. Our Kapha generally elevates during winter.

Kapha in Balance:
- Calm and peaceful demeanor
- Strong immune system
- Physical strength and stamina
- Compassion and loyalty
- Steady and grounded nature
- Good sleep patterns
- Healthy weight and well-lubricated joints

Kapha Imbalance (Elevated):
- Lethargy and sluggishness
- Depression and emotional attachment
- Weight gain and difficulty losing weight
- Congestion and mucus buildup
- Water retention and swelling
- Dullness and lack of motivation
- Slow digestion and metabolism

Kapha Balancing Diet:
- ***Light and Dry Foods:*** Favor steamed vegetables, light grains, and legumes.
- ***Bitter, Pungent, and Astringent Tastes:*** Include spices like ginger, black pepper, and turmeric.
- ***Warm and Spicy:*** Eat warm foods with plenty of spices.

- ***Limited Use of Oils:*** Use oils sparingly; opt for light oils like sunflower or flaxseed.
- ***Stimulating Beverages:*** Drink warm water and herbal teas, and avoid cold drinks.

Foods to Avoid:
- Heavy, oily, and fatty foods, dairy products, sugary foods, and excessive salt

Pitta Dosha Symptoms and Dietary Recommendations

Pitta in energetic essence is similar to the solar plexus and heart chakras. If your soul wound is in the yellow or green aura layers, you tend to have a Pitta imbalance. Our Pitta generally elevates during summer.

Pitta in Balance:
- Strong digestion and appetite
- Good concentration and focus
- Courage and ambition
- Healthy complexion and body temperature
- Sharp intellect and strong memory
- Joyful and contented disposition
- Efficient and organized

Pitta Imbalance (Elevated):
- Anger and irritability
- Impatience and criticism
- Acid reflux and heartburn
- Skin rashes and inflammation
- Excessive body heat and sweating
- Diarrhea or loose stools
- Burning sensations in the body

Pitta Balancing Diet:
- *Cool, Refreshing Foods:* Favor salads, raw vegetables, and cooling fruits like melons and cucumbers.
- *Sweet, Bitter, and Astringent Tastes:* Include sweet fruits, leafy greens, and legumes.
- *Moderate Use of Spices:* Use cooling spices like coriander, fennel, and mint.
- *Dairy Products:* Consume milk, butter, and ghee in moderation.
- *Hydration:* Drink plenty of water, coconut water, and herbal teas.

Foods to Avoid:
- Spicy, salty, and sour foods, ginger, alcohol, caffeine, and fried or oily foods

Vata Dosha Symptoms and Dietary Recommendations

Vata in energetic essence is similar to the throat and third eye chakras. If your soul wound is in the blue or violet aura layers, you tend to have a Vata imbalance. Our Vata generally elevates during spring and fall.

Vata in Balance:
- Creativity and enthusiasm
- Quick to learn and grasp concepts
- Strong imagination
- Flexibility and adaptability
- High energy levels
- Regular elimination and good digestion
- Clear, vibrant skin

Vata Imbalance (Elevated):
- Anxiety and fear
- Restlessness and difficulty focusing
- Insomnia or irregular sleep patterns
- Dry skin and hair
- Constipation and digestive issues
- Weight loss
- Joint pain and stiffness

Vata Balancing Diet:
- ***Warm, Cooked Foods:*** Favor soups, stews, and casseroles. Avoid cold and raw foods.
- ***Moist and Oily:*** Use ghee, olive oil, and coconut oil generously.
- ***Sweet, Sour, and Salty Tastes:*** Incorporate naturally sweet foods like fruits, sour foods like citrus, and salty foods in moderation.
- ***Nourishing Grains:*** Rice, oats, and wheat are good choices.
- ***Warm Beverages:*** Herbal teas, warm milk, and spiced teas (like ginger tea) are beneficial.

Foods to Avoid:
- Raw vegetables, cold salads, dry foods like crackers, and carbonated drinks

DIAGNOSING YOUR DOSHA

I highly recommend finding a local accredited Ayurveda practitioner to diagnose your dosha composition in person. Like Chinese traditional medicine doctors, they take your pulse, look at your tongue, and ask about your dietary preferences and bowel movements. You can search for a professional through the National Ayurvedic Medical Association. The Kerala Ayurveda Academy is an accredited program that offers online consultation if you find it more convenient. Banyan Botanicals offers an online quiz where you can identify your natural dosha composition and which dosha is currently elevated. Once you identify what's out of balance, you can follow their food list recommendations to use diet to return to a balanced state. I have no personal affiliation with Banyan Botanicals, but I find their Ayurveda knowledge base is helpful to my clients who are beginners.

CHAPTER 15

FENG SHUI

Our immediate living and working environments are extensions of our own energy fields, continuously exchanging energies and shaping our well-being. Therefore, it is crucial to ensure that these spaces make us feel comfortable and positive. Feng Shui, an ancient Chinese practice, aims to harmonize individuals with their surroundings, creating a balanced and nurturing environment. As a third-generation Feng Shui master with over a decade of experience, I have Feng Shuied hundreds of homes and buildings, witnessing firsthand the profound impact it can have on your life.

In this chapter, I'll offer a beginner's guide to the general Feng Shui directions, how they correspond to different aspects of life, and the crystals best suited for each area. It's important to note that your personal Feng Shui, influenced by your Birth Element and Kua Number (which differs from Numerology), may suggest different auspicious directions.

APPLYING FENG SHUI TO YOUR HOME

To determine the Feng Shui orientation of your home, stand inside the house facing the front door and use a compass to find the north direction. From there, you can ascertain that south is directly opposite, with west to the left and east to the right. Divide your home into

THE AURA COLOR WHEEL

nine sections, imagining it as a grid of nine squares. If your home isn't perfectly rectangular or square, approximate as best you can. Each section of this grid corresponds to a specific area of your life and is linked to one of the Feng Shui elements (see chart). Here are detailed energies and decor recommendations for each of these Feng Shui directions.

FRONT DOOR

NORTHWEST HELPFUL PEOPLE Metal Gold, Silver, Bronze, Gray, White Circle **Best for: ENTERTAINER**	NORTH CAREER Water Blue, Black Wavy **Best for:** **RESEARCHER**	NORTHEAST SPIRITUAL GROWTH Earth Light Yellow, Brown, Sand Square **Best for: TEACHER**
WEST CREATIVITY Metal Gold, Silver, Bronze, Gray, White Circle **Best for: ARTIST**	CENTER UNITY Earth Light Yellow, Brown, Sand Square **Best for: VISIONARY**	EAST HEALTH Wood Green, Brown Rectangle **Best for: HEALER**
SOUTHWEST LOVE & MARRIAGE Earth Light Yellow, Brown, Sand Square **Best for: REFORMER**	SOUTH REPUTATION Fire Red, Yellow, Pink, Purple, Orange Triangle **Best for: WARRIOR**	SOUTHEAST MONEY Wood Green, Brown Rectangle **Best for:** **ENTREPRENEUR**

East: Health & Family
- *Ideal Function:* Dining room or family room
- *Energy Best for:* Healer Soul Gift Archetype
- *Elemental Energy:* Wood
- *Recommended Colors:* Shades of green, dark brown, blue, black
- *Colors to Avoid in Excess:* White, gold, silver, gray, copper, bronze
- *Recommended Shapes of Decor:* Rectangle
- *Shapes of Decor to Avoid in Excess:* Circle
- *Crystals:* Chrysoprase, emerald, dioptase, fluorite, turquoise

Southeast: Money & Prosperity
- *Ideal Function:* Home office or main entrance
- *Energy Best for:* Entrepreneur Soul Gift Archetype
- *Elemental Energy:* Wood
- *Recommended Colors:* Shades of green, dark brown, blue, black
- *Colors to Avoid in Excess:* White, gold, silver, gray, copper, bronze
- *Recommended Shapes of Decor:* Rectangle
- *Shapes of Decor to Avoid in Excess:* Circle
- *Crystals:* Citrine, green aventurine, cinnabar, dragon blood jasper

Southwest: Love & Marriage
- *Ideal Function:* Master bedroom
- *Energy Best for:* Reformer Soul Gift Archetype
- *Elemental Energy:* Earth

THE AURA COLOR WHEEL

- *Recommended Colors:* Sand, light brown, light yellow, light orange, pink
- *Colors to Avoid in Excess:* Green, dark brown
- *Recommended Shapes of Decor:* Square
- *Shapes of Decor to Avoid in Excess:* Rectangle
- *Crystals:* Carnelian, rose quartz, tangerine aura quartz, rhodochrosite

Northeast: Personal & Spiritual Growth

- *Ideal Function:* Meditation room or study
- *Energy Best for:* Teacher Soul Gift Archetype
- *Elemental Energy:* Earth
- *Recommended Colors:* Sand, light brown, light yellow, light orange, pink
- *Colors to Avoid in Excess:* Green, dark brown
- *Recommended Shapes of Decor:* Square
- *Shapes of Decor to Avoid in Excess:* Rectangle
- *Crystals:* Labradorite, super seven, auralite 23, charoite, sugilite, amethyst, azurite

North: Career Path

- *Ideal Function:* Home office or bathroom
- *Energy Best for:* Researcher Soul Gift Archetype
- *Elemental Energy:* Water
- *Recommended Colors:* Blue, black, white, gold, silver, gray, copper, bronze
- *Colors to Avoid in Excess:* Earth tones, sand, light brown, light yellow

- *Recommended Shapes of Decor:* Wavy
- *Shapes of Decor to Avoid in Excess:* Square
- *Crystals:* Larimar, angelite, kyanite, lapis lazuli, fluorite

South: Fame & Reputation

- *Ideal Function:* Kitchen or living room
- *Energy Best for:* Warrior Soul Gift Archetype
- *Elemental Energy:* Fire
- *Recommended Colors:* Red, orange, yellow, purple, pink, green, dark brown
- *Colors to Avoid in Excess:* Blue, black
- *Recommended Shapes of Decor:* Triangle
- *Shapes of Decor to Avoid in Excess:* Wavy
- *Crystals:* Tiger's eye (red or golden), ruby, garnet, red jasper, green jade, malachite

West: Creativity & Children

- *Ideal Function:* Art room or kid's room
- *Energy Best for:* Artist Soul Gift Archetype
- *Elemental Energy:* Metal
- *Recommended Colors:* White, gold, silver, gray, copper, bronze
- *Colors to Avoid in Excess:* Red, orange, yellow, purple, hot pink
- *Recommended Shapes of Decor:* Circle
- *Shapes of Decor to Avoid in Excess:* Triangle
- *Crystals:* Citrine, amber, lemon quartz, smoky quartz, amethyst

THE AURA COLOR WHEEL

Northwest: Helpful People

- *Ideal Function:* Guest room or living room
- *Energy Best for:* Entertainer Soul Gift Archetype
- *Elemental Energy:* Metal
- *Recommended Colors:* White, gold, silver, gray, copper, bronze
- *Colors to Avoid in Excess:* Red, bright orange, yellow, purple, hot pink
- *Recommended Shapes of Decor:* Circle
- *Shapes of Decor to Avoid in Excess:* Triangle
- *Crystals:* Clear quartz, pyrite, apophyllite, jade Buddha, or any ascended master statues

Center of Home: Unity, Yin/Yang Balance, and Harmony

- *Ideal Function:* Open space or relaxing area
- *Energy Best for:* Visionary Soul Gift Archetype
- *Elemental Energy:* Earth
- *Recommended Colors:* Sand, light brown, light yellow, light orange, pink
- *Colors to Avoid in Excess:* Green, dark brown
- *Recommended Shapes of Decor:* Square
- *Shapes of Decor to Avoid in Excess:* Rectangle
- *Crystals:* Clear quartz, apophyllite, amethyst, citrine, rose quartz

CHAPTER 16

LIVING WITH NATURE'S CYCLES

Living in harmony with nature's cycles, such as the Wheel of the Year, moon phases, and days of the week, plays a vital role in maintaining our aura health. These natural rhythms guide us through periods of growth, rest, and renewal, aligning our energies with the Earth's. Observing these cycles helps us remain grounded, enhances our emotional balance, and fosters a deeper connection with Mother Earth and Father Sky. Apart from the basic natural cycles discussed here, there are other significant astrological events, such as planetary retrogrades or notable aspects, that you might want to track to observe their effects on your energy. I recommend keeping a journal as a reminder. By syncing our activities and intentions with these natural patterns, we can cultivate a sense of peace and well-being, ensuring that our aura remains vibrant and higher chakras connected.

THE WHEEL OF THE YEAR

The Wheel of the Year is a modern pagan calendar that marks the annual cycle of seasonal festivals, or "Sabbats." The Greater Sabbats (turning of the season) or "cross-quarter days" are fire festivals that were often celebrated at the time of the new or full moon, with communities coming together to celebrate around a great fire. They are Imbolc, Beltane, Lughnasadh, and Samhain. The Lesser Sabbats or "quarter days" are the four solar festivals that mark the sun's position in the sky at different times of the year: Ostara, Litha, Mabon, and Yule. Below is a Wheel of the Year chart I created on my altar to remind myself of these important dates while I adjust my diet, Feng Shui decor, and intentions according to the seasons. "N" means Northern Hemisphere and "S" means Southern Hemisphere. You can make a copy of the chart or download a color version at www.helencreatesbeauty.com/pages/auracolorwheelbook.

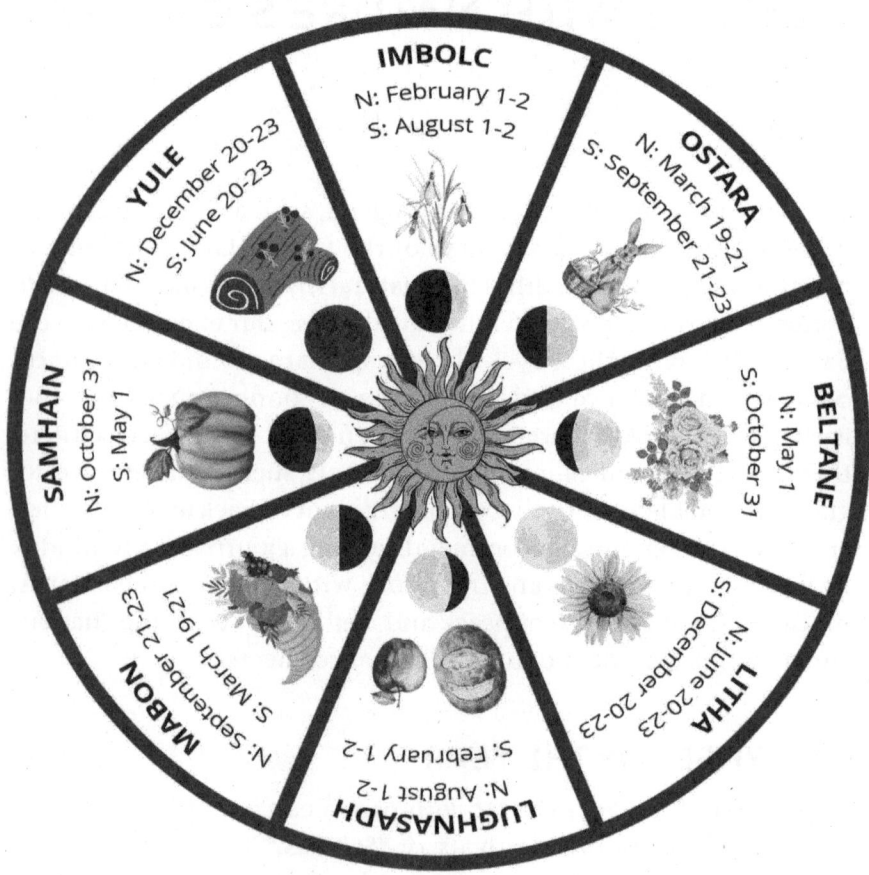

These celebrations mark the transitions in nature and the changes in the seasons, reflecting a deep connection with the cycles of the Earth. They are often associated with various myths, deities, and cultural traditions, and are used by practitioners to attune themselves to the natural world and its rhythms. I've outlined helpful deities, colors, crystals, foods, rituals, decorations, and more to focus on during these Sabbats:

Imbolc

- *Energy:* Waxing crescent moon, purification, renewal, inspiration
- *Deity:* Brigid, Vesta
- *Colors:* White, light blue, silver
- *Crystals:* Amethyst, garnet, white moonstone, onyx
- *Flowers:* Snowdrop, violets, wisteria, jasmine, vanilla
- *Herbs:* Bay leaf, clove, cinnamon, cardamon, basil
- *Scents:* Wisteria, jasmine, vanilla, cinnamon, violet, myrrh
- *Altar Decoration/Symbols:* White flowers, potted bulbs, Brigid's cross
- *Foods:* Seed pastries, dairy products, early spring vegetables
- *Ritual:* Candle lighting, cleansing rituals, making Brigid's crosses

Ostara

- *Energy:* First quarter moon, balance, new beginnings, fertility
- *Deity:* Ostara is the pagan Germanic goddess of spring, dawn, new growth, and Easter. Ostara is usually depicted as a young maiden with joyful energy and adorned in flowers.
- *Colors:* Pastels (pink, green, yellow)
- *Crystals:* Moss agate, aquamarine, rose quartz, amethyst, moonstone

- *Flowers:* Daffodils, honeysuckle, dandelions, tulips, lilacs
- *Herbs*: Lemongrass, meadowsweet, spearmint, honeysuckle, dandelions
- *Scents:* Jasmine, rose, magnolia, sandalwood
- *Altar Decoration/Symbols:* Spring flowers, seeds, eggs, rabbits/hares, birds, ladybugs, bumblebees
- *Foods:* Eggs, honey, sprouts, dandelion greens, strawberries, all spring vegetables, pumpkin, sunflower seeds, pine nuts
- *Ritual:* Plant your seed with a written intention paper

Beltane

- *Energy:* Waxing gibbous moon, fertility, fairies, fire, other worlds, passion, abundance
- *Deity:* Flora, Gaia, The Green Man, The Horned God, Venus, Freya
- *Colors:* Green, yellow, red, white
- *Crystals:* Green calcite, bloodstone, malachite, amber, carnelian, dragon blood jasper
- *Flowers:* Yellow cowslip, lily of the valley, lilac, hyacinth, daisies, peonies
- *Herbs:* Hawthorn, honeysuckle, rosemary, yarrow
- *Scents:* Lilac, frankincense, African violet, sage, mugwort, jasmine, rose
- *Altar Decoration/Symbols:* Maypole, ribbons, garlands, spring flowers, bonfire
- *Foods:* Oatmeal cakes, honey, berries, dairy, strawberries, cherries, spring greens
- *Ritual:* Maypole dancing, bonfire, flower and crystal ritual bath

Litha

- *Energy:* Full moon, joy, creation, manifestation, power, vitality, growth
- *Deity:* Litha, Apollo, Hestia, Athena, Artemis, Helios
- *Colors:* Red, orange, yellow, gold
- *Crystals:* Sunstone, citrine, yellow calcite, tiger's eye, jade
- *Flowers:* All flowers, especially rose, lily, sunflower
- *Herbs:* Calendula, mint, thyme, parsley, chamomile, St. John's wort
- *Scents:* Pine, rose, lemon, orange, lavender, frankincense
- *Altar Decoration/Symbols:* Roses, sunflowers, sun symbols, butterflies, seashells, pinwheels
- *Foods:* Early summer fruits and vegetables, honey cakes, strawberries, honey, lemon balm tea
- *Ritual:* Build a Litha altar and reflect on what you have achieved the first half of the year and write down your intentions for the second half of the year

Lughnasadh/Lammas

- *Energy:* Waning gibbous moon, gratitude, abundance, family, celebration, community
- *Deity:* Lugh, Demeter, Ceres
- *Colors:* Yellow, orange, brown, gold
- *Crystals:* Red calcite, carnelian, peridot, aventurine, citrine
- *Flowers:* Sunflower, passionflower, marigold, hibiscus
- *Herbs:* Basil, rosemary, thyme
- *Scents:* Sandalwood, rose, rose hips, rosemary, basil, passionflower

- *Altar Decoration/Symbols:* Grains, bread, grapes and vines, corn dollies, Lugh's spear, symbols representing your own skills
- *Foods:* Apples, bread, all grains, berries, corn, elderberry
- *Ritual:* Create a blessing and gratitude earth mandala or crystal grid, bake bread

Mabon

- *Energy:* Last quarter moon, harvest, thanksgiving, balance, feasting, cornucopia, reflection
- *Deity:* Morgana, Hermes
- *Colors:* Red, orange, yellow, maroon, gold, bronze, brown
- *Crystals:* Topaz, amber, citrine, lapis lazuli, agate
- *Flowers:* Marigold, chrysanthemum, aster
- *Herbs:* Sage, frankincense, saffron, marigold
- *Scents:* Cedar, sage, pine, clove, cinnamon
- *Altar Decoration/Symbols:* Cornucopia, acorns, pine cones, pinwheels, autumn leaves
- *Foods:* Nuts, wheat, grapes, apples, pumpkin, squash, pomegranate
- *Ritual:* Balance your Yin and Yang energies, give thanks

Samhain

- *Energy:* Waning crescent moon, ancestors, shadow, darkness, divination, offerings, death, rebirth, introspection
- *Deity:* Hecate, Diana, Hades
- *Colors:* Orange, brown, black, dark purple
- *Crystals:* Smoky quartz, black onyx, black moonstone, jet, obsidian, tourmaline

- **Flowers:** Marigold, chrysanthemum, goldenrod, pansies
- **Herbs:** Mugwort, wormwood, angelica, witch hazel, valerian
- **Scents:** Nutmeg, sage, clove, heather, patchouli, sweetgrass
- **Altar Decoration/Symbols:** Oak or other fallen leaves, pumpkins, squashes, acorns, flint corn, cauldron, photos or tokens of deceased loved ones
- **Foods:** Pumpkins, pomegranates, apples, nuts, all root vegetables and winter squashes, beans, apple cider, herbal teas
- **Ritual:** Scrying divination (see Chapter 19), ancestor altar

Yule

- **Energy:** New moon, renewal, hope, letting go, generosity, hearth fire, stillness, resting
- **Deity:** The Oak King, Selene, Aphrodite
- **Colors:** Red, green, white, silver
- **Crystals:** Ruby, clear quartz, bloodstone, garnet, diamond
- **Flowers:** Holly, poinsettia, plum flower, dried flowers from summer
- **Herbs:** Juniper, cedar, pine, ivy, wintergreens
- **Scents:** Cinnamon, bayberry, cedar, juniper, pine, frankincense
- **Altar Decoration/Symbols:** Yule log, candles, snowflakes, pine cones, evergreen wreaths
- **Foods:** Nuts, gingerbread, cider, eggnog, ginger tea
- **Ritual:** Yule log burning ritual

MOON PHASES

Living in harmony with the moon cycles plays a crucial role in maintaining our aura health. The moon's phases influence the ebb and flow of energy within us, affecting our emotions, thoughts, and overall well-being. Each phase of the moon—from the new moon to the full moon and back—symbolizes different aspects of life, such as new beginnings, growth, fruition, and release. By aligning our actions and intentions with these natural rhythms, we can ensure a balanced and vibrant aura while doing less but achieving/attracting more. A moon cycle is 28 days, and each moon phase lasts 3.5 days. The following are the eight moon phases and recommended actions during this moon cycle.

New Moon
- *Activity:* Set intentions.
- *Affirmation:* From a small seed a mighty trunk may grow.
- *Ritual:* Meditate on a new moon evening; write down your intentions for this moon cycle.
- *Crystals:* Black moonstone, clear quartz, fluorite

Waxing Crescent Moon
- *Activity:* Visualize your intentions; plan your steps.
- *Affirmation:* "Who looks outside dreams, who looks inside awakes." — *Carl Jung*[1]
- *Ritual:* Meditate on your intentions, visualize them in real life with details, journal them, or better yet, draw them.
- *Crystals:* Angel aura quartz, rutilated quartz, clear quartz

First Quarter Moon
- *Activity:* Take actions toward your intentions.
- *Affirmation:* "The creation of a thousand forests is in one acorn." — *Ralph Waldo Emerson*[2]

- *Ritual:* Act on your intentions and plans. Keep a progress journal and see how baby steps get you closer to your goals.
- *Crystals:* Peach moonstone, golden tiger's eye, moss agate

Waxing Gibbous Moon

- *Activity:* Focus on your efforts toward your goal.
- *Affirmation:* Create the sequence of goodness; consequences will always be good.
- *Ritual:* Keep a gratitude and compassion journal while focusing on your efforts.
- *Crystals:* Citrine, mookaite jasper, carnelian

Full Moon

- *Activity:* Express yourself; share and communicate your visions and intentions with other people.
- *Affirmation:* There is nothing like you, there was nothing like you, and there shall be nothing like you.
- *Ritual:* Meditate under full moon light; call in your angels, guides, and ancestors; and fully visualize your visions coming true.
- *Crystals:* Rainbow moonstone, blue kyanite, celestine

Waning Gibbous Moon

- *Activity:* Revise and make changes if necessary to make sure your goals and actions are in alignment.
- *Affirmation:* The purpose of life is to know yourself and love yourself and trust yourself and be yourself.
- *Ritual:* Meditate and journal; ask your soul what changes you can make to be in alignment.
- *Crystals:* Blue lace agate, citrine, snowflake obsidian

Last Quarter Moon
- *Activity:* Make room for solitude and reflect, rest, and restore.
- *Affirmation:* Nature does not hurry, yet everything is accomplished.
- *Ritual:* Meditate and journal; write down all the insights you learn from this moon cycle.
- *Crystals:* Garnierite (green moonstone), labradorite, chevron amethyst

Waning Crescent Moon
- *Activity:* Release and let go of what doesn't serve you anymore.
- *Affirmation:* Compassion is the fountain of forgiveness.
- *Ritual:* Meditate and write down what doesn't serve you anymore on small pieces of paper, then bury them in the earth, let them flow away on a stream, or burn them.
- *Crystals:* Rhodonite, rose quartz, chrysoprase, blue chalcedony

DAYS OF THE WEEK

The energy associated with the days of the week holds significant importance for our aura health, as each day carries its unique vibrational frequency and planetary influence. By understanding and aligning with these energies, we can enhance our well-being and maintain a balanced aura. I've outlined some helpful activities, colors, crystals, and so on for each day of the week.

Monday
- *Ruling Satellite:* The moon
- *Deities:* Selene, Artemis, Hecate, Mani, Luna
- *Energy:* Intuitive, emotional, feminine, receptive
- *Ideal Activities:* Rest, inner reflections, set goals

- *Colors:* Gray, silver, light blue
- *Crystals:* Moonstone, selenite, pearl, silver, blue kyanite

Tuesday

- *Ruling Planet:* Mars
- *Deities:* Mars, Aries, Tyr/Tiu
- *Energy:* Warrior, passionate, motivated
- *Ideal Activities:* Take action to achieve goals
- *Colors:* Red, orange, yellow
- *Crystals:* Ruby, garnet, red jasper, carnelian, sardonyx

Wednesday

- *Ruling Planet:* Mercury
- *Deities:* Mercury, Hermes, Odin/Wooden
- *Energy:* Merchant, trickster, scientist, inventor, healthy
- *Ideal Activities:* Business activities, communications, doctors' appointments
- *Colors:* Green, turquoise
- *Crystals:* Green nephrite jade, turquoise, amazonite, chrysocolla, green aventurine, blue topaz

Thursday

- *Ruling Planet:* Jupiter
- *Deities:* Jupiter, Zeus, Thor
- *Energy:* Leader, spiritual seeker, wisdom keeper, traveler
- *Ideal Activities:* Spiritual practices, learning and teaching, travel
- *Color:* Yellow
- *Crystals:* Lapis lazuli, aquamarine, alexandrite, amethyst, sapphire

THE AURA COLOR WHEEL

Friday
- **_Ruling Planet:_** Venus
- **_Deities:_** Venus, Aphrodite, Freya/Frigga
- **_Energy:_** Lover, beautiful, gentle
- **_Ideal Activities:_** Intimate relationships, dating, art—have fun!
- **_Colors:_** Pink
- **_Crystals:_** Rose quartz, emerald, pink tourmaline, rhodochrosite

Saturday
- **_Ruling Planet:_** Saturn
- **_Deities:_** Saturn, Kronos/Cronus
- **_Energy:_** Virtuous, proud
- **_Ideal Activities:_** Shadow work, introspection, planning, organization, restoration
- **_Colors:_** Black, dark violet
- **_Crystals:_** Black tourmaline, jet, shungite, black obsidian

Sunday
- **_Ruling Star:_** The sun
- **_Deities:_** Apollo, Helios, Sol
- **_Energy:_** Brave, masculine, dominant
- **_Ideal Activities:_** Exercise, outdoor activities, creative projects, socializing, relaxation
- **_Colors:_** Red, orange, yellow
- **_Crystals:_** Citrine, sunstone, heliodor, golden calcite, diamond

CHAPTER 17

CRYSTAL HEALING

Crystals are effective as healing tools because they resonate with the inherently crystalline structure of the human body, known as the liquid crystal body matrix. This crystalline basis allows the body to transmit and receive energy and information efficiently. Marcel Vogel, a pioneering IBM researcher and a key figure in crystal healing, discovered that crystals, when paired with focused intention, can restructure the water molecules that compose 70 percent of our bodies, enhancing our health and crystalline coherence.

Crystals also help us connect with Earth's energy. Their colors often correspond to specific chakra energies or aura layers, aiding in aligning and balancing these energy centers through a process called entrainment. This process involves the synchronization of two energy fields, leading to increased coherence and unity. By placing crystals on corresponding chakra points, the same color crystal will activate a certain chakra to a coherent state, and the complementary color crystal will balance the overactive chakra to a harmonious state.

As a certified crystal healer, I advocate various daily practices incorporating crystal energy, which many clients find beneficial. In this chapter, I'll share some of my favorite ways to work with crystals.

WEAR CRYSTALS FOR PHYSICAL, EMOTIONAL, MENTAL, AND SPIRITUAL HEALING

One effective way to harness crystal energy daily is by selecting crystal jewelry that aligns with your desired energy for the day. For example, wear blue lace agate for calmness, amethyst to enhance intuition, golden tiger's eye or pyrite for a confidence boost, and black tourmaline for protection. I personally wear carnelian to strengthen my immune system when I feel a cold coming on. Selenite is excellent for aura cleansing. I keep a selenite crystal bar on my vanity and use it like a comb over my aura, visualizing it clearing my energy field. This practice is significantly enhanced by setting a clear intention.

The crystals mentioned in Chapter 2 can be strategically placed on your body's energy points to activate or balance your energy, depending on whether a chakra is blocked or overactive. If unsure of the state of your chakras, using a pendulum—a small weight suspended on a string—can help identify imbalances. Hold the pendulum over a chakra and observe its motion: smooth, clockwise movement indicates balance; slow movement or a standstill suggests a blockage; and erratic or fast movement signifies overactivity. Based on this, apply the recommended crystals directly on the chakra points for 15 to 20 minutes during a guided meditation session for enhanced effect.

For general energy balancing, I use a layout (see diagram on next page) that includes placing crystals along the chakra centers and arranging clear quartz points in an infinity symbol around the body. This arrangement amplifies the balancing effect. Assistance from someone may be necessary to properly place the crystals, especially on the stomach area. Adjust the number of quartz points based on their size and your specific needs. For specific issues or psychic surgery, I recommend consulting a professional crystal healer.

Crystal Healing

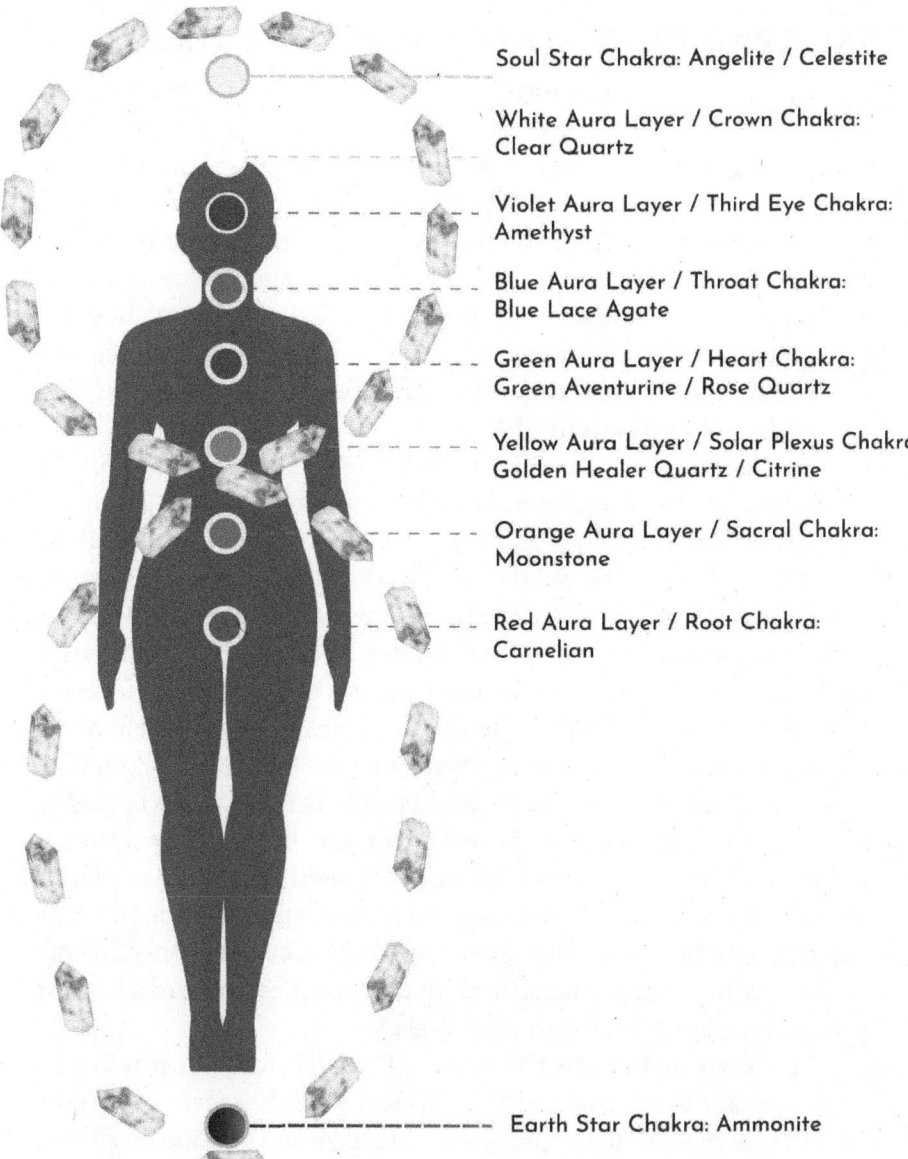

PROGRAM CRYSTALS FOR YOUR INTENTIONS

Crystals can convert one form of energy into another, a process known as transduction, which includes phenomena like piezoelectricity (mechanical pressure into electricity), thermoluminescence (heat into light), triboluminescence (mechanical stress into light), and fluorescence (absorbing energy and emitting light). This capability allows crystals to effectively align their vibrations to specific tasks. When we set intentions, visualize, or program crystals, they translate this input into the energy needed to manifest our goals, sending coherent messages to the Universe to produce tangible results, even if our own state of consciousness is unordered.

Programming a crystal involves directing its energy toward a precise intention or goal, which is useful for long-term carry, healing jewelry, or creating crystal grids. To program a crystal, first cleanse both yourself and the crystal using sacred scents or a crystal singing bowl. Then, in a meditative state in your sacred space, write down your intention. This could be a desire to remain calm during stress or to stay focused on your goals. You may also dedicate crystals to specific aura layers or use them like selenite or clear quartz to cleanse your auric field daily.

For programming, place the crystal on your third eye chakra, visualize living out your intentions, and hold the crystal while engaging all five senses: observe its color, feel its texture, listen to any sounds it makes, smell it, or even give it a kiss. Then, hold the crystal or place it in front of you, visualize entering the crystal, and ask it for any messages it might have. Journaling after meditation can deepen your connection, enhancing intuition and psychic abilities over time, helping you gain insights specific to your goals.

To effectively harness the power of crystals for your intentions, it's important to understand their crystal growth systems. A crystal growth system refers to the process used to form and develop crystalline structures. There are seven distinct crystal systems and one non-crystal system (amorphous) to consider when programming crystals to manifest your intentions. The following chart details these systems, examples of stones, and their best uses for various intentions. When you purchase a new crystal, you can always google it to see what crystal system it is.

Crystal Healing

Crystal System	Appearance	Examples	Energy (Intention)
Isometric/ Cubic	Three equal axes at right angles (90°) and may form cubes, octahedrons, or dodecahedrons.	Halite, Fluorite, Spinel, Pyrite, Garnet, Diamond, Sphalerite, Sodalite, Magnetite, many metals like Silver, Gold, Copper, and Platinum	Stabilizing and grounding. Excellent for structure, reorganization, and clarity. The only crystal form that doesn't bend light rays as they pass through it.
Tetragonal	Three axes at right angles (90°), one axis is unequal.	Zircon, Chalcopyrite, Scapolite, Rutile, Apophyllite, Wulfenite, Tugtupite, Idocrase (Vesuvianite)	Created from rectangles with long and short axes at right angles to each other, tetragonal crystals absorb and transform energy and are excellent balancers and resolvers.
Hexagonal	Three equal axes at 120°, and a fourth at right angles with sixfold symmetry.	Emerald, Beryl family: Aquamarine, Morganite, Heliodor, Apatite, Zincite	Highly energetic, energy balancing and exploring specific issues, and manifestation.

THE AURA COLOR WHEEL

Crystal System	Appearance	Examples	Energy (Intention)
Trigonal	This system is similar to the hexagonal system but displays threefold symmetry.	Smithsonite, Stichtite, Rhodochrosite, Phenacite, Hematite, Septarian, Nodule Agate (all varieties), Corundum (Ruby and Sapphire), Chalcedony (all varieties including Jaspers), Quartz (plus varieties like Citrine, Smoky Quartz, and Amethyst), Calcite (all colors), Tourmaline, Dioptase, Cinnabar, Eudialyte, Pietersite, Pyromorphite	Created from triangles, trigonal crystals radiate energy and are invigorating and protective, rebalancing the biomagnetic sheath. Trigonal minerals reset the metabolic processes in the physical body, allowing the body to reboot itself. Ideal for correcting imbalances and supports immune system.
Orthorhombic	Displays three unequal axes at right angles. May be simple, body-centered, face-centered, or base-centered.	Bronzite, Barite, Iolite, Celestite, Peridot, Chiastolite (Cross Stone), Topaz, Shattuckite, Anhydrite, Tanzanite, Cavansite, Aragonite	Formed from rhomboids, orthorhombic crystals have unequal axes that encompass energy and are useful cleansers and clearers.

Crystal Healing

Crystal System	Appearance	Examples	Energy (Intention)
Monoclinic	This system displays three axes, two of which are at right angles; the third is not a right angle.	Diopside, Jadeite, Jade, Nephrite Jade, Selenite, Feldspar, Mica, Lepidolite, Gypsum (Selenite), Kunzite, Azurite, Malachite, Epidote, Arfvedsonite	Formed from parallelograms, monoclinic crystals are useful for purification and perception.
Triclinic	This system displays three axes, none of which are at right angles.	Turquoise, Rhodonite Astrophyllite, Kyanite (all colors), Amazonite, Larimar, Sunstone, Larvikite (black moonstone)	Formed from trapeziums, asymmetric triclinic crystals integrate energy and opposites and assist in exploring other dimensions.
Amorphous	Non-crystal system. No crystal lattice.	Opal, Obsidian, Shungite, Tektites (Moldavite, Libyan desert glass). Man-made: Goldstone, Opalite, brightly colored slag glass (usually sold as obsidian).	Lacking an inner structure, amorphous crystals allow energy to pass through freely and act rapidly and may be a catalyst for growth. They also relate to the fluids of the body.

CREATE CRYSTAL GRIDS TO MANIFEST YOUR INTENTIONS

This is my personal favorite way to work with crystals. For over a decade I have been creating crystal grid paintings for hundreds of clients to manifest their intentions. I place them on their personal Feng Shui directions to enhance the crystal grid's impacts. At the end of Chapter 1, I shared a story about my client Mary and healing her soul wound in the solar plexus chakra. I created a solar plexus chakra healing and empowerment crystal grid and placed it in the southwest direction of her bedroom, facing her bed. This was based on her personal Kua Number 7, which indicates that her auspicious direction for health and well-being is southwest, not the general Feng Shui southeast direction. I always offer a free personal Feng Shui Birth Element and Kua Number reading for clients who purchase a crystal grid painting from me to identify the best location for optimal intention manifestation. A person's Feng Shui Kua Number is calculated by their birth date and birth gender. While this book focuses on your Soul Aura Color rather than Feng Shui, you can refer to the further reading and resources for more information on Feng Shui Birth Elements and Kua Numbers.

A crystal grid is a set of intentionally selected, energetically aligned crystals forming a geometric pattern for the purpose of manifesting a certain intention. The more specific an intention is, the more focused energy is directed to manifest it. For example, you can have an intention for better health, more money, abundance, prosperity, or a loving relationship. Or you can have a more specific intention like better liver health, manifesting success in your business, or deepening your love relationship with your significant partner.

How Crystal Grids Communicate with the Universe: Through Sacred Geometry

Crystal grids operate through the principle of sacred geometry, a language through which the Universe communicates, mirroring the intricate, geometric energy patterns of Mother Earth. Mother Earth's ley lines are a giant crystal grid itself. By aligning a crystal grid with these sacred patterns, we tap into universal energy, conveying our intentions for physical manifestation. This process is guided by the notion that sacred geometric forms are channels for abstract, cosmic life to intersect with earthly existence, as noted by Robert Lawlor in *Sacred Geometry: Philosophy & Practice*.[1]

When constructing a crystal grid, selecting a geometric pattern that matches your intention is crucial. Each pattern possesses unique energetic properties. For example, the chakra symbols discussed in Chapter 2 can serve as bases for grids aimed at strengthening or healing specific aura layers. I recommend using natural materials like wood, bamboo, cloth, or even paper for the grid base, avoiding synthetic substances such as acrylic or plastic. A selenite etched plate with a sacred geometry pattern is particularly effective because selenite is known for its self-cleansing properties.

There are seven universal sacred geometry patterns:

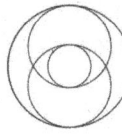

1. The Vesica Piscis

The vesica piscis is a symbol that has deep spiritual significance across various cultures and belief systems. It often represents the intersection or overlap between two realms or dimensions, such as heaven and earth, spiritual and physical, or masculine and feminine energies. It's seen as the fundamental shape from which other geometric forms emerge. Overall, it is a symbol of unity, balance, and interconnectedness.

2. The Seed of Life

This shape is made of seven intersecting circles that represent genesis, birth, and the creation of new energy or ideas; this is the smallest unit of the flower of life.

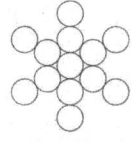

3. The Fruit of Life

The fruit of life shape is comprised of 13 circles radiating out in six directions from the center to the exterior. This shape represents unity and transition between the physical and spiritual worlds.

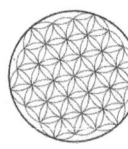
4. The Flower of Life
This shape is made of 19 intersecting circles. The flower of life is thought to contain the building blocks of the entire Universe, both matter and space. Since it is integral to creation, it is the perfect shape for manifesting our intentions through crystal grids, such as healing, love, wealth, and so on.

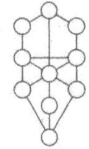
5. The Tree of Life
This symbol can be created from the circles in the flower of life. It is sacred in Jewish Kabbalah and represents divine love and oneness.

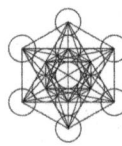
6. The Metatron's Cube
This shape is made from the lines connecting the centers of the parts of the fruit of life shape. It's a symbol of Archangel Metatron. This base is especially effective for angelic communications.

7. The Sri Yantra
This shape is made from nine overlapping triangles surrounding a central point (the bindu). It's a Hindu symbol representing the connection between the Universe and humanity. Ideal for past-life memories and manifestation.

Seven Steps for Creating a Crystal Grid

Here are the steps to create and maintain a crystal grid for manifesting your intentions:

1. ***Set Your Intention:*** Write down your intention on a piece of paper and place it under the center stone of the grid.
2. ***Choose a Base:*** Decide whether to use a crystal grid base or simply arrange your grid on a flat, natural surface.
3. ***Select a Center Stone:*** Choose a center stone that aligns with your intention. Tower-shaped crystals are preferred as they are effective at broadcasting energy.

4. *Select Desired Outcome Stones:* Choose stones that represent the outcome you desire. Place them on the outside circle of the grid.

5. *Choose Way Stones:* Select additional stones, typically crystal points, that represent the energies or attributes needed to achieve your outcome.

6. *Activate the Crystal Grid:*
   - Using a clear quartz or selenite wand, begin by pointing the wand over or touching the center stone.
   - Channel universal love or your specific energetic intention through the wand.
   - Starting from the center, visually or physically "draw" a line to an outer stone, moving clockwise to each subsequent stone, linking them back to the center after each connection.
   - Continue this pattern until all stones are connected and you return to the center.
   - Conclude by directing the wand toward the center of the grid, infusing it with universal energy to activate its purpose. Keep your intention in mind during this activation.

7. *Maintain Your Grid:*
   - Reactivate your grid at least once a month or whenever it feels necessary.
   - If the grid is physically disturbed or crystals are moved, it needs reactivation.
   - Make adjustments to the grid (adding or removing stones) as needed, ensuring you reactivate it after any changes.

This structured approach helps ensure your crystal grid remains potent and aligned with your goals.

Here is an example of a simple yet powerful crystal grid designed to heal, balance, and strengthen all seven chakras, creating a radiant and magnetic aura that attracts synchronicities, opportunities, and the right people into your life. This grid features a Metatron's cube wooden base, as Archangel Metatron resonates with the chakra system, supporting alignment and harmony.

The crystals used include:

- Carnelian for the root chakra
- Orange calcite for the sacral chakra
- Citrine for the solar plexus chakra
- Green aventurine for the heart chakra
- Amazonite for the throat chakra
- Amethyst for the third eye chakra
- Clear quartz at the center for the crown chakra

These crystals are energetically connected with clear quartz Vogel wands, which serve as waystones to amplify and direct energy flow. Named after researcher Marcel Vogel, these precision-cut wands are renowned for their ability to focus and channel life force energy. Their faceted structure acts like a prism, enhancing healing vibrations for spiritual cleansing, chakra balancing, and connecting to higher consciousness.

DISPLAY ENERGY-APPROPRIATE CRYSTALS IN DIFFERENT FENG SHUI DIRECTIONS

Each crystal emits unique energies that can harmonize specific areas of your life when strategically placed using the principles of Feng Shui. By positioning energy-appropriate crystals in the nine Feng Shui directions, which correspond to different life aspects, you can amplify positive energy flow. For instance, if you wish to attract financial abundance, place "money" crystals such as citrine, green aventurine, or cinnabar in the southeast area of your home, as this direction governs wealth and prosperity. Conversely, the southwest direction, associated with love and relationships, would benefit from crystals like rose quartz or rhodochrosite. Please see Chapter 15: Feng Shui to learn more.

MAKE CRYSTAL ELIXIRS AND DRINK UP THE TRACE MINERALS AND ENERGY

A crystal elixir is water infused with crystal energy. There are two ways to make a crystal elixir:

1. *Direct Method:* Crystals directly soak in the water to infuse energy. Check www.mindat.org for toxicity guidance. It takes 4 to 24 hours for the energy to infuse in water. I like to put my crystals in water the night before I go to sleep and drink it first thing in the morning.

2. *Indirect Method:* The crystals will not come into contact with the water; they are simply transferring energy. You place the crystals in a glass container and then place that container within a larger container of water. Nowadays there are lots of crystal water bottles for sale in metaphysical stores; some may include crystals already in the bottle, and you can change them based on your intentions. I have one with a tea infuser in it so that I can have crystal energy in my tea as well. This method is particularly useful for crystals that are not water safe or may release harmful substances.

THE AURA COLOR WHEEL

As a rule of thumb, if you are new to crystal elixirs, it is safer to use the indirect method. In general, all quartz variety crystals are safe using the direct method.

Here are a few crystal elixir recipes I use most often on myself or for my clients. You can get a copy of *Gem Water* by Michael Gienger and Joachim Goebel for more blend ideas.

- *Immune Boost Elixir for Red Aura Layer:* (Direct method recommended): Carnelian, bloodstone, clear quartz, green aventurine, red calcite (or red jasper)
- *Detoxifying/Cleansing Elixir Blend for Red Aura Layer:* Aquamarine, amazonite, tourmaline (in any color), selenite, apophyllite
- *Hormone System/PMS Relief Elixir Blend for Orange Aura Layer:* Moonstone (any variety), rose quartz, chrysocolla, pearl
- *Digestion/Gut Health Elixir Blend for Yellow Aura Layer:* Citrine, amber, topaz (any color), golden healer quartz, mookaite jasper
- *Confidence Elixir Blend for Yellow Aura Layer:* Golden tiger's eye, citrine, emerald, sunstone
- *Stress-Related Issues Elixir Blend for Green Aura Layer:* Blue lace agate, blue chalcedony, Botswana agate, jade
- *Focus and Clarity Blend for Blue Aura Layer:* Rainbow fluorite, clear quartz or stilbite, sodalite or lapiz lazuli, smoky quartz
- *Insomnia Elixir Blend for Violet Aura Layer:* Amethyst, lepidolite, green or blue calcite, lavender rose quartz
- *Intuition and Psychic Ability Blend for White Aura Layer:* Labradorite, rainbow moonstone, azurite, Herkimer diamond or rutilated quartz

TAKE A CRYSTAL BATH TO SOAK UP THE ENERGY YOU NEED

Taking a crystal bath can transfer the crystal energy through your skin into your bloodstream. Therefore, it's another great way to absorb Mother Earth's energy. First, consider whether the crystal you want to use is water safe. As a general rule of thumb, if the crystal's Mohs hardness scale is above 6 and is nonporous, it's water safe. Check with www.mindat.org. All quartz variety crystals are safe to use in a bath (for example, clear quartz, rose quartz, citrine, amethyst, green aventurine), as well as all agates, moonstone, amber, obsidian, calcite, bloodstone, super seven, and carnelian (not safe in salt water). Here are some examples of non-water-safe crystals: lepidolite, hematite, turquoise, fluorite, selenite, pyrite, and apophyllite.

Here are a few crystal bath recipes I use most often on myself or for my clients. You can get a copy of the book *Ritual Baths*, by Deborah Hanekamp, for more recipe ideas.

GROUNDING CRYSTAL BATH FOR RED AURA LAYER

- Smoky quartz
- Black obsidian
- 1 cup Epsom salt
- 2 cups rose petals (fresh or dried)
- 10 drops lavender essential oil
- 3 drops vetiver essential oil
- 1 pot kava tea

EMOTIONAL RELEASE CRYSTAL BATH FOR ORANGE AURA LAYER

- Smoky quartz
- Amethyst
- Citrine
- 3 cups pink Himalayan sea salt
- 3 drops bergamot absolute essential oil
- 10 drops rose absolute essential oil
- 1 pot rose and hibiscus tea

THE AURA COLOR WHEEL

NEW MOON CRYSTAL BATH FOR ORANGE AURA LAYER

Black moonstone

Lemurian seed crystal

1 cup Epsom salt

Red rose petals

5 drops sweet orange essential oil

10 drops lavender essential oil

1 pot cherry blossom tea

FULL MOON CRYSTAL BATH FOR YELLOW AURA LAYER

Rainbow moonstone

Clear quartz

Citrine

3 cups Epsom salt

White sage leaves

1 cup coconut milk

Red and pink rose petals

3 drops palo santo essential oil

1 pot nettle and angelica tea

SELF-LOVE CRYSTAL BATH FOR GREEN AURA LAYER

Rose quartz

Morganite

Pink opal

Eucalyptus leaves

2 tablespoons dragon fruit powder

1 cup coconut milk

1 bunch fresh basil

10 drops rose absolute essential oil

Pink, red, and white rose petals

1 pot passion fruit or rose tea

FORGIVENESS CRYSTAL BATH FOR GREEN AURA LAYER

Rose quartz
Green calcite
Lemon quartz
1 cup sea salt
1 cup oat milk
White rose petals
3 drops jasmine essential oil
3 drops sweet orange essential oil
Yellow orchid flowers
1 pot chamomile or blue butterfly pea flower tea

INTUITION CRYSTAL BATH FOR BLUE AND VIOLET AURA LAYERS

Lapis lazuli
Super seven
Auralite 23
1 cup sea salt
1 bay leaf
1 fennel bulb (chopped)
3 drops patchouli essential oil
10 drops lemon balm essential oil
1 pot sage or blue lotus tea

USE CRYSTALS AS DIVINATION TOOLS

Crystals have served as record keepers of Earth's history since its creation, their intricate crystalline structures naturally encoding information over time. For centuries, people have gazed into crystals to access insights and guidance specific to them—a practice known as scrying. To learn more about this ancient divination method, refer to Chapter 19: Divination Tools.

CHAPTER 18

CONNECTING WITH YOUR SPIRIT TEAM

Spirit guides are ethereal beings who exist in higher dimensions and vibrate at frequencies typically beyond our physical perception, much like the rapid flutter of hummingbird wings, which move too fast for the human eye to see. Connected to us through unconditional love, spirit guides support our spiritual journey and day-to-day challenges. Our ability to sense their presence hinges on our psychic awareness and our own vibrational frequency, which may resonate more strongly with certain types of guides. Their job in the spirit realm is literally to help us. However, because planet Earth runs on free will, if we don't give our permission or have the intention for their help, they will remain invisible to us.

For me, connecting with the spirit realm is a natural progression of daily meditation for a consistent period. At the beginning of my meditation journey, I had no expectation of it at all. I think because of this nonattachment nature, it made it easier to connect with them. All you need to connect with the spirit realm is to trust, be open, surrender, and pray for them to come close to you—but not have attachments or expectations of who and how they will show up. Even though I can connect with the spirit realm, it doesn't mean I can sustain it all the time and tune in and out instantaneously. I still need to be spiritually connected to be able to tune in to this subtle energy realm. But once you've tuned in, I'm sure you will want to go back in all the time. This is a realm of unconditional love and infinite possibilities—it's absolutely beautiful and peaceful.

Everyone, including you, has the ability to connect with Spirit. It is our natural gift. This isn't reserved for the special few. Granted, people who are born with a higher frequency because they have healed more of their soul wounds and learned their soul lessons, or are encouraged to do so as a child, have stronger antennae to receive the signals, but these skills can be developed and trained once we believe them! Remember, beliefs are thoughts, and thoughts are things just like your body—they are all energy!

Connecting with your spirit team for guidance is another method to strengthen or heal any of your aura layers and live your purpose. It's like having a private coach, who's known you all your life, working with you all the time. In my opinion, it's the best method!

In this chapter, I will introduce the nine types of spirit guides and outline five key steps for connecting with your spirit team. Setting the intention to connect and maintaining a meditation practice will naturally draw Spirit closer to you.

NINE TYPES OF SPIRIT GUIDES

Everyone has a spirit team who's been working with them since the second they were born. This spirit team can consist of one of the nine types of spirit guides: angels, ascended masters, ancestors, deities, nature spirits, fairies, animal guides, star beings, and expert guides. Archangels are omnipresent and can be everywhere at the same time, while a guardian archangel is your main spirit guide assigned to you—and only you—when you were born. Your guardian angel can be one of your positive ancestors who transcended the incarnation cycle and remained in the spirit realm. Although all angels are gender-neutral, based on my experiences giving angel readings to clients, some people have two guardian angels as a pair. Or I can describe it as two energies: one is Yin or feminine and nurturing in nature, and one is Yang or more protective and masculine in nature. For people who have one guardian angel, depending on the guardian angel's energy, they typically pair with another spirit guide in the opposite energy nature on top of the person's crown chakra. All the other types of spirit guides change, depending on the stage of your life or any specific projects you are working on at the time. Most people have five to nine spirit guides working with them at a time.

1. Archangels

Based on my personal channeling experience, here's a list of the primary archangels' energies and signs. It's not all-inclusive but serves as a good starting point. When you begin to work with the spirit realm in this way, you can ask their name and add them to your spirit guide journal.

- *Archangel Michael* (main archangel for the Entrepreneur Soul Gift Archetype)

    He who is like God. The angel of protection. The warrior with a sword. Great business partner if you are an entrepreneur; great helper of cord cutting.

    Color: indigo blue
    Animal: falcon, hawk, blue birds
    Crystal: azurite, sugilite, charoite
    Flower: sunflower
    Number: 111

- *Archangel Metatron* (main archangel for the Visionary Soul Gift Archetype)

    Metatron's name came from the Hebrew *Meta Thronon,* meaning "the throne next to the Divine." He was once a human known as Enoch and was a prophet and scribe who gained so much knowledge of the Divine that he ascended to archangel when he passed. He is the angel who governs divine timing and the Akashic Records—all universal events, thoughts, words, emotions, and intent ever to have occurred in the past, present, or future in terms of all entities and life forms, not just humans. He governs the sacred knowledge, geometry. He holds the Metatron cube, which aligns with our chakra systems. It is also the symbol of our heart chakra, where our soul resides. He works with sensitive (rainbow aura) children, empaths, healers, and spiritual teachers of the ages.

Color: white, golden
Animal: eagle, condor, butterfly
Crystal: tourmaline, clear quartz
Flower: white water lily
Number: 999 or 1111

- *Archangel Gabriel* (main archangel for the Artist Soul Gift Archetype)

  The messenger of God. Gabriel helps give birth to children and creative ideas and works with artists of all kinds. When you have a creative block, call on Gabriel for help.

  Color: white, copper
  Animal: dove, raven
  Crystal: citrine
  Flower: lily, jasmine
  Number: 333

- *Archangel Ariel* (main archangel for the red aura layer)

  The lioness of God. She works with nature's cycles, abundance, and balance. She works with animals, plants, and the fairy realm. She governs the law of attraction and manifestation.

  Color: magenta, ruby, pink
  Animal: swan, goose, duck
  Crystal: ruby
  Flower: geranium
  Number: 888

THE AURA COLOR WHEEL

- ***Archangel Raphael*** (main archangel for the Healer Soul Gift Archetype)

  His name translates as "God heals." Responsible for healing of all kinds, he can also be called upon for safe travel. His symbol is a caduceus, the winged staff with two coiled serpents that symbolize the medical profession and are often seen on ambulances.

  Color: emerald green
  Animal: deer, wolf
  Crystal: emerald
  Flower: lavender
  Number: 555

- ***Archangel Haniel*** (main archangel for the blue aura layer)

  The grace of God. Angel of the moon, emotions, and intuition. She helps us develop our innate psychic abilities, especially clairvoyance.

  Color: silvery light blue
  Animal: turtle, dolphin, whale
  Crystal: moonstone
  Flower: blue hydrangea
  Number: 222

- ***Archangel Jophiel*** (main archangel for the orange aura layer)

  The beauty of God. She is the angel who guarded the Tree of Life in the Garden of Eden. Her primary purpose is to help us see the world's beauty and have joy. She also helps us silence the ego's voice (fear and doubt). If you are one of those people who constantly doubts the spiritual information you receive, call upon Jophiel!

Color: yellow, fuchsia
Animal: heron, goldfinch
Crystal: yellow calcite, golden healer quartz
Flower: peony
Number: 444

- **Archangel Chamuel** (main archangel for the green aura layer)

    He who sees (seeks) God. The angel of unconditional love, relationships, forgiveness, soulmates, and twin flames. Please call upon Archangel Chamuel to bring love to any situation or help you find your soulmate. Chamuel is a gentle angel who works in the background and allows you to restore a sense of purpose.

    Color: pink, pale green
    Animal: rabbit, hare
    Crystal: rose quartz
    Flower: pink rose
    Number: 666

- **Archangel Uriel** (main archangel for the Teacher Soul Gift Archetype)

    The light of God. I often see him holding a torch of orange flame. He helps you find your unique purpose and shine your light. Call upon him if you seek inspiration, need creative ideas, or work as an entrepreneur seeking problem-solving.

    Color: orange, ochre, amber
    Animal: blue jay, birds
    Crystal: amber
    Flower: lotus
    Number: 777

THE AURA COLOR WHEEL

- ***Archangel Sandalphon*** (main archangel for the Entertainer Soul Gift Archetype)

    The archangel who connects to the Earth Star chakra. He works with Archangel Metatron to cleanse our chakra system with Mother Earth. He is also the angel of music, sound, and vibrational healing. He sends our prayers to heaven and enhances our clairaudience psychic abilities.

    Color: copper
    Animal: frog, cricket, insects that sing, birds
    Crystal: turquoise
    Flower: daffodil
    Number: 44

- ***Archangel Raguel*** (main archangel for the Reformer Soul Gift Archetype)

    Friend of God. The peacemaker, angel of justice. He also helps with soul contracts (positive or negative) and relationship issues—an angel for resolving conflict and bringing harmony and peace.

    Color: light brown, orange
    Animal: mouse, squirrel, possum, raccoon
    Crystal: aquamarine, larimar, amazonite
    Flower: marigold
    Number: 22

- ***Archangel Jeremiel*** (main archangel for the yellow aura layer)

    The mercy of God. He is the angel of forgiveness, justice, and global peace. He assists us in doing life reviews, spiritual clearing, and removing harmful patterns. You can also call upon him to help you with any lawsuits or legal issues.

    Color: bright orange, gold
    Animal: cheetah, leopard, puma
    Crystal: honey calcite
    Flower: gardenia
    Number: 33

- ***Archangel Zadkiel*** (main archangel for the Warrior Soul Gift Archetype)

  The righteousness of God. He holds the violet flame, transmuting all emotional trauma and negative karmic relationships into positive energy. He helps us forgive even those who have harmed us. Karmic clearing and letting go of the past.

  Color: violet *Flower: violet*
  Animal: beaver, otter *Number: 99*
  Crystal: lapis lazuli

- ***Archangel Azrael*** (main archangel for the violet aura layer)

  He who helps God. Azrael helps us heal any mental or emotional trauma. He is also the angel who helps with the human/animal transitions from the earth plane to the spirit realm. He often appears during life-or-death moments. He helps us with grief.

  Color: light violet, red, rainbow
  Animal: butterfly, dragonfly
  Crystal: sodalite
  Flower: white chrysanthemum
  Number: 55

- ***Archangel Raziel*** (main archangel for the Researcher Soul Gift Archetype)

  The secrets of God. He is the yoga guru of the archangels. He governs esoteric, hidden knowledge of the mystic realms and the law of attraction. He is also a helper in developing your intuitive and psychic abilities, especially your clairvoyant sense and dream analysis. He helps all writers, creatives, yoga teachers, and mediums with their skills.

  Color: gold, rainbow
  Animal: white feather birds, fish
  Crystal: clear quartz
  Flower: iris
  Number: 88

2. Ascended Masters

Ascended masters are enlightened individuals who have achieved a high degree of wisdom and self-mastery, freeing them from the need to reincarnate within the karmic cycle. Residing in the sixth dimension or higher, they assist with human ascension and are found across various cultures and historical periods. Notable figures include Buddha, Guan Yin, Jesus, Mother Mary, Mary Magdalene, and Muhammad. For those interested in learning more about these figures, *Divine Masters, Ancient Wisdom*, by Kyle Gray, offers a comprehensive exploration.

3. Ancestors

Ancestors are those who have lived before us, influencing our lives beyond their physical existence. This includes not only relatives from our paternal and maternal lineages but also influential figures who have shaped our cultural, intellectual, emotional, and spiritual environments. For example, founders of religions, prolific authors, and pioneers in various fields can serve as ancestral guides. Remember, only ancestors who have high vibrations can become a guide, not the ones with unresolved soul wounds and lessons.

4. Deities

Deities across various cultures, especially in polytheistic traditions, like those of ancient Greece, Egypt, Shinto, Santeria, and various Neo-Pagan faiths, are revered as either powerful natural forces like fire, lightning, or the sea, or exalted ancestors recognized for their heroic or virtuous deeds. These deities serve specific roles, aiding in different aspects of human life. Monotheistic and henotheistic systems view these figures differently, often as manifestations or different aspects of a single supreme entity. Personal beliefs greatly influence how individuals experience and interact with these divine figures, which can be deepened through direct meditative experiences. It's also helpful at the beginning of your spiritual journey to learn or read some stories about deities and spiritual beliefs of other cultures, traditions, and individuals throughout history.

5. Nature Spirits

Nature spirits can be the elemental forces like fire, air, water, earth, and ether. They can also be any living creature besides humans and animals on planet Earth, like flowers, trees, rivers, raindrops, clouds, mushrooms, crystals, herbs, and plants as well as all the fairy spirits who reside in this realm. If you are drawn by nature or power places (sacred sites) and ley lines, nature spirits are probably one of your spirit guides. Kything, a conscious act of being in spiritual presence or conscious connection with an object, is a great way to receive messages from nature spirits. Soften your gaze and begin to observe the object with your soul and intuitive senses.

6. Fairies

Fairies are energy beings closely associated with nature, magic, and folklore, especially in Celtic traditions. They are believed to inhabit natural spaces and possess magical abilities, sometimes mischievous, other times protective. Their energy is joyful and prosperous. Gnomes, nymphs, pixies, elves, and devas are some of the fairies I've seen clairvoyantly.

To connect with fairies, spend time in nature, meditate, and visualize their presence with respect. Offering flowers or crystals or creating fairy houses in outdoor spaces may also invite their energy. Working with rituals from nature-based traditions and embracing a playful, openhearted mindset can help you align with the magical essence of fairies.

7. Animal Spirits

Animals embody specific archetypal energies and can act as guides or messengers in the spiritual realm. Sometimes they can be your pets who passed and stayed in the spirit realm. Whether as a sign of guidance or a warning, understanding the spiritual significance of animal encounters can be enlightening. Works like Dr. Steven Farmer's *Pocket Guide to Spirit Animals* can help interpret these messages more deeply.

8. Star Beings

Star beings are extraterrestrial entities from different star systems who assist in humanity's spiritual ascension and planetary evolution. Individuals who feel a connection to otherworldly origins, such as Starseeds, may find that certain cosmic entities resonate deeply during meditative practices aimed at discovering one's star origin. Here is a list of planets, star systems, and Starseed civilizations I have channeled: Alpha Centauri, Andromeda, Atlantis, Arcturus, Avalon, Blue Avian, Blueprinters, Hadarian, Hathor, Lemuria, Lyra, Mars, Maldeck, Mintaka, Orion, Reptilian, Pleiades, Polarian, Sirius, Spica, Vega, and Venus.

This is just a starting point. You may discover new information yourself as you connect with your spirit team and have a direct experience with their energies during meditations. Dolores Cannon is a famous channeler of star beings and has published numerous books on this subject if you feel drawn to discover more. If you want to further your understanding with spirit guides, *The Seven Types of Spirit Guides: How to Connect and Communicate with Your Cosmic Helpers*, by Yamile Yemoonyah, is a great resource.

9. Expert Guides

Expert guides are those who come into your life during a specific situation where you need expert guidance. They act as temporary spirit guides to support specific endeavors. For example, during a channeling meditation when I questioned whether to write a book, the spirit of Herbert Spencer, a 19th-century English philosopher known for applying Darwinist principles to societal evolution, appeared to guide me on writing about soul evolution. It's common for professionals, such as surgeons during operations, to be accompanied by a team of spirit experts who specialize in medical fields. Same applies to athletes competing, artists creating, and teachers or leaders public speaking. I can see clairvoyantly expert guides behind them. These spirit guides are accessible to anyone seeking to enhance their skills or knowledge in a particular area. By reaching out to these spiritual experts, you can tap into their vast reservoir of expertise, ready and willing to assist.

FIVE STEPS FOR CONNECTING WITH YOUR SPIRIT TEAM

The following are the five key steps for connecting with your spirit team. They include giving permission, trusting your abilities, surrendering to divine timing, taking guided action, and expressing gratitude.

1. Tune in and give permission.

Before attempting to connect, ensure you are in a restful and calm state, ideally right after meditation. It's essential to approach this without a rushed mindset or specific expectations, as these can hinder genuine connections. Our guardian angel is assigned to us to assist us for our soul's evolution the moment we are born. Archangels are omnipresent and ready to give us guidance. However, because planet Earth runs on free will, if we don't ask and give permission for divine intervention, they can't help us. Therefore, the first step to connect with your spirit team is to ask and give permission for them to help you. Here's a simple invocation:

> "Dear guardian angel, archangels,
> and spirit beings of the highest good,
> who are currently working with me,
> please come close now and give me guidance
> on _____ (any specific issue you seek guidance on)
> or make me feel your energy
> (if you just simply want to feel their presence).
> I am open to receive what is the highest good for all.
> Please show me messages, symbols, or signs
> that are easy for me to understand.
> My heart is full of gratitude,
> thank you, thank you, thank you."

Notice if there is any energy shift in you, around you, or in the room you are in. Notice your left side, right side, above you, and below you. Depending on your innate and developed psychic abilities, you may feel it in different ways. For example, I feel heat in my body, especially my palms, then I see colors and visuals in my third eye because my clairsentience, clairvoyance, and claircognizance abilities are the strongest. Some of my students have heard something or smelled a certain scent, which signals their spirit teams are close by, because their primary psychic abilities are clairaudience and clairsalience. Those abilities rarely happen to me when I'm tuning in to my spirit team but occasionally occur when I'm doing a reading for others. That's another way I know how my spirit team likes to work with me.

The truth is that most of them are here with you all your life, and they really want to find a way to communicate with you that is easy for you to understand. Keep noticing any messages, signs, or symbols coming your way in the following days. Colors, numbers, clouds, or animals are some of the most common signs. Your guidance will be revealed to you. I also like to do some automatic writing or drawing right after the connection and see what comes through.

2. Ask for a sign and trust your psychic abilities.

One of the most frequent questions asked by my students in the beginning of their spirit connection practice is, "How do you know this guidance you receive is from your spirit team and not just from your mind?" My answer is this: messages or guidance from your spirit team always sound true, coming from a place of unconditional love; you feel good and inspired after receiving it, even if sometimes it doesn't make sense immediately. The answers from yourself can come from two parts: your mind, which is your ego, or your heart, which is your soul. The messages from your soul have the same vibrational resonance with spirit guidance—it is pure love. Remember, your soul is your higher self, which is your true inner light, that divine spark within you where you and God are one, so trust it. Messages from your spirit team and your soul feel open, gentle, and filled with love! I often feel a rush of warmth moving me to tears. However, the messages from your mind are from your ego, and they are rooted in fear. If they sound like "If you don't do this, then that might happen," then you know they are fear based. The guidance from your ego always sounds like some kind of urgency and the need to control. It feels like contraction in the body.

Connecting with Your Spirit Team

Another common question I had issues with during the early time of working with Spirit was "How do I know I should trust it (both the message and their existence)?" Remember, I didn't even believe in angels when I first started meditating. I remember thinking, *You are literally asking me to ask for spirit guidance every time I need to make a decision?* And now this is what I do every day! It's not an easy transition, but I assure you it's a worthwhile one. Life is so much simpler when you know and trust this: the Universe has your back! And your spirit team knows whether you are trusting their guidance! Remember, they are here with you all the time, regardless of whether you feel their presence or not.

In the beginning when I was trying to establish a connection, I asked my spirit guides for signs telling me they were near to give me confirmation. One time, I asked if my guardian angel was with me, and if so, could he or she show me an orchid, because orchids were my father's favorite flower. He planted a lot in our patio where I grew up, and we would go to the local orchid garden to drink orchid tea every Sunday. Those memories are very meaningful to me. I waited and had almost forgotten about this request; at the time I wasn't that committed yet. The next few days when I was cleaning up a closet, a dry orchid flower fell out from a notebook. My body felt a rush of warmth and I burst into tears. I felt nothing but truth and love that it was a sign from my guardian angel. My guardian angel knew that if he showed me a sign like this unexpectedly, I would for sure recognize it as a sign and not as just another orchid flower! Because I live in Southern California and flowers are abundant here all year round. He sure made it special—a dry orchid flower falling out from my yoga teacher training notebook!

That night, I prayed to know his name. He told me his name is "羽," a Chinese character that means feather. I can sense he has more of a masculine energy. He has a pale blue to white aura, and he has worked with Archangel Haniel since I was born. I hadn't written Chinese characters for a long time, since I'd moved to the U.S. 20 years earlier. But that character showed up in my third eye vision and moved my hand to write it down in my automatic writing journal, which I call "my date with my angels."

Just as I was writing this story, another dry orchid flower fell onto my lap in my backyard. Tears filled my eyes. I knew in my bones I had shared my truth with you. And to add the cherry on top, I opened Instagram and the first video I saw was an artist painting orchid flowers.

I hope this inspires you to start connecting with your spirit team and trust them! Ask for a sign from them and stay open and receptive, and they will show you something special that only you would know how to decipher! You will know when you are spiritually connected to your spirit team when you notice the message you need to hear pop up on a website or social media feed while you're browsing, you hear a song with the exact lyrics you need, you see a license plate on a car that contains a message for you, and so on.

3. Surrender to divine timing and form.

This step is hard for most people, especially for an impatient person like me. You pray and trust, but you still haven't received an answer or any guidance. Then you start to doubt and think, *Is this really working?* Let me assure you, divine guidance has its own timing and may come in different forms than you expect. You can't rush it.

There are several reasons why you may not receive spirit guidance immediately. The first one is that right now is not the best time for you to know the answer. No matter how urgent we view our situations, it still may not be the right time for you to know. In addition, if what you are asking or requesting is impacting more people or is bigger in scale, the Universe needs to move pieces of the puzzle to make it work for you and everyone else's highest good.

Second, check in with yourself and see if you haven't been connected spiritually lately. Remember, in order to keep our soul connected with Mother Earth and Father Sky, our auric field needs to be balanced to activate our Earth Star, Gaia Gateway, Soul Star, and Stella Gateway chakras. Just like any intimate relationship, you need to show up daily to cultivate the connection. If you haven't done any spiritual or energetic practices for a while, chances are you might be disconnected from the spirit realm. That's why I emphasize the importance of a daily meditation practice. I do the Inner Light Meditation every day; you should try it too.

Last but not least, there may be an inconvenient truth that you need to be aware of. Our psychic abilities function best when we are in an energetically neutral state. If we are in a fearful state or have attachments to particular outcomes, it's hard for us to receive clear guidance. You should either get yourself back into an energetically neutral place to tune in again or have a reading from another professional. Even though I tune in to my spirit team daily, sometimes it still helps to get a reading from another professional. Because they are outsiders, it's easier for them to be in an energetically neutral state to give you a more accurate reading. Of course, you need to find a professional whom you trust and resonate with.

Another aspect of surrendering is the form of what you asked for. For example, if you ask for abundance, it might not come in the form of money; it might come in the form of help from your family or neighbors, it might be a loving hug or understanding from someone, or it might be a free meal. Give gratitude for any forms of abundance that come your way.

When I surrender, spirits deliver.

4. Take guided action.

I need to tell you a truth: you need to take action toward the divine guidance you have received, even if sometimes it doesn't make sense to you at the beginning. It doesn't have to be immediately; you can let it sink in and then take conscious action. But if you don't take action toward them, you might not receive any more guidance later.

Taking soul-aligned action is the most important step after receiving guidance. Most of the time we don't receive the whole divine plan in one go. Only after we take that one step toward our spirit guidance will we receive the guidance for our next step forward. It really takes courage, because we don't know it all and sometimes it doesn't even make sense. It requires a commitment to fully trust your spirit team and your soul's ability to receive intuitive guidance.

THE AURA COLOR WHEEL

I compare spirit guidance to the headlight of a car. You know that you want to drive from Los Angeles to New York City, and when you're driving at night, you can't really see too far ahead—you only know that's the general direction you are heading toward. Spirit guidance is like that. It shows you the next step forward like the headlight of the car; maybe it shows you a few feet ahead of you, but it won't show you the whole way. You know you're getting there, but you don't know exactly how or when. Spirit guidance requires you to let go of control.

When you have practiced and formed a trusted relationship with your spirit team, you know when there is a sign. I remember two years ago I asked my spirit team what my next step should be in building my business. I wrote it down and created a crystal grid for this intention. Then one day when I was scrolling my e-mail inbox, I saw an e-mail from Hay House's writer community. I had no idea what that was and didn't even remember I had signed up for their e-mails. I just knew that I needed to open that e-mail and I needed to join the writers' club. I wasn't sure if I was going to write a book (although I had thought about it or if so, what it would be). I just knew it was a sign and I had to take action, and I did. Guess what? Two years later, I was writing this book with Hay House. I'm not going to lie, when I submitted the proposal, I knew I was going to win the contract, not from the ego or being prideful, but from the heart. I know this is divine guidance.

After you have taken the first small step, Spirit will guide you to the next. If you haven't received clear guidance, you can ask for a sign. If you keep seeing angel numbers (double or triple digit numbers) like 111, 222, 77, 88, and so on, that means the actions you have taken are on the right track and your spirit team is here with you. When I take the first step toward guided action, I often find the Universe responding in surprising ways. I might flip to the exact page of a book that holds the wisdom I need, my computer screen may open to the task I need to focus on, or even a simple cup of tea reveals a message in the tea bag's quote. It's as if the answers are waiting to be discovered, aligning perfectly with my intentions. When you pay attention to these messages from the Universe, it makes your life much easier and more in flow, versus striving or pushing to achieve your goals.

5. Practice gratitude.

Your spirit team doesn't need your gratitude—their job here is to assist you no matter what. But gratitude is the frequency of love. Being grateful when you receive guidance from your spirit team will put you in the vibration of love, which matches their vibration; therefore, your connection is strengthened. I always say, "Thank you, my dear spirit team, for revealing to me what I need to know right now."

Keeping a daily gratitude journal is a great practice too. At the end of each day, even the most difficult days in your life, write down three to five things you are grateful for from the day before going to sleep. These are the blessings you can count on, and your spirit team will bring you more of that!

CHAPTER 19

DEVELOPING YOUR PSYCHIC ABILITIES

Developing your psychic abilities can enhance your intuition, help you sense the subtle energies of your aura, and allow you to receive guidance from the spirit world. It strengthens your capacity for self-diagnosis and self-healing of any aura imbalances or dis-ease, while also deepening your connection to the messages from your soul and spirit team, supporting your continuous spiritual growth.

Psychic abilities allow you to sense and interpret information from the nonphysical world. Everyone has these innate abilities; they are not exclusive to a select few but are like muscles that require training to strengthen. Unlike the magical education in fictional worlds like Harry Potter, most schools do not offer classes in psychic development, which means these natural skills often remain undeveloped.

From birth, individuals exhibit psychic potential. For example, in China, it is common for Feng Shui consultants to observe babies' reactions when brought into a home to gauge the presence of negative energies. A baby playing joyfully suggests a harmonious environment, whereas crying upon entry might indicate the presence of adverse energies. As we age, the emphasis on logical and rational education can diminish our connection to these psychic capabilities, often causing us to lose touch with this intuitive aspect of ourselves. The main psychic abilities, which we'll explore in this chapter, include the clairs, psychometry, relational sympathy, channeling, precognition, astral travel, and telepathy.

THE CLAIRS

There are seven different types of "clairs" that utilize many of our senses, such as seeing, hearing, feeling, smelling, and more.

- *Clairvoyance (psychic seeing)* is the ability to "see" (perceive) images in your mind's eye. You can be in meditation and suddenly images come to you about a specific topic or issue or even about someone else. This is very powerful in me; pretty much all my paintings come through my psychic seeing. Like Vincent van Gogh once said, "I dream my painting and then I paint my dream."[1] This depicts the power of clairvoyance. You can use visualization and meditation to strengthen your clairvoyance skills. People who have a strong violet aura layer powered by the third eye chakra tend to have strong clairvoyance. They are the Visionaries, Artists, and Researchers.

- *Clairaudience (psychic hearing)* is the ability to hear voices that aren't present in the physical realm. Please don't mistake this psychic ability for a psychological disease. Sometimes certain mediums can actually hear their guides speaking to them. People who have a strong blue aura layer powered by the throat chakra tend to have strong clairaudience. They are the Entrepreneurs, Reformers, and Teachers.

- *Clairsentience (psychic feeling)* is the ability to sense feelings above the normal threshold. For example, if someone around you is in a lot of pain, you can feel their suffering deeply too. People who have a strong green aura layer powered by the heart chakra and orange aura layer powered by the sacral chakra tend to have strong clairsentience. They are the Healers, Entertainers, Warriors, Artists, and Reformers.

THE AURA COLOR WHEEL

- *Clairtangency (psychic touching)* is the ability to detect psychic information through your hands. I like to place crystals in different bags, touch them, and guess which crystal I am holding. People who have a strong green aura layer powered by the heart chakra tend to have strong clairtangency. They are the Healers, Entertainers, and Warriors.

- *Claircognizance (psychic knowing)* is the ability to "know," or direct knowing. It's when you just know something way beyond the level of the mind, and you can't explain how you know it. People who have a strong yellow aura layer powered by the solar plexus chakra tend to have strong claircognizance. They are the Visionaries, Entrepreneurs, and Healers.

- *Clairgustance (psychic tasting)* is the psychic sense of clear tasting. We like to say that people who possess this ability have strong taste buds. All culinary experts have it. I remembered a channeled reading experience for a client where I tasted sweetness in my mouth suddenly without eating any sweets. I asked my client if eating sweets meant anything to her. She told me her grandma would make all kinds of desserts for her family and that was one of her favorite childhood memories. We knew that her grandma's spirit was near. People who have a strong orange aura layer powered by the sacral chakra tend to have strong clairgustance. They are the Artists, Entertainers, and Reformers.

- *Clairsalience (psychic smelling)* is the psychic sense of clear smelling. Spirit guides may also present themselves with a certain scent or odor in order to help identify them. I am personally very sensitive to flower scents. Whenever I smell peony, I know Archangel Jophiel is nearby. Peony is my favorite flower, and Archangel Jophiel is one of my main guides on my spirit team. People who have a strong red aura layer powered by the root chakra tend to have strong clairsalience. They are the Researchers, Teachers, and Warriors.

PSYCHOMETRY

This is the ability to discover facts about a person or event by touching their inanimate objects. I found this psychic ability highlighted in thrift stores or historic homes. A friend of mine inherited her grandma's home filled with history and memories. I remember walking into the house and was immediately drawn to a ceramic dish with hand-painted flowers on it. I held it and immediately "saw" in my third eye a lady in her 60s painting this dish in a garden. She was wearing a flowy floral dress. I felt a sense of warmth and joy. I could tell she was painting this dish as a birthday gift for her granddaughter. Her granddaughter used it to put jewelry in and treasured it. Talking to my friend confirmed my psychic impressions. She was very surprised by how I received that accurate information. I told her, "Your grandma's energy is within this dish." People who have a strong red aura layer powered by the root chakra tend to have strong psychometry ability. They are the Researchers, Teachers, and Warriors.

RELATIONAL SYMPATHY

The ability to sense others' needs and desires is known as relational sympathy. Considerate people, especially mothers, tend to have this psychic ability. They know people's needs before they verbally express them, just like mothers taking care of babies before they can talk instinctively know what they need. People who have a strong green aura layer powered by the heart chakra tend to have strong relational sympathy, which is similar to clairsentience. They are the Healers, Entertainers, and Warriors.

CHANNELING

This is the ability to translate and communicate messages and information from the spirit world into the physical world. Some people do this by rough translation, where they receive messages in a subtle way and give their own interpretation of what the messages mean. I channel clients' spirit teams on a regular basis. To me, channeling is a full sensory experience. I first feel energies around me—it can be a temperature change or tingling sensation. Then I ask any spirit guide who wishes to speak to come forward and give me the message. I am familiar with different types of spirit guides' energy. I can tell quickly who is speaking, or sometimes they speak as a collective. Most of the time I see colors, images, or even movies in my third eye and an inner voice speaking to me. I try my best to transcribe that speech. Sometimes I also have strong emotions arise in my heart chakra or physical sensations. Occasionally I smell or taste something.

Automatic writing (see Divination Tools blow) is a form of channeling. People who have a strong blue aura layer powered by the throat chakra tend to have a strong channeling ability, which is similar to clairaudience. They are the Entrepreneurs, Reformers, and Teachers.

Trance channelers are people who can do what's known as embodiment, when their human self steps aside and they begin to channel directly from the spiritual source without any or little knowledge of what's being said.

PRECOGNITION

This is the ability to foretell the future or a future timeline. Please note that precognition isn't as set in stone as people like to think it is. This is because precognition relies on the person's ability to perceive the continuation of a current timeline. For example, we often think that when a psychic or medium is seeing the future, it's set in stone and will always happen. What mediums often don't tell you is that they're playing a game of probabilities, that they're actually reading into your future based on the current state of your energy and your current behavior patterns.

I like to practice my precognition skill by predicting the traffic lights or what will happen in the near future if everything stays in the current pattern. People who have a strong violet aura layer powered by the third eye chakra tend to have strong precognition, which is similar to clairvoyance. They are the Visionaries, Artists, and Researchers.

ASTRAL TRAVEL

This is the ability of your consciousness to leave your physical body and travel around. We all astral project when we sleep, but some people can do this when they're awake and completely aware of what's happening. You can practice this during meditation. Some of my students have astral travel experiences where they see their soul in their Soul Aura Color. This is a great time to ask your soul (higher self) for guidance. People who have a strong violet aura layer powered by the third eye chakra tend to have a more heightened ability to astral travel, which is similar to precognition and clairvoyance. They are the Visionaries, Artists, and Researchers.

TELEPATHY (KYTHING)

This is the ability to read thoughts and messages in other people or living spirits (like plants or animals) or perceive them from the collective consciousness. Sometimes people think they might be going crazy because they have foreign thoughts in their heads. But what's really happening is that they can perceive the thoughts of the collective in their own head. Try this with your loved ones. I love practicing this with my daughter. People who have a strong blue aura layer powered by the throat chakra tend to have an enhanced telepathy ability, which is similar to clairaudience and channeling. They are the Entrepreneurs, Reformers, and Teachers.

DEVELOP YOUR PSYCHIC ABILITIES WITH SPECIAL QUARTZ FORMATIONS

Quartz crystals are renowned for their ability to enhance psychic abilities. Here, we explore three unique quartz formations particularly effective for this purpose: the Channeler, Transmitter, and Dow crystals. Each of these quartz formations offers unique pathways to enhance psychic development and spiritual alignment, making them invaluable tools for anyone looking to deepen their connection to the Universe and their own inner wisdom.

THE AURA COLOR WHEEL

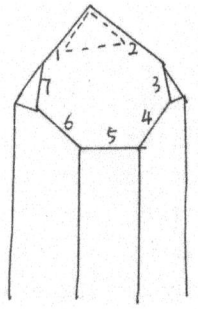

1. Channeler Crystal

The Channeler Crystal is easily recognizable by its main face, which features seven edges, coupled with a smaller three-edged face directly opposite. This 7-3 configuration is significant as, in Numerology, seven is associated with mystical experiences and three with transformation. Channeler crystals are used to facilitate a deep connection to universal wisdom. To utilize this crystal, place it over your third eye during meditation to allow insights, symbols, or visions from the spiritual realm to flow into your mind.

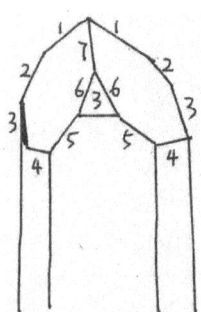

2. Transmitter Crystal

Transmitter Crystals feature a unique 7-3-7 formation, with two seven-sided termination faces flanking a central three-sided face. These crystals enhance meditation depth and strengthen the connection between your conscious self and your higher self, aiding in accessing deeper intuitive guidance and aligning with your soul's purpose. They are instrumental in integrating spiritual insights into daily living.

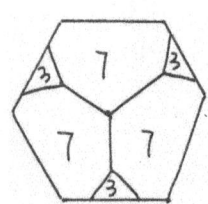

3. Dow Crystal

The Dow Crystal, named after JaneAnn Dow, a noted channeler and crystal healer, exhibits a distinctive 7-3-7-3-7-3 pattern, where each face alternates between having seven or three edges. This formation merges the properties of both Channeler and Transmitter crystals. Dow Crystals are particularly powerful in dissolving the perceived barriers between the internal and external worlds, emphasizing the interconnectedness of all things. They balance the mind, body, and spirit, aid in recognizing one's divine nature, and promote spiritual growth. These crystals are excellent for chakra balancing and removing energy blockages and are profoundly effective in meditation, particularly in connecting with the principles of sacred geometry.

DIVINATION TOOLS

Divination tools are the tools we use to receive messages from the spirit realm. You can get a direct download from your claircognizant psychic ability or during meditation, as well as with the following tools.

Automatic Writing or Drawing

Automatic writing, also called psychography, involves writing or drawing in a trancelike state to channel messages from your spirit guides or your own subconscious mind. To practice this:

- After meditation, when you're calm and centered, begin writing or drawing without censoring thoughts for 10 to 15 minutes.

- Review what you've produced for any symbols, messages, or intuitive insights. Over time, patterns or messages that may be initially confusing become clear.

For example, a client of mine after a guided meditation session with me drew many triangles. At the time, she couldn't understand what that meant. But later on, she realized that the triangle is a symbol of the fire element, and it indicated her relationship with Bridget, the fire goddess from her Celtic origin.

Another way to do automatic writing is to receive guidance from either your soul or your spirit team. Try using the following questions as a prompt:

- Do you have any messages for me?

- Ask a specific question you need guidance about.

- Are you coming here to assist me with a lesson I need to learn or am learning?

- Do you have any messages for the people in my life (family or friends)?

Feel free to add your own! Once you develop a relationship with your guides, you will know the messages are channeled through them instead of from your mind. They typically sound true, loving, and full of wisdom.

Pendulum Dowsing

Dowsing is the art of using a pendulum to receive guidance from your spirit team. To start, grab your pendulum. If you don't have a pendulum, any necklace or string with a heavy enough charm on it will do. Cleanse yourself, your sacred space, and your pendulum before you begin. Sit within your sacred space and formulate a set of three to five "yes" or "no" questions about which you'd like to receive guidance or information. It may be helpful to write these in your journal, so you know exactly what was asked when you go back to reference the reading.

Grip the end of the string, opposite the sacred object, between the thumb and index finger of your dominant hand (the hand you write with). If you are ambidextrous, just pick up your pendulum with whatever hand feels most natural to you.

Ask (aloud or silently) to be shown your "yes" answer and note the manner in which the pendulum swings (for example, forward and backward, side to side, clockwise, counterclockwise, wildly, slowly, and so on). Then repeat this step, asking to be shown your "no" answer. Do not move the pendulum intentionally, but let it move according to the subtle energy currents of your body.

Practice divining with your pendulum by asking general questions to which you are not emotionally attached. When you are neutral about the outcome of the divination, you will obtain clearer insights, as they will not be influenced by your desires. You may want to start by asking super-simple questions to which you know the answer, such as, "Is my name [insert your name here]?" or "Do I live in [insert city name here]?"

Finally, try asking your pendulum the questions you'd like to receive guidance on and take a moment to record and make notes about the answers you receive in your divination journal.

Assessing Chakra Balance with a Pendulum

When you get familiar using a pendulum for yes or no questions, you can also use it to check your chakra energy as balanced, blocked, or overactive. Cleanse your pendulum with intention, holding it under running water or passing it through the smoke of sage or incense. Sit quietly and set an intention to connect with your or another person's chakra energy field for healing or guidance. Ensure you're in a peaceful, quiet environment where you won't be disturbed.

Hold the pendulum a few inches above each chakra area, starting from the root chakra and working your way up to the crown chakra. Observe the pendulum's movement to detect if your chakra is:

- *Balanced:* The pendulum will likely swing in a steady, clockwise circle.

- *Blocked:* If the chakra is blocked, the pendulum may barely move or could move erratically or in a counterclockwise direction.

- *Overactive:* For an overactive chakra, the pendulum may swing in a wide, fast circle, indicating excess energy in that area.

Note patterns for each chakra. If unsure, ask your pendulum direct questions about each chakra, such as "Is my root chakra balanced?" to get a clearer answer. Thank your pendulum, and cleanse if desired. Using a pendulum takes practice, and interpreting the energy can be intuitive, so trust what you feel and observe during each session.

Muscle Testing

Muscle testing, or kinesiology, is a reliable diagnostic tool that is often used in alternative medicine, such as energy healing like Body Code, Emotional Code, and Theta Healing. When the body is in balance and happy, your muscles feel strong. When there is fear, pain, resistance, poor mental health, self-doubt, or worry, the body reacts differently and your muscles feel weak. When you agree to something subconsciously, your muscle strength is higher than when you disagree. When your subconscious mind disagrees, it will make your body and your muscles feel weak.

Muscle testing is like the bridge between your conscious and subconscious mind. Just because you consciously know something to be wrong for you, or you disagree with it, doesn't mean that your subconscious mind agrees.

The Sway Test Technique is more friendly for beginners. Stand up with your feet together, arms by your sides and your eyes closed. Say "yes, yes, yes" and you should sway forward. Say "no, no, no" and you should sway backward. You can also say, "My name is . . . (your real name)." Then say, "My name is (a name of the opposite sex)." Think about someone or something you love and then think about someone or something you don't like. If you aren't testing correctly, try drinking water. If you are testing opposite after drinking water, then just go with that.

Once you have calibrated your muscle testing, you are ready to move on to diagnosis and start asking questions. Formulate a set of three to five "yes" or "no" questions about which you'd like to receive guidance or information from your spirit team. Most people find this diagnostic technique the easiest as you are working with your own muscles and energy system.

Cartomancy

Cartomancy is the art of reading oracle, tarot, Lenormand, or affirmation cards to receive guidance and wisdom. It is one of the divination tools for us to communicate with the Divine.

I highly recommend you cleanse yourself (with burning sage or palo santo), your card deck, and your sacred space before you begin your reading. Intuitively choose a deck you feel drawn to work with today. Feel free to set some crystals around you that help enhance your intuition, such as amethyst, Herkimer diamond, clear quartz, or labradorite. Sit in your sacred space, take some deep breaths, and focus your mind on a current issue in your life that you'd like to receive guidance on.

When you're ready, shuffle your deck a few times and draw three cards. You can choose from these three-card layouts or make up your own intuitively. Most oracle decks come with spread-reading guides.

- *General Guidance:* Past, present, future
- *Decision-Making:* Origin (why I am here), action (what I should do), best outcome (best outcome from this action)
- *Love and Romance:* You, your relationship, your partner
- *Self-Discovery:* You, your path, your potential
- *Action Plan:* Your influence, outside influences, things to consider

Spend some time meditating on your reading and interpreting the messages you receive. Have a close look at the images and symbols in your cards and make notes of any intuitive messages or thoughts that come to your mind, even if the messages sound irrelevant or don't make sense at first. The more you work with a certain deck, the more intuitive guidance you will receive and understand from it.

Scrying with Crystal, Water, or Fire

Scrying with crystals, crystallomancy, or any reflective surface like water, fire, or candle flames is the art of gazing into a crystal, water, or fire to receive guidance and wisdom. Crystal balls are one of the most common tools for scrying, but no worries if you don't have one. You can just as easily use a piece of black obsidian, some tumbled clear quartz, or just about any other transparent or translucent crystal you feel drawn to. My personal go-to is clear quartz, honey calcite, Lemurian seed crystal, or black obsidian.

A special type of quartz formation that I like to use for scrying work is called a time-link crystal or portal/window crystal. This type of formation can be formed on any type of quartz crystal like clear quartz, citrine, smoky quartz, amethyst, and so on. A time-link crystal can be recognized with a parallelogram-shaped facet (diamond-shaped facet) in the main face of the crystal (see photos that follow). The diamond shape can be slanted toward the left (past time-link crystal), to the right (future time-link crystal), or in the middle (both past and future time-link crystal). Past time-link crystals share useful information for past-life healing as well as for healing your ancestral line (even on a DNA level). Additionally, they can help you access information about the past in the Akashic Records. Future time link-crystal crystals stimulate intuition, bringing useful information for decision-making. Additionally, they can help you access information about the future in the Akashic Records.

Past Time-Link Citrine

Past and Future Time-Link Smoky Quartz

Future Time-Link Clear Quartz

Developing Your Psychic Abilities

Once you have the chosen crystal, cleanse yourself, your sacred space, and your crystal, using either sacred scent or sounds from crystal or Tibetan singing bowls. Sit within your sacred space and formulate an open-ended question about which you require guidance or information. Dim the lights and place a small source of light, like a candle or Himalayan salt lamp, off to one side where it will not interrupt your field of vision. Gaze at the crystal and allow your eyes to move in and out of focus. Allow your mind to absorb any images or symbols that appear within the crystal ball.

When you feel you have received the information you need, cleanse your crystal once again. Take a moment to write in your journal about the images or symbols that appeared within your crystal ball, body of water, or fire. Then attempt to interpret the meanings of the images and symbols that were presented to you. I like to do automatic writing after I do scrying.

You can refer to Dr. Steven Farmer's *Pocket Guide to Spirit Animals* to understand the messages if you see animals. Or if your guides are like mine and like to show you sacred geometry or symbols, draw them out and image google them to see what you find. Trust that the result you click on are the messages you need to see.

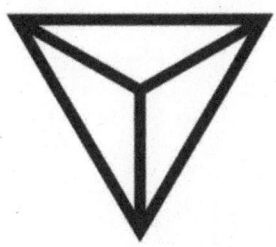

One time during my meditation connecting with my spirit team, I asked if there was a name I could call them. Then I drew the above symbol in my journal. I image googled this symbol, and it turned out to be an ancient Germanic symbol with an isosceles or equilateral triangle pointing downward, with a "Y" in the middle connecting the three points of the triangle. If viewed from a three-dimensional view, it is a two-dimensional projection of a tetrahedron (pyramid) viewed from directly above one of its vertices. It is called the Dragon's Eye, according to *The Book of Signs* by Rudolf Koch. That's what I've called my spirit team since then—the Dragon's Eye—when I have wanted to invoke them to come near me. The Y symbolizes the choice between good and evil, and the three equal parts represent the balance among love, power, and wisdom.

A Little Bit of Symbols, by Henry Reed, Ph.D., may also come in handy. Eventually, you can build your own library of interpretations of symbols and signs, because everyone's energy is different and your intuition speaks to you in a unique way.

EPILOGUE

FLOWING WITH YOUR RAINBOW

I hope that engaging in meditation, crystal healing, connecting with your spirit team, and developing your psychic abilities will remind you that you are a spiritual being, connected to everything and everyone around you, and that your essence transcends the limitations of mere human experience. This realization illuminates the answers to the three fundamental questions we explored in this book:

1. "Who am I?": You are a spiritual light being.
2. "Why am I here?": Your soul's purpose is to evolve, utilizing your innate strengths to serve, heal your soul wounds, and learn your soul lessons. This information is encoded in your Soul Aura Color, which changes and evolves as your soul grows. Through this journey, you return to the full spectrum of rainbow light.
3. "How can I be happy?": Happiness comes from knowing yourself at a soul level, making choices that align with your soul's evolution, and expressing your most authentic self with courage. Like Mahatma Gandhi once said, "Happiness is when what you think, what you say, and what you do

THE AURA COLOR WHEEL

are in harmony."[1] The Aura Color Wheel system serves as a dynamic self-awareness tool, facilitating reflection on your soul's journey. It is not about fixating on a particular Soul Aura Color, but rather the evolution journey and how you can get back into a balanced harmonious state. Ultimately, we all embody the full spectrum of light from every aura layer—a state of transcendence.

When your thoughts and actions resonate with your soul's purpose, you become a magnet for high vibrational well-being across physical, mental, emotional, and spiritual realms. You experience physical vitality, mental clarity, abundance, passion, joy, love, peace, and fulfillment. You establish a profound spiritual connection with source consciousness, fueled by boundless unconditional love. Ultimately, you flow with your rainbow aura, experiencing true freedom. In this state, you transcend human suffering—fear, grief, guilt, shame, insecurity, jealousy, anger, hatred, worry, doubt, pessimism, and boredom—elevating into an omnipresent light being of eternal joy. It is my deepest joy to imagine that one day all of us will live our soul's purpose to our full potential with joy and fulfillment.

Becoming Light

You are a channel of light,
As above, so below.
When you flow,
You channel the heavens,
and create on earth.
Like in nature,
No need to hurry or worry,
Everything is accomplished.
You are nature,
You radiate, attract, and glow.

ENDNOTES

Introduction

1. Rumi, Jalal al-Din. *The Essential Rumi* (New Expanded Edition). Trans. Coleman Barks and John Moyne. San Francisco: HarperOne, 2004.

2. Winfrey, Oprah. Oprah Winfrey's Master Class Quotes. April 3, 2011. https://www.oprah.com/own-master-class/oprah-winfreys-master-class-quotes/all. Retrieved on June 29, 2024.

Chapter 3

1. Leloup, Jean-Yves, and Jacob Needleman. *The Gospel of Thomas: The Gnostic Wisdom of Jesus*. Rochester, VA: Inner Traditions, 2005.

Chapter 13

1. Cayce, Edgar. Edgar Cayce on meditation and prayer, Edgar Cayce's A.R.E.—Association for Research and Enlightenment. https://edgarcayce.org/edgar-cayce/readings/meditation-prayer/?dfg_page=2. Retrieved on July 10, 2024.

2. Brach, Tara. *The World in Our Heart*, April 25, 2012. https://www.tarabrach.com/the-world-in-our-heart-audio/. Retrieved on July 10, 2024.

Chapter 16

1. Jung, Carl. *C.G. Jung Letters, Vol. 1: 1906–1950*. Princeton, NJ: Princeton University Press, 1973, 33.

2. Emerson, Ralph Waldo. *Essays*. https://archive.vcu.edu/english/engweb/transcendentalism/authors/emerson/essays/history.html. Retrieved on July 10, 2024.

Chapter 17

1. Lawlor, Robert. *Sacred Geometry: Philosophy & Practice*. New York: Thames & Hudson, 1982.

Chapter 19

1. Source undocumented, but it is generally attributed to Vincent Van Gogh.

Epilogue

1. Source undocumented, but it is generally attributed to Mahatma Gandhi.

FURTHER READINGS AND RESOURCES

Meditation and Spiritual Wisdom

Chopra, Deepak. *Total Meditation: Practices in Living the Awakened Life.* New York: Harmony, 2020.

Das, Ram. *Remember, Be Here Now.* New York: Harmony, 1978.

Easwaran, Eknath. *The Bhagavad Gita.* Tomales, CA: Nilgiri Press, Blue Mountain Center of Meditation, 2007.

Easwaran, Eknath. *The Upanishads.* Tomales, CA: Nilgiri Press, Blue Mountain Center of Meditation, 2007.

Patel, Kamlesh D. *Spiritual Anatomy: Meditation, Chakras, and the Journey to the Center.* New York: Balance Hachette Book Group, 2023.

Ayurveda

Frawley, David. *Ayurvedic Healing: A Comprehensive Guide.* Silver Lake, WI: Lotus Press, 2001.

"More Than a Dosha Quiz," Banyan Botanicals. https://www.banyanbotanicals.com/pages/dosha-quiz.

Rose, Sahara. *Eat Feel Fresh: A Contemporary, Plant-Based Ayurvedic Cookbook.* New York: DK, 2018.

Rose, Sahara. *The Idiot's Guide to Ayurveda.* New York: DK, 2017.

Feng Shui

Diamond, Marie. *Feng Shui Your Life: A Beginner's Guide to Using Your Home to Attract the Life of Your Dreams.* Carlsbad, CA: Hay House Publishing, 2023.

THE AURA COLOR WHEEL

Living with Nature's Cycles

Boland, Yasmin. *Moonology: Working with the Magic of Lunar Cycles*. Carlsbad, CA: Hay House Publishing, 2016.

Leavy, Ashley. *Cosmic Crystals: Rituals and Meditations for Connecting with Lunar Energy*. Beverly, MA: Fair Winds Publishing, 2019.

Northrup, Kate. *Do Less: A Revolutionary Approach to Time and Energy Management for Ambitious Women*. Carlsbad, CA: Hay House Publishing, 2020.

Uhl, Cassie. *The Zenned Out Guide to Understanding the Wheel of the Year: Your Handbook to Honoring the Eight Seasonal Celebrations*. New York: Rock Point, 2021.

Crystal Healing

Gienger, Michael, and Joachim Goebel. *Gem Water: How to Prepare and Use More Than 130 Crystal Waters for Therapeutic Treatments*. Rochester, VT: Earthdancer Books, 2008.

Hall, Judy. *The Ultimate Guide to Crystal Grids: Transform Your Life Using the Power of Crystals and Layouts* (Volume 3). Beverly, MA: Fair Wind Press, 2017.

Hanekamp, Deborah. *Ritual Baths: Be Your Own Healer*. New York: Morrow Gift, 2020.

Leavy, Ashley. *The Beginner's Guide to Crystal Healing: Learn How to Energize, Heal, and Balance with Crystals*. Beverly, MA: New Shoe Press, 2022.

Pearson, Nicholas. *Crystal Basics Pocket Encyclopedia: The Energetic, Healing, and Spiritual Power of 450 Gemstones*. Rochester, VT: Destiny Books, 2023.

Hudson Institute of Mineralogy. www.mindat.org.

Spirit Guides

Bernstein, Gabrielle. *The Universe Has Your Back: Transform Fear to Faith*. Carlsbad, CA: Hay House Publishing, 2020.

Campbell, Rebecca. *Letters to a Starseed*. Carlsbad, CA: Hay House Publishing, 2021.

Canon, Dolores. *Three Waves of Volunteers and the New Earth*. St. Louis, MO: Ozark Mountain Publishing, 2011.

Day, Christine. *Pleiadian Initiations of Light*. Newburyport, MA: New Page Books, 2010.

Gray, Kyle. *Divine Masters, Ancient Wisdom*. Carlsbad, CA: Hay House Publishing, 2021.

Marciniak, Barbara. *Bringers of the Dawn: Teachings from the Pleiadians*. Rochester, VT: Bear & Company, 1992.

Yemoonyah, Yamile. *The Seven Types of Spirit Guides: How to Connect and Communicate with Your Cosmic Helpers*. Carlsbad, CA: Hay House Publishing, 2020.

Further Readings and Resources

Psychic Abilities and Divination

Choquette, Sonia. *Trust Your Vibes: Live an Extraordinary Life by Using Your Intuitive Intelligence* (Revised Edition). Carlsbad, CA: Hay House Publishing, 2022.

Farmer, Steven. *Pocket Guide to Spirit Animals*. Carlsbad, CA: Hay House Publishing, 2012.

Koch, Rudolf. *The Book of Signs*. New York: Dover Publications, 1955.

Reed, Henry. *A Little Bit of Symbols*. New York: Sterling Ethos, 2016.

Self-Discovery

Bloch, Douglas, and Demetra George. *Astrology for Yourself: A Workbook for Personal Transformation*. Lake Worth, FL: IBIS Press, 1987.

Buchanan, Michelle. *Numerology Made Easy: Discover Your Future, Life Purpose and Destiny from Your Birth Date and Name*. Carlsbad, CA: Hay House Publishing, 2018.

Bunnell, Lynda, and Ra Uru Hu. *Human Design: The Definitive Book of Human Design: The Science of Differentiation*. Carlsbad, CA: HDC Publishing, 2011.

Chestnut, Beatrice, Ph.D., and Urania Paes, MM. *The Enneagram Guide to Waking Up: Find Your Path, Face Your Shadow, Discover Your True Self*. Newburyport, MA: Hampton Roads Publishing, 2021.

Frawley, David. *Astrology of the Seers: A Guide to Vedic/Hindu Astrology*. Silver Lake, WI: Lotus Press, 2000.

Hu, Ra Uru. *Global Incarnation Index: Incarnation Crosses*. Santa Fe, NM: Jovian Archive Corporation, 2001.

Riso, Don Richard, and Russ Hudson. *The Wisdom of the Enneagram: The Complete Guide to Psychological and Spiritual Growth for the Nine Personality Types*. New York: Bantam, 1999.

Rudd, Richard. *The Gene Keys: Embracing Your Higher Purpose*. London: Watkins Publishing, 2013.

Schulman, Martin. *Karmic Astrology: The Moon's Nodes and Reincarnation* (Volume 1). New York: Samuel Weiser, 1975.

Schulman, Martin. *Karmic Astrology: Joy and the Part of Fortune* (Volume 3). New York: Samuel Weiser, 1978.

ACKNOWLEDGMENTS

I extend my heartfelt gratitude to my spirit team, who have entrusted me with channeling the Aura Color Wheel self-discovery system to shed more light in the world and continue to support me on my spiritual journey.

My deepest thanks go to those who have loved and supported me: my parents, with special mention to my father, now one of my spirit guides, who always encouraged my interests and curiosities and called me his light. To Jose M. Plehn, my dear husband and soul family member on this earthly journey, thank you for supporting my dreams and encouraging me to be my most authentic self. My mother-in-law, Cecilia Dujowich, is like my second mother, always supporting my work and helping with family responsibilities.

I am profoundly grateful to all my spiritual teachers who have guided me on this path, including Shiva Das, Ed Zadlo, Dr. David Frawley, Ashley Leavy, Rebecca Campbell, Kyle Gray, James Van Praag, Dougall Fraser, Charles Virtue, Peroshini Naidoo, Morwenna Bugano, Vianna Stibal, Deepak Chopra, Eckhart Tolle, Gabrielle Bernstein, and more.

To all my fellow creative entrepreneur coaches who had helped me on my business growth journey, including Kate Northrup, James Wedmore, Jennifer Finley, Emily Jeffords, Bonnie Christine, and more—thank you for exemplifying the courage to pursue your soul's purpose and inspiring others to do the same.

I am also thankful to my fellow spiritual lightworkers who provided valuable feedback and supported the development of this book, including Ashley Leavy, Cassie Uhl, Nicholas Pearson, Miranda Norman, and others.

Acknowledgments

A special thanks to the incredible team at Hay House, especially Reid Tracy, Kelly Notaras, and the editors who selected my book proposal for the contract. My wonderful editors, Lara Asher, Lisa Cheng, and Monica O'Connor, have helped transform this book into a better version for the world.

To all my students and clients who have trusted me as their guide to their soul's purpose and healing journey. You inspire me to be a better human and teacher.

To all the lightworkers who have come before me and those who will come after me, thank you for making the world a brighter place by aligning with your soul's purpose and serving as beacons of light for others on their spiritual paths.

ABOUT THE AUTHOR

Helen Ye Plehn is the founder of Helen Creates Beauty and the creator of The Aura Color Wheel: A System to Identify Your Soul's Purpose through Your Soul Aura Color. She is the author of *Flowing with My Rainbow Chakra Affirmation Deck*. Her signature Flowing with Your Rainbow Course based on the system has named her a Visionary Educator on MSN.com.

She is an aura intuitive, certified crystal healer, angel channeler, third-generation Feng Shui master, certified yoga and meditation instructor, intuitive painter, and spiritual teacher. She is also an Ayurveda practitioner, Vedic astrologer, Theta healer, and passionate Flamenco dancer.

Helen's spiritual awakening began in 2011 after a psychiatric ER visit due to severe anxiety and depression. After more than a decade of daily meditation practice, spiritual wisdom education, and a deep quest for her soul's purpose and happiness, she founded Helen Creates Beauty, LLC, to further develop and offer her soul's gifts.

About the Author

She is highly clairvoyant and sees colors as energy. As a professional artist working with colors daily, combining art, Feng Shui interior design, and various spiritual healing modalities, Helen helps her clients live with purpose, joy, and fulfillment.

She resides in Southern California with her husband and daughter. She has an undergraduate degree in psychology and social work, a master's degree in interior architecture and design, and has published three academic peer-reviewed articles and four conference papers during her Ph.D. studies in tourism and hospitality management at Temple University in Philadelphia. Her doctoral area of research was human sensory experience design.

Connect with Helen at **www.helencreatesbeauty.com**, **www.auracolorwheel.com**, **@helencreatesbeauty** on Instagram, Facebook, TikTok, and Pinterest, and the Aura Academy by Helen Creates Beauty YouTube Channel: **https://www.youtube.com/@auracolorwheel**.

Hay House Titles of Related Interest

YOU CAN HEAL YOUR LIFE, the movie,
starring Louise Hay & Friends
(available as an online streaming video)
www.hayhouse.co.uk/louise-movie

THE SHIFT, the movie,
starring Dr. Wayne W. Dyer
(available as an online streaming video)
www.hayhouse.co.uk/the-shift-movie

* * *

AURA ALCHEMY: Learn to Sense Energy Fields, Interpret the Color Spectrum and Manifest Success, by Amy Leigh Mercree

CRYSTALS365: Crystals for Everyday Life and Your Guide to Health, Wealth, and Balance, by Heather Askinosie

RAISE YOUR VIBRATION: High-Vibe Tools to Support Your Spiritual Awakening, by Kyle Gray

UNBLOCKED: A Revolutionary Approach to Tapping into Your Chakra Empowerment Energy to Reclaim Your Passion, Joy and Confidence, by Margaret Lynch Raniere and David Raniere, Ph.D.

YOUR LIFE IN COLOR: Empowering Your Soul with the Energy of Color, by Dougall Fraser

All of the above are available at your local bookstore,
or may be ordered by contacting Hay House.

* * *

TRANSFORM YOUR DAY— ANYTIME, ANYWHERE

With the **Empower You** Unlimited Audio *App*

❝ ★★★★★ **Life changing.**
My fav app on my entire phone, hands down! – Gigi ❞

Unlimited access to the entire Hay House audio library!

You'll get:

- 600+ soul-stirring **audiobooks** to expand your mind
- 1,000+ **meditations** for restful sleep, morning focus, and gentle healing
- Bite-sized audios **under 20 minutes**—perfect for busy days
- **Exclusive talks** you won't find anywhere else
- **Daily affirmations**
- Fresh content added **every week** to fuel your journey

New audios added every week!

❝ Driving, yard work, and housework have been **transformed**!
– Ruffles27 ❞

Scan the QR code to start listening or visit **hayhouse.com/unlimited**

CONNECT WITH
HAY HOUSE
ONLINE

🌐 hayhouse.co.uk   f @hayhouse

📷 @hayhouseuk   🦋 @hayhouseuk.bsky.social

♪ @hayhouseuk   ▶ @HayHousePresents

Find out all about our latest books & card decks • Be the first to know about exclusive discounts • Interact with our authors in live broadcasts • Celebrate the cycle of the seasons with us • Watch free videos from your favourite authors • Connect with like-minded souls

---

'The gateways to wisdom and knowledge are always open.'

Louise Hay